Cornell Studies in Anthropology

BANG CHAN

*Social History of a Rural
Community in Thailand*

Cornell Studies in Anthropology

This series of publications is an outgrowth of the program of instruction, training, and research in theoretical and applied anthropology originally established at Cornell University in 1947 with the aid of the Carnegie Corporation of New York. The program seeks particularly to provide in its publications descriptive accounts and interpretations of cultural processes and dynamics, including those involved in projects of planned cultural change, among diverse tribal and peasant cultures of the world.

Buurri al Lamaab: A Suburban Village in the Sudan
BY HAROLD B. BARCLAY

Huaylas: An Andean District in Search of Progress
BY PAUL L. DOUGHTY

Bang Chan: Social History of a Rural Community in Thailand
BY LAURISTON SHARP AND LUCIEN M. HANKS

A priest of Bang Chan
Photo by Ewing Krainin

BANG CHAN

Social History of a Rural Community in Thailand

LAURISTON SHARP *and*
LUCIEN M. HANKS

Cornell University Press   Ithaca and London

This book has been published with the aid of a grant from the Hull Memorial Publication Fund of Cornell University.

First published 1978 by Cornell University Press.
Published in the United Kingdom by Cornell University Press Ltd.,
2-4 Brook Street, London W1Y 1AA.

International Standard Book Number 0-8014-0858-X
Library of Congress Catalog Card Number 77–90910
Printed in the United States of America
Librarians: Library of Congress cataloging information appears on the last page of the book.

To Ruth and Jane

Contents

Illustrations

Maps

Preface

In planning this account of the development of the village of Bang Chan, which had its beginnings over a century ago outside the capital city of Thailand, we sought to provide for the interests of both general readers and specialized scholars. The former, we hope, may move along the mainstream of the story as sampans move along Bang Chan canal during the rainy season, directly and easily. Their passage need not be troubled by the references and footnotes. Wherever possible the technical vocabulary of anthropology has been avoided, although there will be stretches of the journey, as in the section in Chapter 2 headed "Economics, the Social Order, and Kinship," in which the channel may seem to be silting up or choked with weeds, as though the dry season had arrived. We believe such muddy sections will prove useful for an attempt to understand the workings of Thai cultural behavior and only hope they will not deter general readers from proceeding on their way.

Other readers may be our colleagues in the study of Thailand and Southeast Asia or in our discipline of anthropology. These students will wish to track down references, question our assertions, and search out evidence for our judgments. We welcome them to the footnotes and the references. Most of the references deal with conventionally published materials, listed in the Bibliography. Exceptions are unpublished field notes cited with initials plus date: "HMH 12/20/52." These notes are available in the files of the Cornell University Thailand Project and the Human Relations Area Files in New Haven, Connecticut. Our colleagues and students who have kindly made their field notes available and the initials by which they are identified in the files at Ithaca and New Haven are listed on the following page. (Some of our Thai colleagues have chosen to use idiosyncratic initials rather than the conventional ones.)

AE	Aram Emarun	KJ	Kamol Janlekha
CIW	Loebongse Sarabhaja	KY	Yāūd Nakorn
HMH	Hazel M. Hauck	SM	Singto Metah
HPP	Herbert P. Phillips	SS	Saovanee Sudsaneh
JK	Jadun Kongsa	VIC	Vichitr Saengmani
JRH	Jane R. Hanks		

The initials LMH and LS designate the authors.

For the further aid of diligent colleagues we have scattered transcriptions of the Thai words here and there throughout the text. The transcriptions follow the phonetic system developed by Mary R. Haas and Heng R. Subhanka (1945) with a few changes. We have chosen to neglect tones and the glottal stop. Long vowels will be indicated by a superimposed bar, $\bar{a}$, $\overline{ae}$. The open o we write au, approximated in the au of English $auto$ and $taut$. Where some confusion may be possible, as in our transcriptions of certain final consonants or semivowels, the reader may refer to the Glossary, where some of our transcriptions are given in Thai. In general we have not tried to transcribe many proper names, writing Bangkok rather than Bāngkaug, Bang Chan rather than Bāng Chan, though some readers may be surprised to see Srisuriyawongse transcribed as Srīsurijawong. We shall let these eccentric forms stand naturally as they fell from the pen.

When there is no real problem of meaning, we shall also be somewhat relaxed in our translations. We know that a wat is normally a complex of buildings that is both more and less than a temple and perhaps better thought of as a kind of monastery. And its inhabitants may not be priests in some technical senses of the word (most of them are not elders, and there are no sacraments in Theravada Buddhism). But "temple" and "priest" are commonly used by many English-speaking Thai; through the years, in this as in so many other matters, we have fallen in with common usage, and we continue with it here, hoping that we shall not too greatly discomfort the fastidious.

In this work we have sought to complement or supplement other published studies of Bang Chan or the larger cultural context of Thailand which were carried out by associates during the period of our own work, from 1948 into the 1970s, and which are thus pertinent to an understanding of the village in its areal and temporal setting. So we note among books and monographs dealing directly with Bang Chan the work of Rose K. Goldsen and Max Ralis (1957), Jane R. Hanks (1963), Lucien M. Hanks (1972), Hazel M. Hauck et al. (1956, 1958, 1959), Kamol Janlekha (1957), Herbert P. Phillips (1965), Lauriston Sharp et al. (1953), and Robert B. Textor (1973a, 1973b). A neighboring Siamese village is described by Howard K. Kaufman (1960), and James B. Hendry (1964) makes comparisons with a village in southern Vietnam. Works by our students on the larger Thai scene include studies of other Thai villages by John E. deYoung (1955), Jasper C. Ingersoll (1963), and Konrad Kingshill (1960); of Thai economics by Eliezer B. Ayal (1969) and James C. Ingram (1955, 1971); of government and administration by Charles F. Keyes (1966, 1970), Akin Rabibhadana (1969), and David A. Wilson (1962, 1970); of educational development by David K. Wyatt (1969); and of the Chinese by G. William Skinner (1957). Finally, Frank J. Moore (1974) has provided us with the latest in a series of handbooks concerned with the polity and society of the Thai nation.

A project such as the Bang Chan study resembles a May Day dance. Some erect the pole with its streamers while others tamp down the turf, teach the steps, choose the music, or prepare the May wine, and still others form the audience, encouraging all to do their best. Each is indispensable. So with our sponsors, fellow workers, advisers, students, friends, and informants: every one contributed in some special manner to the achievement of the final result. Though they share no responsibility for the present text, we hope they may gain some satisfaction from having contributed to it.

Our financial sponsors for the work in Bang Chan were the Carnegie Corporation of New York, the Rockefeller Foundation, the Wenner-Gren Foundation for Anthropological Research, the U.S. (Fulbright) Educational Foundation in Thailand, the Social Science Research Council, the American Philosophical Society, and Cornell University. In Thailand we enjoyed the cooperation of the Ministry of Agriculture, the Ministry of the Interior, the Ministry of Public Health, the Ministry of Education, the University of Agricultural Science (Kasetsat), the Siam Society, and, early on, the American Embassy in Bangkok.

Our colleagues in research who constantly enhanced our understanding of details and the context of the Bang Chan scene were

Anusith Rajatasilpin, Aram Emarun, Jane R. Hanks, the late Hazel M. Hauck, Jadun Kongsa, Kamol Janlekha, Loebongse Sarabhaja, Herbert P. Phillips, Saovanee Sudsaneh, Singto Metah, Tasanee Hongladaromp, Robert B. Textor, Titaya Suvanajata, Vichitr Saengmani, and Warin Wonghanchao. Among our many friends and advisers we depended particularly on the late Phrayā Anuman Rajadhon and Siribongse Boon-Long.

For assistance in the preparation of the manuscript we are particularly indebted to Jane R. Hanks, who helped to clarify ideas and prose far beyond the call of duty. Both Loebongse Sarabhaja and Warin Wonghanchao supplied indispensable last-minute information, while Robert B. Textor, David K. Wyatt, and Akin Rabibhadana made important criticisms of the manuscript. The maps were the imaginative work of Jeanne McWaters and Emily Elman. Ewing Krainin kindly provided five of the photographs.

Finally, to the people of Bang Chan, who patiently submitted to our prying questions while at the same time providing warm hospitality, we say a fervent *khāub khun māk*.

L. S.
L. M. H.

Ithaca, New York
North Bennington, Vermont

BANG CHAN

*Social History of a Rural
Community in Thailand*

CHAPTER 1

Departure

The Road to Bang Chan

Go any day in Bangkok to that great intersection of streets and canals called the Water Gate (Pratū Nām). There the locks hold the fresh water of a vast network of up-country canals and prevent it from pouring out into the tidal canals of Bangkok. Buildings stand between the waterways and the streets and can be entered from either side. Within them big and little vendors sell anything that anyone will buy: golden buckles, squid, Thermos bottles, melons. These days most customers thread their way from the street among rows of country women sitting on their heels next to baskets of prickly durians. A few years ago people were found mainly on the canal side. One then saw the cluster of boats for hire, family skiffs, and slow tubby grain boats scurrying to make way when the steam passenger launch approached from Bāngkapi canal, its decks bristling with eager disembarkers. Today more people take the bus on their way to and from the countryside.

Red, blue, green, and white buses park in tired rows along the curb, and those who cannot read the signs on the front must ask some driver lounging on a passenger's bench which bus goes north to Minburī. The dark glasses hiding his eyes make it difficult to judge whether he really knows; if not, the boy ticket taker polishing the hood of another bus may know. The bus is just leaving, so we dash for the rear step, where hands stretch out to help us climb aboard.

We add to the lurching crowd of passengers. Two boys standing next to a deeply tanned woman reach for a handhold to avoid being thrown into a basket of chickens. Instead they bump against an elderly man wearing a worn brown felt hat of European style. His toes are slightly protected by his canvas shoes, but unguarded bare feet extend from the khaki pants of the man sitting next to him. Between shoes, bare feet, sacks, and baskets the youthful ticket taker picks his way skillfully to collect his fares. Like a drillmaster, he whistles "Go!" to the driver after each stop. Those who climb aboard seem grateful for the breeze that blows through the open sides.

Houses thin out, and along the shaded highway the bus picks up speed, dodging perilously around pushcarts and bicycles and on-coming trucks. Inside the woman's basket, the chickens begin to stir and cluck, attracting the gaze of a bobbed-haired girl who was leaning quietly against her seated father. The ticket taker relaxes against the back of the driver's seat and makes a bantering remark to his colleague. His ease is suddenly broken by a woman's call to stop the bus. She and an adolescent boy clamber over baskets, laps, and feet to the exit. The bus pauses a minute while the ticket taker mounts to the roof and hands a bicycle to the waiting boy. Another shrill whistling starts the bus off again.

After the man with the European hat swings down in front of a glistening temple near the southeast corner of Don Myang airport, the bus turns east onto a branch road. Dyked *padi* fields extend on both sides to island-like clusters of trees and beyond to other clusters stretching toward the horizon. Green shoots of transplanted rice stand above a glistening carpet of water. Children with blue school uniforms file along the dykes toward some farmhouse in one of the clusters. A group of highway workers pauses from digging with mattocks to exchange a passing shout and laugh with the bus driver. Occasionally we pass a raw, mounded road leading to a new house with stucco trim; the residents commute daily to the city. The newly planted trees, the glistening automobile, and the urban clothes have not yet quite blended with the country scene.

An hour's ride has brought us some thirty kilometers to a row of open-fronted stores and a small rice mill at the broad bridge across Bang Chan canal. Here the bus pauses for us to descend, and then is off. The noises of the countryside rush to fill the silence left by a roaring motor. Somewhere a paddle dropped in the bottom of a boat pierces the stillness. A white egret circles to a landing on a distant dyke. Nearby a second one settles, and both stand motionless on their long legs.

Over a plank across a watery ditch we move to the stores. In a café two chess players and several kibitzers look up from their game to watch us approach. The stocky, white-haired proprietor smiles and asks what we have brought him from Bangkok. We reply that the zookeeper would not let us bring him that tiger today because another man asked for it earlier. The proprietor laughs at the excuse and moves to hold the sampan near the little dock so that we may climb aboard.

We paddle under the highway bridge in a northerly direction along the watercourse winding past teak-paneled houses set back among the trees. Wading in the shallow brown water along the ill-defined bank, a black-haired girl plunges a basket cone into the muddy bottom and reaches through the open top to catch a darting fish. A naked toddler stands on the bank watching her. The schoolteacher on his way home drives his skiff swiftly along and greets us with a brief question. "We are going to the temple," we reply before he is out of earshot. Next we pass the schoolhouse, whose long, flat roof sits like a lid on an empty container; the flagpole stands naked in the vacant school yard. On the veranda of a pile house opposite the school an old woman plaits a mat while her grandchildren play tag among the posts beneath the house. The acrid odor of chicken dung blows by as our boat passes.

We disembark at the temple. Before our eyes appear the customary features of a country temple compound: the sanctuary (*bōt*) where priests make their devotions, the congregating hall (*wihān*) where villagers listen to sermons, the cremation platform, the monks' quarters, all set about a court facing the canal. Rather than bearing an air of tidy sanctity, the compound seems neglected. Though the gilded cosmic serpent gleams on top of the congregating hall, built by village contributions in the 1930s, the weathered boards in the building point to the beginnings of decay. Even on the fifty-year-old sanctuary the ceramic decor is defaced, and surrounding columns lurch as if disarranged by some destructive demon. Mangy dogs sniff in the refuse under houses. Across the weed-filled courtyard, a cluster of temple boys pauses from swimming to watch us. We call to ask for the abbot or head priest, and a boy with dripping shorts runs along the walk to show the way. We pause in a musty passage between two buildings, and the boy disappears into a doorway through which a softly chanted prayer reaches our ears. In a moment the boy is back with news that the head priest has not yet returned from Bangkok but is expected back before sundown.

Seeing a group of yellow-robed priests sitting cross-legged on a veranda, we make obeisance. They reply to our salutation with cordial smiles; one politely asks if we intend to spend the night in Bang Chan. "Just visiting for the day," we reply.

Back at the edge of the canal we pass a shelter where an elderly woman is lighting a fire to begin the evening meal for three men who lie in faded clothes napping on the plank floor. The temple houses and feeds them remnants of the food received by the priests. If Buddhism offers a theme of preservation, it consists in giving to sustain life. Otherwise no one gains merit by holding back decay from material things.

From the temple the canal leads our boat under a rickety footbridge past a row of closely spaced dwellings. In one a young woman, working at a sewing machine, modestly continues her work as if we were not there. Tall trees arch over the canal, and the monsoon is a refreshing breeze. A man, chopping bits from a chunk of wood, pauses to call out, "The water is rising well! I have finished transplanting all my fields and the two additional ones I rented this year. This is a good time to visit, if you want, for I'll have time to talk. Farther up the canal you'll see my son cutting grass for the buffalo."

Beyond the grove we are again in the open fields. The water stands clear and warm, a few inches deep, around the precisely planted rows of rice shoots. The farmer's son can be seen clipping grass along a dyke. The canal continues on past farther groves and farther farmhouses. In the remote distance a single blue hill rises from the plain and above it floats a towering thundercloud.

The Community

This is Bang Chan, whose households and fields merge with neighboring communities as do the turgid waters of the canals. We might paddle for days through the network of waterways in Thailand's central plain and still feel ourselves in Bang Chan. The succession of rice fields, shaded wooden houses, and thatched huts is punctuated by occasional open-sided stores, temples, and schools. Bang Chan's school and temple roofs are distinctive, however, and stand as beacons for those returning homeward from their journeys. The country people who call Bang Chan home are those who send their children to the local school or who visit the temple on holidays.

Of course, a few farmers who live only some minutes away from the temple prefer occasionally to take their bowls of food and their flowers an hour's boat trip to Ku temple or in the other direction to Bam Phen temple. In Bang Chan the headmen of the hamlets (*mūbān*) can tell the approximate geographical boundaries of their jurisdictions; at least they claim to know who lives where. A dozen or so hamlets are grouped into a commune (*tambon*) under a chief (*kamnan*), who is elected by the hamlet headmen from among themselves. In fact, the name Bang Chan stands officially for a commune rather than for the community of a school and a temple. On some maps the name also appears as Bang Chan Canal Village or Bān Khlaūng Bāng Chan (L. M. Hanks 1972:7). People living on the west side of Bang Chan canal live officially in commune Kannā Jao, while those on the east live in commune Bang Chan. If they must visit the district offices (*amphōe*), the west siders go a half day's journey to Bāngkapi, while the east siders go three or four miles to Minburī. There they go on official business to pay taxes, register births, vote in elections, and collect salaries if they work for the government. If occasionally they transfer land or must defend their rights at law, the district offices may also provide these facilities.

To discover what was going on in this village community, the research group established geographical boundaries for its work, somewhat less arbitrary than the government's administrative boundaries. Bang Chan, for purposes of research, became in 1948 the 1,600 people in the seven hamlets in the neighborhood of the temple and the nearby school: hamlets 5, 6, 7, and 8 in Kannā Jao commune and 4, 5, and 6 in Bang Chan commune. Probably 95 percent of the children at the school came from this area and 90 percent of the regular worshipers at the temple. The area of the community is shaped more like a pronged fork than a circle, for the homes of the inhabitants cluster along branching canals in a northerly direction. To the south, outside of Bang Chan, a predominantly Moslem hamlet performs its devotions at its own local *surao*, so called because it is too small and flimsy a structure to be dignified by the name *masjid*. This hamlet also maintains a vernacular school where after regular school hours children learn to read scripture in Arabic. A few households of the faithful lie scattered about in Bang Chan as well, where they live amicably enough among Buddhists.

Beginning in 1949 three censuses, at intervals of four years, were

taken in the seven hamlets that we call Bang Chan. Each enu-
meration was conducted by a different set of workers, and not all
data are strictly comparable. Definition of residence, for instance,
varied, so that a son who worked for a season in Bangkok may have
been counted in one census and omitted in another. Thus Tables 1
and 2 must be regarded as involving approximations, particularly
where differences are small or trends inconsistent.

The apparent stability of our census figures disguises a flux of
population in this area. Janlekha (1957:29) found that by 1953, 38 (13
percent) of the 288 households present in 1949 (excluding the temple)
had disappeared and 48 (17 percent) had been added. Of the 38 that
disappeared, 11 disintegrated or merged with other households after
a death or some other social disturbance. Twenty-seven households
(9 percent) moved away from the community. This loss to the
community grows in significance in Janlekha's sample of 104 farming
households, where 26 (25 percent) disappeared between 1949 and
1953 (ibid.: 78). The movement seems to have abated somewhat
between 1953 and 1957, when 23 moved into the community and 24
(8 percent) disappeared.

While we lack exact annual figures for comparison, the average
rate of migration for the period we have covered varies between 2 and
6 percent per year. Although the lower limit may be small, the upper
limit suggests a rather large, restless, and mobile segment of the
population. This we might expect in an urban community but not in
one where more than 85 percent of the households work in agriculture, where more than 70 percent are farm operators, and where less
than 15 percent are laborers without landholdings (ibid.: 45). Such a
migration rate might also be expected where the land is mainly

Table 1.   Summary of demographic data from three research censuses of Bang Chan

Demographic data	1949	1953	1957
Total population	1,608	1,696	1,771
Population density per square mile	320	340	352
Sex ratio (males to 100 females)	107.2	102.3	95.7
Crude estimated annual birthrate	20.3	24.9	20.0
Fertility ratio	428	525	368
Households	288	298	297
Average number of persons per household (excluding temple)	5.5	5.6	5.9

Table 2.   Age and sex data from three research censuses of Bang Chan

Age	1949				1953				1957			
	Male	Female	Total	%	Male	Female	Total	%	Male	Female	Total	%
0–4	78	85	163	10	116	103	219	13	87	90	177	10
5–9	108	101	209	13	100	105	205	12	87	123	210	12
10–14	98	109	207	13	118	103	221	13	86	92	178	10
Total ages 0–14	284	295	579	36%	334	311	645	38%	260	305	565	32%
15–19	109	84	193	12	83	97	180	11	94	123	217	12
20–24	93	77	170	11	92	72	164	10	107	88	195	11
25–29	58	57	115	7	60	74	134	8	80	80	160	9
30–34	52	44	96	6	46	51	97	6	62	67	129	7
35–39	45	50	95	6	37	43	80	5	41	49	90	5
40–44	47	35	82	5	42	45	87	5	46	44	90	5
45–49	44	34	78	5	43	35	78	4	41	30	71	4
50–54	28	31	59	4	35	28	63	3	40	30	70	4
Total ages 15–54	476	412	888	56%	438	445	883	52%	511	511	1,022	57%
55–59	23	27	50	3	27	29	56	3	25	31	56	3
60–64	22	15	37	2	27	24	51	3	29	28	57	3
65–69	14	8	22	1	15	11	26	2	18	14	32	2
70–74	8	8	16	1	9	6	15	1	12	9	21	2
75–79	2	7	9	1	6	7	13	1	8	3	11	1
80–84	3	4	7	0	2	5	7	0	3	4	7	0
Total ages 55–84	72	69	141	8%	86	82	168	10%	95	89	184	11%
Total population	832	776	1,608	100%	858	838	1,696	100%	866	905	1,771	100%

worked by tenants. Here only 30 percent of the land is operated by tenants, who constitute 38 percent of the farm operator households. Of the remaining 62 percent of farm householders, 22 percent work their own land exclusively, while 40 percent rent some portion of the land in addition to their own holdings (ibid.: 57). Two-thirds of this population own land.

The changes in residence and occupation between 1948 and 1953 have been analyzed by Janlekha (1957: 90–92). He points to an occupational group of marginal farmers and farm laborers as the main source of these changes (ibid.: 44–46). They are found living in little thatched dwellings interspersed with the paneled teak houses of the more prosperous. We judge that during the years 1953 to 1957 fewer variations in the fortunes of such people cast them out of the village and brought others like them to their places in Bang Chan.

Yet always the people on these lower levels of the economic scale are shifting and changing their residences or their means of livelihood or both.

The Cornell Thailand Project

Field research in Bang Chan began in 1948 as an initial phase of the Cornell Thailand Project. This project, in turn, was part of a larger Cornell University program of comparative studies of cultural change which had been inaugurated in 1947. The program offered instruction and training on the campus and in the field on the problems of changing cultural behavior in nonindustrialized societies; but as a necessary concomitant, at a period before Point IV or other large-scale government or private technical-aid programs had been organized, the Cornell program also provided for a coordinated investigation of the tide of modern technological and other cultural influences, indigenous and foreign, flooding into village communities of such regions as Thailand, India, Peru, and the American Southwest. Separate studies in these and other widely scattered areas not only would provide discrete descriptions of the cultural life of local communities in the context of their differently developing regions, but would also focus on a common problem: How may the ramifying influences of the present, most of them stemming ultimately from the Atlantic civilization, affect the future of peasant communities and of the agrarian societies of which they are a neglected part?

After initial field investigations, staff members of the Cornell Thailand, India, Peru, and Navaho projects worked together in a series of seminars dealing with the problems of cultural transfer, cultural continuity, and cultural change. Cases were collected and analyzed for their relevance to the problems of facilitating the introduction of agricultural, industrial, medical, and other innovations into areas where such technologies were wanted but were deficient by modern standards (Spicer 1952). Training and research seminars in cultural anthropology were conducted among the various cultures of the American Southwest for American and foreign social science students and those trained in technological or natural science fields (Bunker and Adair 1959). Common reference points and strategies were developed for the cross-cultural study of change (Goodenough 1963) and programs of experimental intervention were proposed for the areas with which we were concerned (Smith 1951, 1955). A manual for field workers was prepared in order to guide program participants in the common problems of observing and recording cultural change (Leighton and Sharp 1952).

In 1948, with the aid of the Thai Ministry of Agriculture, Sharp had visited many village communities in the economically important rice-producing central plain between Ayutthayā and the Gulf of Siam. It became clear that, given the information, resources, and background data available at the time, a large-scale survey meeting scientific sampling and other statistical criteria could not be successfully undertaken. Under these conditions, Sharp decided that the changing behavior of rural Thai could best be studied in selected rural communities viewed in relation to their surrounding areas and the national society. For his own work, he wished to find a village engaged primarily in commercial rice cultivation which was predominantly and actively Buddhist and which would be increasingly subject to influences from the capital, Bangkok, which for over a century and a half had been a principal channel for the introduction and transmission to the Thai people of new techniques, forms of social organization, and ideas. Bang Chan seemed to meet these criteria and, in addition, to promise excellent cooperation on the part of both farmers and officials of the region, a promise that was fully realized.

With the assistance of Kamol Janlekha, the first Thai trained in agricultural economics, the study of Bang Chan began in September 1948. At the same time, the Cornell Thailand Project was able to provide financial and other support to John deYoung and Singto Metah for a comparative study of the northern village of San Pong, near Chiengmai.

Rice produced by the farmers of Bang Chan and San Pong which was not locally consumed was then being purchased by the Thai government at its own price for resale as a form of indirect taxation of the producer; yet no Thai official knew what it cost a farm family to produce a ton of padi, or unhusked rice (Silcock 1970). Except for Janlekha, there were no agricultural economists in Thailand, and few economists of any kind, to work on rural development problems. Indeed, before 1948 no one had conducted long-term detailed research in any single Thai farming community. This does not mean that valuable data on various aspects of Thai culture were not available. For nearly fifty years the pages of the *Journal of the Siam Society* had presented learned observations on folklore, history, numismatics, the arts, and other topics, contributed by eminent Thai and foreign scholars. Ten generations of Catholic missionaries and four Protestant generations had produced extensive accounts of Thai life. Travelers' observations in Thai or Western and Chinese languages had yielded further descriptions of the Thai cultural scene, as had the memoirs and records of diplomats and merchants. The Thai government had even employed two foreigners in the early 1930s to conduct rural economic surveys of the country. But Westerners who through command of the language had access to documentary material in Thai were rare; and Thai scholars were few and overmodest. All of these ante bellum writers, with their varied skills and interests, contributed significant data for those seeking to know how Thai behaved and why; but following the Pacific war of 1941–1945, a need for studies of village communities and of their relations to their regions and to the larger polity and society of Thailand became only too evident.

In Bang Chan, with the cordial help of the villagers, almost a year was devoted to the gathering of basic information by the first two investigators, Sharp and Janlekha, who were joined in midcourse for five months by Metah from the north when deYoung left San Pong. From time to time Thai government officials and students visited Bang Chan and some participated for short periods in certain aspects of the field research. A village schoolmaster, Khru Jāud, kept a diary in which he recorded local events from an inside view as he experienced them or heard of them. Paddling up and down the several miles of village canals, the interviewers talked informally with villagers, listened as villagers talked with each other, observed and took part in daily activities, collected copious genealogies, and completed schedules for a sample of over a hundred farm households to provide information on the technology and economics of rice production and distribution and related activities. Many of the findings of this first year of work were published (see Sharp 1967).

In 1952 a new phase of multiple studies began in Bang Chan as Sharp introduced to the community several more specialists and students, Lucien and Jane Hanks among them. Also in Bangkok and elsewhere in the country, students associated with the Cornell Thailand Project had embarked on a series of studies that would help place Bang Chan in a setting of other villages, other ethnic groups, and the nation at large. However rice farmers may have been affected by these contacts, Thai village and related studies proliferated and perhaps profited as a beginning was made and reports on the work of the project were prepared for publication. Articles, monographs, and doctoral dissertations dealt from a local or national point of view with such topics as national economic policy, government, social organization, education, religion, health, nutrition, child welfare, personality, and history; neighboring and distant village communities were studied for comparison and contrast, and studies of ethnic minorities, including the Thai-Islam and the ubiquitous Chinese were produced (Sharp 1967).

In a large and diversified storage compartment for unpublished material on Bang Chan lay our notes for a book on social change. We used the 1948–1949 study as a base for viewing the new that was appearing monthly in the community. This base served admirably in handling certain economic or technological subjects. Sharp could vouch for the number of new radios, electric generators, fiberglass taxi boats with outboard motors, and home enterprises; similarly government services formerly unavailable could be charted as they appeared during the period of observation. Some changes in consumer habits lent themselves to such quantifying treatment; and there were other areas of life in which change could be documented.

But there were also important aspects of Bang Chan cultural behavior in which the presence or absence of change was difficult or impossible to identify in a short time. How could it be determined whether or not there was an increasing secularization of life or an increasing differentiation between the religious and the secular; or whether there were changes in the internal power structure of the village, or in family structure and kin relations? As Sharp worked through the genealogies obtained in 1949, changes in kinship organization failed to appear, but it could not be determined whether or not crucial data were missing. In dealing with education, Hanks found himself unable to detect much more than incidental change in Bang Chan's primary school without tracing education back at least as far as 1935, when the central government first erected a school building. A search for changes in the temple took one back even further, for in 1901 certain priests of the local temple began serving as teachers in a nationally organized education system. Gradually the dates of refer ence receded backward from 1949 to 1892, the year in which the Bang Chan temple was first founded. From this point, an attempt to add a few more decades to the village history seemed well worth the effort, and we resolved to trace Bang Chan as far back in time as possible. Sharp's data from 1949 suggested that we might have to go back at least a century. A return to the village in 1957 for further historical data supplied many missing items and a fairly continuous history that dates back to the 1840s and 1850s, when the first settlement occurred on the present site of Bang Chan.

The Destination

The venture upon which we embark in this study is to be called *social history*. The label best fits our plan to consider miscellaneous actions, happenings, or events in a temporal sequence. A broader frame might masquerade as the "evolution" of Bang Chan, but with less than twelve decades in the record the label becomes absurd. Were there a central character or even a central theme, continuity might suffice to dub this a biography of Bang Chan, but the implication of a structured maturation misrepresents this amorphous community. History presumes a less artful approach and the freedom to be discontinuous.

The continuities and regularities of an individual's life history, the patterned growth or development of a biography, are implicit in the folk-urban model, which sees the cities of agrarian societies growing out of tribal or peasant villages and continuing to be nourished by their surrounding rural countrysides. This scheme, which sees an urban type of civilization born from a folk culture, hardly applies in our case. Bang Chan is the unwanted child of Bangkok, not its rustic parent. Secondary urbanization, some aspects of the great and little tradition, the urbanizing spread of progress (Redfield 1962:326–356) approximate the Thai scene well enough; and Bang Chan inhabitants are peasants according to most of Redfield's definitions (1956:27–34). However, the polarity between the city and the village becomes in the central rice plain of Thailand a flow between Bangkok and Bang Chan. Having come from the city, the residents fish for a while, then grow rice, then grow it commercially in response to urban demand, and eventually return to the city as it engulfs them, having entered and then retired from peasantry. Occupations change continuously: so when people fish, we call them fishermen; when they grow rice, farmers; when they keep stores, storekeepers; and when they move to Bangkok, or Bangkok moves to them, they are city folk again. The patterns offered by the folk-urban schema furnish only limited aid to understanding, while history allows our data more freedom to show the shape of local change.

Calling our venture *social history* also raises problems, for historians pride themselves on the scrupulous use of documents. Bang Chan has few, and most of them were never consulted. A visit to the district office in Minburī revealed a thousand neatly tied bundles of yellowing land deeds. In the deeds were listed changes of ownership that had long been forgotten in Bang Chan, but more serious for our study were the transfers of ownership that were acknowledged in Bang Chan but unrecorded at the district office. Some land disputes and criminal actions reached the district courts, and the court record might have offered interesting data that witnesses in Bang Chan had forgotten; but we lacked the clerical staff of translators to deal with these records. The notebooks of hamlet headmen helped us begin our census counts but were often unreliable on births and deaths and who lived where. Aside from the notebooks of a few traditional doctors or curers (*māu*), documents were hard to find, even though many people were literate. In that community the written word was not important. Farmers never drew up agreements that determined a continuous, inescapable obligation. People contracted with each other, but the agreement needed constant mutual effort and care to keep it alive. When a party to an agreement failed to meet its implicit or explicit terms, the agreement ended. It was unwise to contract with untrustworthy persons. Bang Chan's past could not be traced through the contents of mildewed envelopes in musty storage chests. It had to be found, if at all, in the spoken word.

For precedent to call our study history, perhaps we must turn back to such primitive practitioners as Herodotus. They, too, accepted stories by witnesses and by witnesses of witnesses, using their best judgment to validate a statement, but often being unable to affirm or deny its accuracy. When finished with this gathering of tales, they wrote what they had learned about the attributes of a given people or event. This was history, and we too shall tell what we have learned from the stories told to us by our village friends about Bang Chan's past.

At best, however, this guise fits the modern social scientist awkwardly. In the classical accounts of foreign peoples certain naivetés inevitably appear, for those historians spoke a foreign language, if at all, with a heavy Greek accent. When identical words appeared in their own and another language, they were unaware that the meaning might have changed. When made aware, rather than recognize a variant usage, they condemned the barbarian stupidity. Idioms were rarely understood in their efforts to make literal translations. They thought always in their mother tongues. Their accounts would fail to meet the standards of a world better skilled in empathy, semantics, and linguistics.

Today our account of what happened poses other problems. While we have become accustomed to cognates and idioms, much still resists translation. Two languages may offer no exact equivalents, and approximate substitution rubs away the richness of the original. Thus we might translate the Near East tabu on eating pork into a fear of disease; something of the horror is captured, but the overtone of nauseous contamination is missed. More context is needed to make the word as well as the custom meaningful. So the ethnographer does not translate but seeks to convey the world together with something of the language that goes with it. Then the untranslatable becomes understood without need for translation.

Yet the problem of balancing the equation has only shifted. The ethnographer still must address his audience, which now expects to be transposed vicariously. He wears a mask that enables him to perceive a world through the eyes of an alien people. Through the mouth of the mask come familiar words describing what he sees. He begins with curious tales of the rice goddess and her pregnancy, which produces rice; he tells of disease caused by spirit possession and its cure by exorcism. All this is accepted well enough, but when he says these foreigners live only in the present and have no history, the audience grows restless. Someone shouts into the ears of his mask, "Why, they must have history! Everybody has history. They have culture inherited from their parents and grandparents, don't they? Ask them whether they do the same things as their parents."

Through the mask the ethnographer replies, "Yes, they say they do many things in the same way their parents do. Other things they do quite differently. They say it depends."

"That proves it," asserts the skeptic. "They have continuity with the past just as we ourselves cannot escape our forebears."

Then the ethnographer adds, "They say, though, that they pick what they wish from the past, learning only that. Parents do not give them anything automatically. They have to ask parents for what they wish. The elder generation gives only upon request. If no one asks for this or that, it simply disappears and is forgotten."

The skeptic is still dissatisfied. "They just don't realize what they have received from their past. Ask them about their language, their agricultural rites. They didn't even notice these things."

"They admit having the same language as their parents," the ethnographer reports. "They learned it from their parents before they could really choose. It was useful so they kept on speaking it. If they moved to another country, it would not be useful. They would have to learn another. As for agricultural rites, no one bothers to learn about them unless he needs them for farming."

The skeptic, however, remains unconvinced, still muttering, "Whether they know it or not, they have continuity with the past. So they have history."

In such a dialogue, we return to the same ontological problems that the classical historians faced. While they assured skeptical audiences that distant people were human beings with barbarian attributes, so we seek to make clear that Bang Chan farmers can be rational, normal human beings and still have no history. How can we and the classical historian convince an audience?

The chief differences lie in the paradoxes and conflicts that result from our urge for empathy. Before their audiences the classical historians did not worry about misjudging an alien people or failing to convey some subtle meaning. If Herodotus reported that the Massegetae drank blood, anyone in Greece knew they were ignorant barbarians. That ended the matter. Today the ethnographer presumes that all people act as normally and rationally as any other. His experience from living months or years with a people convinces him. As for the Massegetae, our contemporaries would be constrained to explain perhaps that these people considered blood a source of needed vitality, or that blood substituted for scarce water. He excuses their distasteful customs by showing their utility. When people lack history, the ethnographer assumes the normality of this lack. However, he stands between the contradictions of two worlds with rational people in both. When he writes a history of a people without history he has imposed a judgment of his own culture on the scene, which he thus distorts as much as when he offers a poor translation of a phrase.

While one people may feel as confident of the existence of history as of the existence of their own minds and bodies, this does not guarantee its reality. History, like demonology and witchcraft, can never be demonstrated to another people unprepared to admit its existence. The proofs serve to convince only those already convinced. He who habitually thinks with another set of symbols cannot communicate. In this sense history is a "collective idea" of certain peoples. An ethnographer with doubts about the existence of history is not acting in good faith when he frames his observations of society as history.

Another may argue that the existence of history is irrelevant. Nevertheless, its presence as a collective idea may influence reactions to the new as well as to the old. Bang Chan farmers may establish the uniqueness of their generation by selecting only what they "wish" from the coffers of the older generation. This may give them greater flexibility in meeting the new than is given to other people who sense the past pressing heavily upon their shoulders. At least, here is a hypothesis to be tested, even if many years lie ahead in Bang Chan and elsewhere before the test can be made.

These unanswered and perhaps unanswerable questions indicate our timidity and self-consciousness in this undertaking. The classic historians, however, furnish us with bracing examples of dauntlessness. Their travels along unguarded routes took a great deal more courage than an hour's bus ride to Bang Chan. Their innocent judgments rendered their work no less valuable. Our last count of historians done away with by their critics shows the number to be small. So we approach twelve decades of Bang Chan aware that time and history may exist only in the heads of some men, and may be dim or absent in other heads. Nonetheless, we shall impose on our findings our own chronological ordering along with our assumptions of temporal flow from past to present. If the remainder of our judgments be made as innocently as those of the classical historians, we shall have at least described what appeared to happen.

CHAPTER 2

The Dispensable Ones

We may think of Thailand's central plain as a rectangle measuring some 235 by 120 miles with its long axis running north and south.[1] Down the middle of this flat surface cuts the mother of waters, the Māc Nām, running from the northern hills to the mudbanks of the south, where her waters cross into the Gulf of Siam.[2] Like a good mother, she sends her water to nourish everything along her course. Each year in flood she renews the gray-black soil of the plain for many miles to east and west with a fresh layer of silt. Before these plains became a succession of padi fields, her waters revived the tall grasses and canes along her banks and tributaries, as well as the bushy thickets of the scrub jungle found on somewhat higher ground (LS 10/22/48).[3] In the bottoms of pools dried, baked, and hardened in the hot season, her floodwaters restored the green of desiccated vegetation at the edges and stirred the vitality of the fish hibernating in the moist clay beneath.[4] As ponds filled with water from rains as well as floods, elephant and deer herds, together with the tigers that always follow, moved out again from the hills on the horizon to fresh pasture in the plains. Then the weaverbirds could build their nests in the thickets and cranes moved inland from the riverbanks and seashore in search of fish.[5] Here the pause in the annual cycle, caused in temperate zones by cold, is caused by tropical monsoon heat.

Human residents of the plain were scarce before 1850. An occasional group of Khā hunters dwelt on the edge of some permanent pond, dibbling a patch of rice on its bank, but most such hunting groups preferred the uplands.[6] The Thai clung to the main watercourses, avoiding the plains between. They even named the plain east of Bangkok Sāen Sāeb, or 100,000 Stings, hence a wilderness to be avoided. The mosquitoes and scorpions mattered less, however, than the inconstant water supply, for the water that flowed so

abundantly for seven or eight months across the entire plain all but
vanished for the rest of the year. Of course, a family might have
stored enough in big earthen jars to last through the dry season, but
the Thai found it far more convenient to dip water from a river as
needed. Besides, the larger rivers afforded daily fishing and bathing
throughout the year. Along the riverbanks, with many neighbors at
one's side, the Thai could live without fear that elephants would
trample a house or flatten a garden. So they built their houses and
moored their boats along the rivers, and rarely did anyone venture
the twenty miles or so from the capital city out into the plains toward
Bang Chan's present site.

These central Thai had adapted their living to the water. Sir John
Bowring, with pleasant memories of the scene where he successfully
concluded a commercial treaty, described his approach to Bangkok
in 1855:

But the houses thicken as you proceed; the boats increase in number; the
noise of voices becomes louder; and one after another temples, domes, and
palaces are seen towering above the gardens and forests. . . . On both sides
of the river a line of floating bazaars crowded with men, women and
children, and houses built on piles along the banks, present all objects of
consumption or commerce. Meanwhile multitudes of ambulatory boats are
engaged in traffic with various groups around. If it be morning, vast
numbers of priests will be seen in their skiffs on the Meinam with their iron
pots and scripts, levying their contributions of food from the well-known
devotees. [Bowring 1857, 1:392–393]

Not a road but a river served as the avenue for travel and trade as well
as the source of food and domestic water and the catchall for waste.
Had Bowring remained a few weeks longer, he would have witnessed boatloads of merry people dousing each other with water at
the New Year's Festival (Song Krān). In the full moon of May on the
Lord Buddha's birthday (Wisākhabūchā) he would have seen all the
temples on the shores aglow with lanterns. In November on the
night of Lāūj Krathong he would have seen the water itself illuminated by thousands of miniature boats bearing candles and sins
down toward the sea. Over these waters moved also the king with his
mighty officials and soldiers in caparisoned barges and swiftly paddled men-of-war.

After the excitement of Bangkok, most early travelers along the
river seem to have been bored by the monotonous succession of
gardens, padi fields, and clusters of houses. Monsignor Jean Baptiste
Pallegoix (1854:84–97) was always relieved on his trips during the

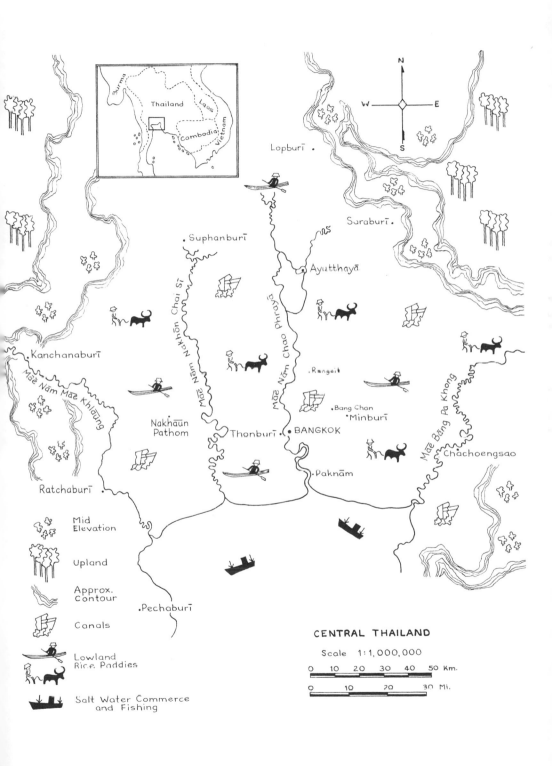

CENTRAL THAILAND

Scale 1:1,000,000

Mid Elevation

Upland

Approx. Contour

Canals

Lowland Rice Paddies

Salt Water Commerce and Fishing

1830s and 1840s to find a pleasant town of four to six thousand souls where life was not quite so dull as in the river villages. Two decades later, Adolf Bastian (1867:20–48) headed downstream and later remembered chiefly the villages where he showed his pass to a hospitable governor or stopped to spend the night near a few thatched houses. People of this region, too, lived facing the river with their backs to the forbidding plain.[7]

Whether or not the Thai scene appealed to Europeans, residents were happy to have peace. By the time of King Rama III (1824–1851), little more than two generations had lived along the Māē Nām since the last invasion by a foreign army. This peace had begun when Phrayā Tāksin (1768–1782) reestablished the Thai state after the Burmese sack of Ayutthayā and regained the vassal principalities of the north. His successor, King Rama I (1782–1809), then founded the capital at Bangkok, drove the Burmans from the western and southern provinces, and held them in check along the western hills (Hall 1955:389–399). Subsequent friction with the British gave the Burmans little time or strength to reengage the Thai. On the other hand, the British at Penang also disturbed the flow of tribute from the Malay rajahs to Bangkok, and there the maintenance of Thai sovereignty continued to be a problem into the second half of the nineteenth century (Hall 1955:443–452; Vella 1957:59–77). Yet these matters to the south scarcely disturbed the peace of the center.

A much more serious threat came from the east, where the unified and aggressive Vietnamese were contending for sovereignty over the intervening states (Hall 1955:372–375; Vella 1957:111–112). Though the kings of Cambodia tried to prevent invasion by sending tribute both to Hué and Bangkok, any move that might be interpreted as favorable to the other power was answered with threatened invasion by the affronted rival. The contest also concerned the Laotian principalities to the northeast, where secret missions proffered military aid to the vassal who would revolt. From Luang Prabāng through Vientiane and Xieng Khouang to Phnom Penh the country was uneasy (Hall 1955:400–401; Vella 1957:94–118; Wyatt 1963).

Rama III turned to fortifying the east. A chain of forts was erected and cities were hastily fortified; the naval arm was strengthened with new ships; soldiers were drafted to man the defenses (Thiphakarawong 1934b:246). A plan was devised to make these eastern forts more accessible to Bangkok by connecting the Māe Nām river system with the Bāng Pa Kong River, which drains the eastern borderlands. A connecting canal would save the defenders at least two days in reaching such points as Battambāng and Siemreap, for instead of following three sides of a rectangle, they would have a direct route without exposure to winds and tides. The *Chronicle of the Third Reign* relates for 1837:

Moving to the second month on the fourth day of the rising moon, his Majesty decreed that Phrayā Srīphiphat Rātanarātchakosa become director and hire Chinese to dig a canal from Huamāk to Bāng Khanak of 1,337 sen, 19 wā, 2 sok in length, 6 sok in depth, and 6 wā in width [about 34 miles in length, 10 feet deep, 40 feet in width]. . . . The digging was not completed until the year of the Rat, the second year of the decade, 1202 of the Sakrād [1840/41]. [Thiphakarawong 1934b:179][8]

This canal, which then ran through the plain to the east of the capital, was known as Sāen Sāeb (Thiphakarawong 1934a:70). Every basket of clay carried up from the oozing pit on the back of a Chinese coolie and dumped upon the dyke was accompanied by the bites, nips, and stings of the myriad creatures living along the way. The pains of some five thousand hired Chinese transformed the wasteland of the 100,000 Stings into a land for living.

Both Rama III and his famous successor, Rama IV (1851-1868), encouraged the settling of this region. At a point west of where a little rivulet, now known as Bang Chan canal, entered Sāen Sāeb canal, a parcel of 2,000 *rai* (800 acres) of land was given to an august member of the Bunnag family. Probably this land was given by King Rama III to Chao Phrayā Phraklāng (Dit Bunnag), who had served with distinction as foreign minister, and indeed had functioned also as prime minister (Bowring 1857, 1:441). Among his many services, Chao Phrayā Phraklāng had helped restore the sovereignty of Bangkok over the Malay provinces of the south; after suppressing a last major rebellion in Kedah and Kelantan in 1839/40, he had returned in triumph with many prisoners of war (Vella 1957:67-69; Thiphakarawong 1934b:118-119). The king turned over a number of the prisoners to him as a reward for his services, and they became retainers for his estates.[9] Then when he or his son, Chao Phrayā Srīsurijawong (Chuang Bunnag), prime minister under Rama IV, wished to settle people on his fief, these former prisoners of war or their descendants were moved to the new land. The people in

question were Moslems "from Saiburī" (presumably Kedah or Kelantan), and some of their descendants still live today on the land
where their forebears had settled (LS 12/31/48; LMH 9/18/57). They
report that His Excellency directed them to dig a mound above the
floodwaters and build him a residence. At the same time they were to
construct huts in the vicinity, and to raise garden produce and
animals to feed their master during his periodic visits. Perhaps his
house bore some resemblance to another country residence of Chao
Phrayā Srīsurijawong which Carl Bock reached late one night in
1881:

After an hour's absence he [the servant] returned with a servant of the
second governor who told me that the first governor was at Radburi on a
visit to the ex-Regent, whose summer palace was at my disposal—a white
washed building on the wall of which was a tablet with English letters
engraved as follows, "His Excellency the Prime Minister of Siam. A.D.
1861." It was a small building of two stories, a very modest residence for so
wealthy and great a man; and judging by the dilapidated state it was in, it
could not have been inhabited for years. The staircase was almost eaten up
by white ants, and the air inside was foul, as if the windows had not been
opened for ages. [Bock 1884:81]

For some years, we are told, the prime minister came to his residence
near Bang Chan. Later he seems to have come infrequently. His
descendants did not use the house, and it gradually crumbled.
Today there remains only the mound known as the Governor's
Mound (Khōk Chuan) alongside the lotus pond formed when the
earth was removed (LMH 8/18/57), with fields owned by a landlord
known as Nāj Chyd Bunnag (KJ 9/12/49).

   Near this point a group of Laotian prisoners of war was settled by
the "second king" (wāng nā or uparād) under Rama IV, who seems
also to have assisted the move to populate the region. The then
second king had taken an active part in the rebellion at Vientiane in
1828 and returned with many prisoners of war (Vella 1957:83–84).
After being forced to witness the punishment of their leaders, they
began a new life as slaves in various palaces (LMH 11/31/53, 7/16/
57). After twenty or more years of life in Bangkok, some of these
people were moved out of the city to build a village on the banks of
Sāen Sāeb canal and to maintain themselves with rice grown in the
lowland behind their houses (LMH 7/6/57, 7/22/57, 7/23/57). Not far
from them a second village of Moslem prisoners of war was also

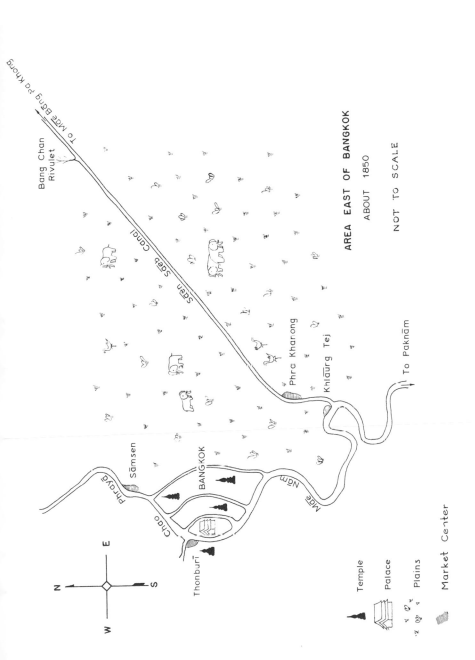

AREA EAST OF BANGKOK

ABOUT 1850

NOT TO SCALE

Temple

Palace

Plains

Market Center

begun. So the banks of Sāen Sāeb canal were populated under royal direction. We believe all these settlements were made between 1841 and the middle 1850s.[10]

From City to Wilderness

In the 1850s one could follow the east bank of the Māe Nām a mile or so upstream from the grand palace in Bangkok and reach a small suburb of a few hundred houses called Sāmsen. Here the river was thick with sampans, large sailing barges, and junks from across the sea. Even at that time the main handlers of commerce were Chinese, and we may infer that a sizable portion of Sāmsen's residents were Chinese. William Skinner observed, "It is perhaps significant that the oldest and largest Hainanese temple in Bangkok is located in Samsen near the old wharf from which all upriver traffic begins" (1957:84). Skinner further suggests (p. 136) some of the activities of Sāmsen in describing the Hainanese: "[They] were hand sawyers, market gardeners, fishermen, domestic servants, waiters, tea shop operators, and, not infrequently, coolies, miners, and peddlers. They were the poorest of all the [Chinese] speech groups, and their general low standing was undisputed."

The first resident of the area we know today as Bang Chan came from Sāmsen (LMH 7/30/57). His name was Chāem. He grew up in a Sāmsen family with two older brothers and an older sister. Our records tell us only that his mother was a gardener, though whether she grew rice or was a market gardener is not specified. The father is not mentioned at all. Possibly he was a Chinese immigrant who married a Thai and gardened or fished for a living. When the oldest boy was a young man, the father died or disappeared, leaving the mother with no land to work (JRH 2/18/54).

We do not know how long the family remained in Sāmsen after the father's disappearance, but before long the eldest son moved out with his wife, his mother, and a younger brother along the newly opened Sāen Sāeb canal. The sister married and settled with her husband in Sāmsen, where she is said to have become rich and thereafter visited her kinsmen in the country. Chāem, the youngest, married and moved in with his wife's parents, who were also gardeners (JRH 2/18/54). He did not remain in the city long; within a few years Chāem set off with his wife and mother-in-law along Sāen Sāeb canal.

To go from Sāmsen to Sāen Sāeb canal required going down the Māe Nām to Phra Khanong, below Bangkok, where the larger boats entered. Yet there may also have been a more direct route via such smaller waterways as the Sāmsen and Bāngkapi canals.[11] Once on the broad canal, the boat must have paused to visit at the hut where Chāem's brothers and their mother were living, yet he chose not to stay long with them. Turning north from the main canal into a rivulet, he passed the country residence of Chao Phrayā Srīsurijawong, where in the hot season the going must have been difficult because of weeds.[12] A part of the stream was so jammed with vegetable debris that the water itself ran underground (LS 12/31/48). There Chāem dug a channel through tangled roots and mud a foot or two thick in order to slide his boat along. Subsequent heavy rains and floods would wash the stream bed clear down to the old clay base. Near a point where the sluggish stream branched, he found a slight rise and stopped there. This spot offered a natural mound that might stay dry a little longer than surrounding areas during the floods. Besides, he would have at least two streams for fishing, and with the Moslem village downstream and the Khā hunters to the east, he would not be cut off entirely from human association.

As the new settlers unloaded their basket of milled rice, cooking pots, and sleeping mats in an opening where the tall dry grasses stood, a house was one of the least of their problems. In a few hours Chāem with his sword could cut enough bamboo from the nearby thicket for the frame, while the two women gathered and peeled rattan-like canes to bind the pieces together. Some rushes (*prȳ*) formed the roof and walls. Inside, a platform of bamboo provided a sleeping place above the dirt floor and the coming floods.[13] All could be built in two days; and the following year they would know how high to heap up the soil for a more permanent mound. Nor was food a problem. The rice would not last until they had harvested their first crop, but they could trade some of the abundant fish for more. Fuel for the fire was everywhere, and when the rains came, plants could be gathered to eat with the rice and fish.

Their problem, the problem of all handcraft subsistence economies, was to husband and manage their labor to meet daily needs through the annual cycle and at the same time to make life more efficient and comfortable. For instance, during the dry season a

Bang Chan canal
Photo by Lauriston Sharp

woman might fish, if there were a basket-like cone (*sum*) to plunge
into the mud. Then she could seize a wriggling fish through the open
end and toss it into a second basket in which the catch was collected.
Yet it took most of four days to cut, prepare the reeds, and weave two
such baskets. It was equally important, before the rains came, to cut
and then burn the brush of a small patch of land for the rice plot and
clear away the gnarled roots of grass and weeds, and at least a week of
work was required for three people to prepare the soil properly with
hoes. When the rains came and the seed that had been planted with a
dibble stick began to grow, there still remained weeds to pull, and
when the grain was almost ready for harvest, someone might have to
stand guard all day with a pellet bow to drive away the weaverbirds
from the ripening crop. Then came the tiring though joyful work of

harvesting, threshing, winnowing, and milling before a single mouthful was ready for cooking.[14]

Before any of this could be done, one had to have harvesting and threshing tools; at least one winnowing tray, preferably two or three, to carry and clean the grain; baskets to hold it; a mortar and pestle for pounding off the husks; and a place built for dry storage through the year. For such equipment weeks more of labor must be invested. In the meantime, four hours a day were constantly required for one person to gather the fuel, strike the spark, coax the fire, carry the water, and boil the rice dry enough for eating.[15] Then during the first year when the padi supply ran low, all hands had to turn to for extra days of fishing before sending one person with a boatload to the nearest market. It would take at least a day, probably two, before the boatman returned, for the neighboring people had plenty of fish, and the best place to trade was in Bangkok. All these activities dealt with subsistence and had little to do with acquiring textiles and pottery or such comforts as a sleeping mat, a headrest, fish soy for a more savory meal, even an oil lamp for an emergency at night.

In some twelve-odd hours of tropical daylight, three able adults were none too many to make a bare living in this out-of-the-way spot. Of these working days, many were reduced in effectiveness by fevers, storms, and accidents. A single elephant could trample the rice patch flat; a single storm could blow the house down. The provision of labor, not of material resources, was the problem; and it is no wonder that an enduring tradition developed that material wealth in Bang Chan should be measured not in material possessions, but in the number of productive workers included in a household over a long term (LS 12/31/48). One might gamble labor in hand against the promise of future labor. Chaēm gambled but without great success, for only six of his fourteen children survived to maturity.

Economics, the Social Order, and Kinship

We may pause in our narrative to ask how one person might acquire the labor of others in this part of the world. The question is pertinent in view of the scarcity of workers, and we may wonder why Chaēm and his brothers failed to share their labor. Cooperation would seem to have been the obvious solution for their needs; then all might have lived somewhat more comfortably than they did in that array of separate households in which only parents, spouses, and children shared the rewards of joint labor. Our answers must be drawn from generalities concerning the organization of Thai society and the kinship system as well as the economic scene.

To acquire labor in Thailand, then as now, one simply offered certain working conditions and rewards in return for the services that one sought. In Chāem's day a householder or an employer might offer only food, lodging, and clothing for a domestic servant, a waiter in a teahouse, or a hand on a fishing boat. In return the offspring, the widowed mother-in-law, or the employee would be available any time he or she was needed. If one wished time off, he would ask for it or find a substitute. A married man might ask his wife or child to carry on during his absence; an older child might ask a younger. Should working conditions look more favorable elsewhere because of fewer demands or more adequate living conditions, the employee, the still capable parent, or the child past adolescence might announce his intention to leave. If the head of the house or employer wished him to stay, some of the duties might be shifted to another person or other rearrangements made to relieve him.

Here are no ethnological mysteries. The system has the familiar shape of Adam Smith's free enterprise: each person bargains in the open market for the best arrangement he can make, and if this is not satisfactory, he may move elsewhere. An employer invests food, clothing, and shelter in return for services. An employer's investments vary in the amount invested, the risk involved, the time before a return can be expected, and of course the amount of return. A parent asks a child to carry the teacups to the restaurant next door or a faithful servant to take the family gold to the goldsmith. A boat owner lends his sampan to a neighbor for an afternoon's fishing or his seagoing junk for a trip to China. Thereby he has fished or made the trip to China, and these labors will be approximately rewarded. In this market, labor, services, and goods flow between related people rather than between institutions. A principal feature of Thai society is the ubiquity of this kind of transaction, and the ease with which relationships can be broken off.

A parent considers his children in somewhat the same way an employer views his workers. Bearing and bringing up children are troublesome, particularly for the mother, and parents look forward to a return for their trouble. A Bang Chan woman said, "Having children is a lot of trouble. Babies are afraid of noises and cry a lot.

Some say having no children is comfortable; some say that having none is bad because there will be no one to feed parents when they are old." Another observed, "Nāng Jū never married. It was too much trouble to have children. Unmarried persons live all right. She is living with a younger brother and a girl on her parents' land" (JRH 2/12/54).

At each stage of growth, farm children begin a new chore commensurate with their mounting strength. They carry wood, tend the buffaloes, and bring in sheaves of grain from the field to the threshing floor; when fully grown, a girl may plow while a boy uproots rice seedlings. A farmer's moment of greatest pleasure and profit comes when all of his children are working at home in his fields. This is the return on a parent's investment. In adopting a child, a man declared, "I want a girl for cooking, a boy for farmwork, and later to be ordained into the priesthood" (JRH 12/18/53). The return on a parent's investment is about right when a twenty-one-year-old son, after a youth of farmwork, enters the priesthood. Parents thus give one of their valuable workers to the temple and gain merit for a better existence in their next incarnation. Should a son leave home before coming of age and without entering the priesthood, the returns are thin. Should he become a priest, then resign from the priesthood and return home to work again for his parents, the return is more ample than expected. One looks forward to a daughter's labor until marriage and the "milk money" that her husband or his parents pay her mother for the milk that the bride once drank at her mother's breast. If she marries young or elopes, the return is small; if she brings a husband into the home to help with the work, the return increases.

On these long and risky investments, parents try to increase their security. They bury the umbilical cord and placenta under the house to keep the child from "wandering" (*paj thiaw*). Disobedient children are told that someone will come and take them away from their homes. Adolescents are constantly admonished to stay at home and not wander: "If a boy wanders, and his friends invite him to do wrong, he agrees at fifteen or sixteen because he is too young [to know right from wrong]. Better not wander. But sometimes he disobeys and goes. Parents do nothing but murmur and grumble a lot. If a girl wanders, people will gossip; she is meeting a boy" (JRH 6/17/53). Under these circumstances, wandering always hints at delinquency.

Another device to counter the risk that children may leave home occurs during the topknot-cutting ceremony and the ordination for the priesthood, when songs may be sung concerning the pains the candidate has caused his parents: "[At birth your mother] is losing her soul and feels so frightened, despairing, and suffering that she throws herself up and down as if her mind were badly wounded by the poisoned arrow of a hunter. She is uneasy and moans loudly as if a big mountain had fallen upon her. She does not think of her pain but tries to save your life. You are grown up by her affection and care . . ." (SS 5/18/54). The child to whom this song is addressed, even the young man of twenty-one, is overcome by emotion and is likely to break into tears, though a few minutes later they may be dried by laughter at a comic interlude: the singer improvises a song about a troublesome child who will not stop crying; the child refuses food, he does not want to be held in his mother's arms, no distraction works, the parents are desperate, and the child finally stops when he accidentally finds a bottle of Pepsi-Cola.

The child may be an asset to be transferred for a longer or shorter period as a favor to another person. So children are passed to grandparents, who may be lonely, or to some aunt or uncle who wants an extra hand to watch a two-year-old during harvest week.[16]

Children who become liabilities may be given away: "Her parents were very poor hired laborers and had many children. That girl was always sick, so her parents came to me and offered her to me. I felt pity for her and accepted her. She cooked before and after school and helped generally" (JRH 12/18/53). Delinquent or sickly boys (and healthy ones too) may be given to the local temple; as temple boys (*dek wat*) they serve the priests their meals, accompany them on their daily rounds, and may be cured of their failings by association with the benign temple.

If we glance again at the household of Chāēm's parents, we are able to understand something of the difficulty experienced by Chāēm and his brother in uniting cooperatively. Chāēm's father's death or disappearance ended the usual tacit parent-child arrangement. Dead men give no favors, so all the children were free to go their ways. The father's valuables were simply divided equally among the surviving children. There remained behind no vacant seat or office to be filled, for there was no corporate body, only an aggregate of implied contracts between individuals. Hence there could be neither succession nor inheritance of rights and property. Each interested party began anew with whatever assets he might have received from other survivors, children normally dividing the dead parent's property in equal shares.[17]

The same principle of investment reappears in the relations between siblings. The older provides the younger with favors and expects a return in services. Though the contract is unverbalized, its form is quite clear. If Chaem's older sister acted as many older sisters still do in Bang Chan, she carried him many a day on her hip to the Sāmsen market, bought a cowrie shell's worth of sweets, and gave most of them to him. Later some afternoon at home he might reciprocate by fetching a coconut shell of water for her to drink and by rubbing her back as she lay stretched on a mat. Chaem's eldest brother probably took the younger one to a shadow play in the market and the next day directed him to load the boat with fishing gear. A Bang Chan man described life with his younger brothers and sisters this way: "When I said something, my younger brothers listened to me and believed me, and they never argued with me. . . . Before telling them to do any kind of work, I first thought: 'That person ought to do that'; 'this person ought to do this.' Therefore there is nothing about which to have any conflict. . . . Whenever there was entertainment somewhere, I took them with me. My younger siblings loved me a lot" (HPP 7/22/57).

Though the favors and services vary widely from day to day, even five-year-olds may feel the responsibility of providing benefits and may work hard to favor a younger one. Because a child's ability to grant favors is limited, he or she can usually hold the allegiance of only one younger child, and so children in a family tend to form into pairs of adjacently aged siblings. On the other hand, disobedience is usually the responsibility of the younger: "If my children quarrel, I see who is wrong. If the younger boy or girl is wrong, I beat them; if it is the older boy or girl, I do not beat them. This is to prevent the younger ones from not respecting the older ones. Also I teach the younger ones always to say phī [in addressing the older]. The older girl and the older boy get the same respect, and they should protect their younger brothers and sisters" (JRH 7/7/53).[18] These are not only the normal ways of acting; they are felt to be the necessary ways to maintain order in a household, which otherwise would ring with petulant quarrels. So fundamental is the hierarchy of age that parents of twins, though one be but a few minutes older, carefully train the younger to obey the elder.

We suspect that when the household of Chaem's father dispersed, the decision for the two older brothers to move off together was easily made. They had long worked in harmony. As for Chāēm and his older sister, the differences in sex predisposed them to move gradually apart after puberty, when girls' work becomes more clearly distinguished from boys' work. Finally, her marriage separated them somewhat more.

Chāēm's mother has remained outside of discussion until this moment because speaking of her involves comparing the values of two or more investments. As a married woman, she was a partner in her husband's enterprise. After his death she might have continued to work in his stead, just as many Bang Chan widows manage the farms of their spouses and set their children to working in the fields. If the widow had owned a house and land, she would have held them for or given them to her daughter and son-in-law in return for care during her old age. Probably she had none. With few resources, she was forced to relinquish her position as an investor of favors and become a person who offered her services. If she had brothers or sisters to whom she might turn, she did not seek or accept their favors. Evidently her eldest son was best prepared among her children to offer her food and shelter in return for her help in starting a new household.

One usually acquires labor by investing favors in another who then becomes a client, an employee, or a kind of child or younger sibling. The price is set by the market, and each patron, employer, parent, or older brother must husband his assets so as to be able to increase his favors when the price of services rises. A Bang Chan woman observed: "Rich people are glad to have a baby because they have money to feed the child; but poor people worry about too many children" (JRH 11/3/53). So when hard times come, all must reach less often into the rice pot, or some must move to other patrons. An employer addressed his factory hands: "Whoever can get a better job, paying more money, then let him go and get this other job. Whenever the time comes that money is good again, I want you to come back and help me again" (HPP 7/17/57). So groups grow with prosperity and decrease in size during hard times.

A second contractual device for securing labor is marriage, phrased as a partnership of equals in a new enterprise. To enter such a partnership each side ordinarily attempts to contribute equal amounts. When the resources are said to be considerable, families employ a go-between for the difficult equating of contributions. In Bang Chan the consent of the bride and groom together with the knowledge of their astrological compatibility set the necessary conditions for negotiations. The parents would fix the amount of land, the size of the house, the kinds of furnishings that each must contribute toward the new household. All must be satisfied that these incommensurables reach a balance in which a house built by the groom's family equals the land given by the bride's family. On the appointed day of the marriage, the groom's party, with the final items of the wedding contract in hand, comes to the bride's parental house, shouting like soldiers assaulting a fortress. The bride's kinsmen stoutly defend their stronghold with barriers manned by clowns, who exact an entrance fee from each of the groom's party, as though these latter inevitably were not contributing enough. Then the terms of the contract are carefully counted and approved by witnesses before the bride is permitted to come forth. After ceremonial blessings and feasting, the newlyweds are installed as partners in their new establishment.

It is a fortunate couple that has house and land at the start. More often the parents can provide only a little to help them, and the couple must set about earning the remainder needed. Then the newlyweds offer their services to a parent or some other kinsman until they can amass the farming equipment and the buffalo necessary to operate their own rented house and land. Couples that can expect no help from their kinsmen elope and simply pay the bride's parents a price of "forgiveness," which may include a token of milk money for the trouble of raising the bride. Such a couple without resources must find someone who will accept their services in return for help in getting started. Of course, just the desire of two persons to join together may suffice for a marriage, and such contracts involve no payments or exchange. Two poor people may start this way, and the usually poor minor wife of a rich man enters matrimony happy for the shelter a husband can provide. Divorce, too, is simple when no joint property need be divided, but complex when former spouses and their kinsmen haggle over the division of joint property.

Chaēm and his sister seem to have had no assets other than hands and backs to bring to marriage, yet the sister was said to have become rich. She may have married a poor man who became rich; she may have become a second wife of someone already rich; or if, as a poor girl, she were chosen by a rich man, her potential role as partner might be minimized so that she became a kind of servant and childbearer for her husband's family. As for Chāēm himself, he seems to have found a humble family that contracted for his services through marriage to their daughter.

The Thai phrase *khrāub khrua*, which is usually translated as "family," means literally "cover arrangement of the hearth" and seems to connote no special membership in a group other than those who eat from a single common fire. A Thai household usually includes parents and their unmarried children, for bearing (or raising) children is the ordinary means of acquiring labor.[19] Often it includes one or two persons more: a parent, an aunt, an uncle, a younger sibling, or, as with Chāēm when he first married, a son-in-law.[20] However, one also finds households in which an unmarried woman has taken in her nephews, or in which two or three unrelated lonely people have clubbed together.

My uncle and Phrayā Urupong served in the same regiment in the army. Phrayā Urupong had higher rank than my uncle. When my uncle was discharged from the army, he had no way to earn a living, so Phrayā Urupong gave him some land for cultivating durian. It was near the Rama VI bridge in Thonburī. In the house lived more than ten people: my father; my mother; mother's sister; her husband who is the uncle from the army and who had no children but who adopted some of my mother's younger sister's children; and my six brothers and sisters. [LMH 12/8/53]

We can infer the distribution of favors, beginning with Phrayā Urupong and going first to the uncle and his wife, and from them to the wife's sister and her husband. Each person in a chain redistributes to his own group the food and clothing received, and delivers their services according to the needs of the superior. So a Thai household is a family only in a special sense. It does not necessarily raise children or provide for the aged. It lacks predetermined standardized roles; rather, within the house, roles tend to be improvised and permit much latitude for variation within a broad range of minimum role requirements. This vague system of kin or kinlike relationships is really an assemblage of individually contracted and variable arrangements that provide participants with basic needs. For a cluster of such kin, or for two or more clusters around separate hearths in one house, we shall use the word "household" in preference to "family."

If these are the essential transactions occurring among all Thai, what special meaning, if any, does kinship have in the Thai situation? Thai kinship is heavily influenced by these voluntary contractual relationships. They give to each family relationship a certain twist that is entirely lacking in our own kinship system. Our relatives are acquired by birth. We are required to display special decorous manners toward another because he or she is a grandparent, a cousin, or an aunt. Whether we enjoy our meetings or not, the prescribed conduct must continue for better, for worse, for richer, for poorer, till death us do part. Indeed, we may appeal to the law when certain crucial expectations are unfulfilled.

On the other hand, if a person of our culture volunteers the identical services that a nephew performs for his uncle or aunt, the net effect of a "real" nephew–uncle relationship is accomplished. In two particulars only does this relationship differ from a kinship tie: It is voluntarily contracted and may be voluntarily terminated, while a kinsman's services should continue indefinitely in an inescapable relationship.

Somewhere between this prescribed obligation of our kinsmen and this voluntary contract lie the obligations of a Thai kinsman. There are many ways to become a sibling or a parent by Thai standards. Furthermore, one who acts like a parent *is* a parent and will continue to be a parent until he chooses to act in some other way. In this sense the Thai construe their kinsmen, yet the idea of a continuing and fixed obligation is not altogether absent.

Like nature in its abundance, the Thai kinship system offers hundreds of potential kinsmen. Siblings include cousins, potentially in all degrees, the wives of these cousins and the cousins of these wives, as well as the husbands of these cousins and the cousins of these husbands. The parents of all these cousins are aunts and uncles, and the cousins' children become categorized with grandchildren. The Christian and Islamic brotherhoods of man scarcely exceed the possible range offered by the Thai system.[21] How does one select among them?

First comes shared experience. Chāēm and his siblings were thought to have the common experience not only of growing up together in the same household but also of developing in the same womb. Thus the Thai distinguish immediate siblings from that indefinite mass of possible siblings. Sometimes when two siblings seem exceptionally devoted, people explain that they were siblings in a previous incarnation. In fact, common experience as neighbors, pupils in the same school, or recruits in the same regiment forms a relationship that may become as intimate as that between near kinsmen.

But common experience is not enough. The underlying exchange of services and favors must exceed a calculated quid pro quo and work toward an easy flow of mutual help with no final date for reckoning the balance. To the extent that an investor in or reciprocator of services lays aside all conditions for ensuring his gain, love and respect dominate the relationship. These two people, then, whatever their origin, "become" kinsmen.

Now my second and third brothers are grown up, and when I ask them to do some kind of work, they go and do it. They never disobey, and when there is no disobedience, there is no hatred. Formerly whenever there was entertainment, I took them with me. My younger siblings loved me a lot. [HPP 7/22/57]

In my family my younger brother once fought with me. Father was away, but when he returned, he stopped the quarrel. If father had found us quarreling, he would have to punish the younger brother, because he disobeyed. He must pay respect. [LMH 12/17/57]

From these examples it can be seen that kinsmanly love means giving favors and that respect means obedience to orders and willingness to be ordered.

Even the relationship of mother and child is phrased as love that showers care and favors upon a child, who reciprocates with obedient respect. The common experience starts with conception; a mother begins to nourish a child from that day with her own blood, after birth with her milk. The father contributes sperm to form the body, but the body is but a vehicle for several souls of obscure origin which enter with the first breath after birth.[22] These souls may be complete strangers to both parents, as shown by the wish of pregnant mothers: "May the soul of my child be that of a divine spirit and not of a criminal." Then after normal birth the midwife, holding the newborn, formally asks, "Whose child is this?" Though we know of no parents who refused to accept their child, this ceremony implies the forming of a contract with the infant. Thus kinship, instead of being a set of relationships given by birth, is acquired. Furthermore, the element of investment of favors by a parent reappears again and again. A priest recited a sermon at Bang Chan about the Rice Mother (Māe Pōsob), the goddess who brings the crop:

The word 'mother' means one who can provide children. Mother is the person to whom we should pay gratitude. Human beings and animals owe a great deal to rice; so rice is approved to be called 'mother.' Mothers love children so that the red color of blood is turned into the white of milk in order to show her innocence, as in the following poem:

> Mother's mind is as merciful as Phra Phrōm.
> Mother's milk is like the moon feeding the world.
> Mother's hands are as high as the sky.
> Mother's mouth is like the sun shining.
>   [SS 2/10/54]

Because of these boundless favors, children should respect their mother by obeying her, and the texts of songs from the life-cycle rites reiterate the obligation. The debt to a father, while less dramatized, comes from his work as provider for the household.

If kinship can be easily contracted, it can also be easily dissolved. Instances of the reorganization of contemporary Bang Chan households after the departure of a parent are numerous:

My son's first wife had a house and lands, but she died. His second wife was a hired girl in the house when she became pregnant. I told my son to take her as a wife, but he didn't do it. She was not beautiful; now she lives in Bangkok. I don't like his present wife; she talks too much and you can't trust her. She had five children before marrying my son, and they are all living in Bangkok. She keeps a lot of money to send them. . . . My son should be rich. I wonder where all the money goes. [JRH 1/29/54]

The son's household grew from the death of one wife, an extramarital affair, and marriage with a woman who resolved to leave her children. The mother accused the new wife of secretly spending money from the venture jointly shared with her husband on children of another husband who lived elsewhere. Such an offense has broken many a household apart, for a parent is expected to use only his or her individually owned assets to support children by another spouse who makes no contribution to the present household. Happy are the husband of an industrious and devoted wife, the wife of a dutiful husband, and the parents of respectful children.

Despite flux, kinship hints at permanent obligations. The woman of the foregoing case left her five children in Bangkok but continued to send them money. Chāem's older brother did not abandon his mother in the Sāmsen market to beg for a living. People say an adopted child is more likely to desert his parents than a natural child. Beneath the easily contracted arrangements lie symptoms of a kinship system with fixed obligations.

Though some government posts may once have been passed on patrilineally, and the patriline is emphasized by elite urban families, in the countryside farmers incline toward a matrilineal reference. Mother's mother (*jāj*) is somewhat closer than father's mother (*jā*), and it is this term for mother's mother that tends to be extended to very old but unrelated women as a form of polite address.[23] An uncle or aunt who is a father's younger sibling and who works intimately with a nephew or niece may be called mother's younger sibling (*nā*), ignoring the relationship through the father (JRH 11/26/53). Newly married couples tend to live near if not with the bride's parents; the house and hearth customarily go at death to the youngest daughter.[24]

The clear kin designations of elder and younger echo the duties of patron and client. The respect a parent accords his elder siblings is carried on by his own children, who in turn call the children of these elder aunts and uncles elder sibling (phī), regardless of relative age. Terminology further marks off one's own household from all others by allowing no aunt to be categorized with mother or uncle with father. Parents are uniquely addressed, and in their household age clearly subordinates the younger to the elder.

In the kin nomenclature, an individual's sex is recognized only after marriage and then only by a person's spouse and children and by the children of younger siblings. In other words, it would seem that in kinship a distinction of sex is unimportant until a person reaches maturity and produces children; elder aunt or uncle, grandfather or grandmother contrast with the cousin or sibling or children of those whose sex is not indicated. Male and female become distinct with age.

We shall come to see that the households that banded together to move to Bang Chan were usually those of siblings. Should some cousin happen to join the group, all were well aware that he was more distantly related than the siblings of the same parents. A sibling who was cousin beyond the second degree usually did not join them. In practice, if not in theory, the obligations among siblings extend mainly to the children of one's own parents, less definitely to the myriad possible cousin-like siblings.

Adam Smith anticipated that free economic intercourse would lead to peace and harmony among nations. Perhaps he conceived the thesis by observing that when individuals enter freely into transactions with each other, such intercourse may lead more frequently to love and respect than to hate and antagonism. In the Thai situation, when love and respect grow, the parties to the relationship are kinsmen, whether acquired by accident of birth or by voluntary association. These kinsmanly qualities may be more readily and usually nourished through years of experience in a common household than when left to chance associations in a world of mobile people. Yet when uncertainties vanish as a result of long association, the partners too become kinsmen. Thereafter one cannot quickly forget the other, even though circumstances change. The links of kinship are less likely to be broken than are others. Kinship softens the brittle edges of sheer opportunism, at the same time that it provides a more permanent tie that more readily frames the relationships and defines the mode of conduct between people.

Neighbors in the Wilderness

Chaēm, his wife, and his mother-in-law experienced many of the hardships, successes, and failures undergone by settlers of the American frontier, yet they did not consider themselves pioneers. They were not developing a land for the future, nor did they anticipate that someday, through their efforts and those of others who would join them, the wilderness would be transformed. They had little pride in the possession of the land they occupied, partly because all land belonged to the king, and they owned only a small acreage by squatter's preemption. Partly the land was worthless as a commodity just because of its vastness, and only years later did anyone petition for a title deed. They felt no drama in penetrating the untouched land, and instead of seeking an idyllic spot far out in the distant vastnesses, they moved just beyond their nearest neighbors, as close to the thoroughfare as possible.

If Chaēm saw himself in these terms, he might have said, "I am a poor man who could not make a living in the city. So I had to move to this desolation."

However primitive we might consider Chaēm's living arrangements, his urban habits clearly distinguished him from his Khā neighbors. Both Chaēm and the Khā peoples probably lived in houses of the same material, fished, and raised a little rice, and

Chǣm doubtless hunted from time to time.[25] But when a household member needed a new loincloth or scarf to cover his shoulders, no one in Chǣm's household was prepared to spin and weave it. If mother-in-law cracked the pot, she might patch it but did not press out a new one. When Chǣm broke his knife, there was no smith at hand to anneal the pieces. In these respects the Khā were self-sufficient while Chǣm, like any helpless city person, had to run to the market. But this became his pride, to have a more finely woven scarf, a more uniformly glazed pot, and a sword of better quality than any the bush people had. He built his life on the assumption of a market, and until the Khā discovered what the traders would buy, until they had learned the language of the market and could haggle over price, they had not acquired the habits that would place them on a level with Chǣm.

Chǣm also felt superior to his Moslem neighbors, though their standard of living probably surpassed his. They, as the slaves of a wealthy man, enjoyed some special advantages. They could use the lumber and tools left over after they built the residence of His Excellency. They must raise animals and vegetables for His Excellency's table, but when the season was good, nothing prevented them from enjoying a few of these eggs and ducks.[26] The presence of many households simplified house building, the preparation of fields, and the harvesting of crops. Not many years after settling, these Moslem people built their first surao for sabbath prayers. But Chǣm was not a slave. Though his actual land was worthless on the market, his right as a free man (sakdi) to hold ten acres or twenty-five rai of the king's land and the small measure of honorary authority this gave him placed his station clearly above that of these villagers. His twenty-five rai compared unfavorably with the honorary four hundred rai of minor government officials and could only emphasize his insignificance alongside Chao Phrayā Srīsurijawong's twenty thousand, yet it distinguished him clearly from slaves. Of course, the retainers of this great man could scarcely complain about the severity of their bondage. His Excellency was in residence with his entourage only a few days in the year, and at these times they served his needs and might petition him for certain favors as well. On a still further score Chǣm counted as a blessing his rebirth into the Buddhist faith. Though both Buddhists and Moslems suffered from the rats and birds that ate their rice, from the elephants and the storms, and though both took life in fishing, Chāēm knew of merit (*bun*) and sin or demerit (*bap*). Only in some future existence did Chāēm expect that his Moslem neighbors might accumulate sufficient merit to be reborn Buddhists.

When he had paddled past this Moslem village and headed his boat along the broad Sāēn Sāēb canal toward Bangkok, Chāēm knew that he was just a humble man from the wilderness who must address respectfully his superiors living in the city. Only in some future existence might he be reborn with enough merit to spend his whole life in the city. There he would not have to work hard under the sun and rain, the clouds of mosquitoes and the threats of wild animals. When city people had to purchase necessities in the market, they did not need to spend a day boating on the canal. They could make merit at the temples and dispatch the ghosts of the dead with proper rites. On New Year's, visitors would come saying blessings and invite them to join the gay crowds on the great river to see the fireworks. Their karma (*kam*) did not destine them to live by fishing, or set them apart from people's cheerful gatherings and banter. Chāēm had to accept his role as the uncouth one, bear his suffering, and resolve to live virtuously.

CHAPTER 3

Newcomers

Chāēm's small household survived in the wilderness along the middle reaches of the rivulet that was to be Bang Chan canal, the first known settlers on that site. If others had preceded them in the days before the Fourth Reign, like sterile seeds underneath a spreading tree, they never took root or left a trace after the annual floods. Chāēm's survival was probably a matter less of courage than of dogged effort and good luck. Or, as his fellow Buddhists would say, Chāēm had sufficient merit to reach a weed-choked backwater and not die of bites, disease, or exhaustion before help came.

Within a few years Chāēm's two older brothers had forced their sampans up the rivulet and agreed to join him. Perhaps the fishing was better in the natural streams than in the newly dug canal, where food, water, and the living fish had not yet reached a balance. Perhaps someone had bought the fishing rights for the main canal and sent the poachers scurrying to the backwaters.

The eldest brother, named Tō, came not only with his wife and Chāēm's mother but with two sons and a blind co-wife. Despite her handicap, she could help prepare a meal by pounding seeds in a mortar and swing the hammock of a sleeping baby, thus relieving other hands for more complex chores. The second brother, Thēp, came with his wife and their infant son. Tō planned to locate across the stream, while Thēp chose a site next to Chāēm; the three thus put the wilderness to their backs and human habitation within sight through the doorways. Tō summoned the strength (*khāū raeng*) of the other two households to raise a mound and sink the corner posts of a new hut. At the end of each day the women of his household prepared a meal to reward the workers and make them eager to work again on the morrow. When the thatch for the roof and walls was tied into place, the same crew moved at Thēp's invitation to repeat their labors for him. As host he would then feast his workers.

In a few days a tiny hamlet arose in the wilderness. The nine adults and five children could then make life flow more smoothly, and not just because new hands increased the working force; gaiety too lightened the joint tasks, and numbers reinforced courage when a trumpeting herd of elephants moved close. Yet these numbers could not entirely extinguish the fear of the wilderness. One day during the first rainy season Tō's blind wife, alone in the hut with the children, was startled by a rustling in the thatch overhead followed by a splash in the floodwater outside. Her cries drew help only slowly, and then no one could find a trace to explain what had happened. They guessed it was only a crocodile on the roof, but as crocodiles were infrequent in the area, let alone on the roofs, she remained unconsoled by this explanation and beseeched Tō to let her return to the more populated shore of Sāen Sāeb canal. Tō acquiesced, but she came back a year or two later with her infant son, conceived by Tō before she had left; she then needed the help of her co-wife's eyes to raise the child (LMH 7/24/57).

Though mutual help was commonplace within a household, no contract bound together the households of the hamlet. The fisherman from each household sculled his own catch home in his own boat, dried the fish on leaves provided by his own helpers, sold these wares to a merchant of his own choosing, and spent the earnings on his own wants. Such arrangements certainly sufficed for these three households, but even larger hamlets with fifty households may develop no corporate arrangements. The concept of the commonweal, which expeditiously organized hundreds of communities in North America and Australia and furnished a basis for enforceable authority, rarely took root in this moist tropical heat. The three brothers did not even erect a common dock where they could tie their boats and unload their fish, or set aside common land to grow the rice needed equally by all. Of course, the three households might one morning jointly build a bridge, which would have facilitated their visiting and sped help in an emergency. A few months later, however, if a lashing parted or a bamboo pole crumpled, no common will would impel anyone to step forward to repair it. To agree to meet and cut a few more bamboos some other morning would be far easier than to organize an authority to erect and maintain a permanent bridge in the hamlet.

Authority in Thailand, rather than rising from a group's agreement to some impersonal, overriding rule that applied to all alike, is personal and individual, or, more accurately, the attribute of a social position. The king, the governor of a town, the head of a household, all stand ready with the appurtenances of their positions to provide some kind of benefit for anyone ready to give wanted services. Here is the political aspect of the search for labor described in Chapter 2, for each person who contracts to provide services acknowledges the authority of his benefactor. Instead of being the administrator for an impersonal corporate system, the patron becomes the center of radiating reciprocal agreements with his individual clients. The number and kinds of benefits that he provides depend upon his resources and the market. No uniform standards apply to all; each contract is reached by separate bargaining, and should patron or client come to regret the terms, either may seek to modify or end the relationship.[1]

No one of the three households could muster sufficient benefits to induce another to become a client. The differences in wealth among them were too slight. Tō's household, with its four adult members, was probably better equipped than the other two. He had worked longer and had evidently accumulated more resources, or perhaps he was just more generous and compassionate than his two brothers when he married a helpless blind woman as his second wife and adopted a boy as his son. On the basis of household size, Thēp, with only his wife, was poorer than Chāem, whose household included two adults besides himself. None of them seems to have expanded his household except with his own progeny. Only if one brother were the lone possessor of a boat or some essential gear would the other two have found some advantage in becoming his clients, but in fact each had his own boat, gear, and appointed house. In discussing common problems with his brothers, Tō, backed by the aging mother who lived under his roof as well as by his own seniority, could probably carry his points with little resistance. At meals in a brother's house, respect dictated that Tō be served first with the best portion, though not necessarily before the elder woman. A child might also present the betel tray to an aging grandmother and then out of deference to her toothlessness offer to pulverize the areca nuts. Neither this respect nor this deference, however, empowered Tō or the grandmothers to command the resources of another household; this right belonged exclusively to the husband and wife who jointly headed each household.

Mutual help occurred on the basis of exchange (*tog raeng, chaj raeng*). Each had a garden and a rice plot of approximately the same size as the others', so that it was easy enough to clear the weeds and harvest each field in succession. Labor given was returned in equal measure. Similarly, a household that ran short of rice or salt might borrow and return a like amount later.

When unique needs arose, a household simply had to hire labor, just as Tō and then Thēp summoned the labor (khāū raeng) of the other two brothers to help build their huts and repaid these services with a bounteous meal. Of course, one summoned the most experienced carpenter of the hamlet to repair the cracked prow of a sampan[2] and the most experienced basketmaker to advise on the weaving of a basket of a new shape. Since the summoner of labor need not return the labor with his own hands but need only show himself able to compensate others for their services properly, summoning is more honorific than exchanging labor. But as in many a pioneer community, the urge for self-sufficiency and thriftiness and fear of imposition (*krēng chai*) counterbalanced any possible reckless proclivity to hire workers.

At the same time common interests and sympathies neutralized the formal isolation of independent households. When a herd of elephants approached and only one person knew the proper manner of asking the guardian spirit Lord of the Place (Chao Thī) to turn them away, this specialist acted promptly. When Chāēm's child died, the appropriate specialist stepped forward to recite the verbal formula that forces the spirit to depart promptly so as not to disturb the living. They simply buried the body, rather than arrange an expensive cremation at a distant temple. Compassion rather than expectation of reward prompted Tō's blind wife to agree to hold the infant of Thēp's wife for a few hours, while its mother helped Thēp weed the garden. Chāēm and his household may have liked to have his old mother spend a rainy day with them because she told good stories, and she liked to see Chāēm's mother-in-law. Tō, returning from a hunting expedition with a wild pig, called for all to take the

day off, butcher the game, and prepare a local feast. Thus a neigh-
borliness arose within the hamlet that moved well beyond a mere
exchange and hiring of services.

The authority of government seems to have rested lightly on the
hamlet of the fishermen. To be sure, Pallegoix in the mid-nineteenth
century describes rather onerous burdens for the ordinary man:

These people working at corvée, which is called *khao düen*, are held to three
months of services per year. They are employed at building fortresses,
pagodas, and palaces, deepening canals, making dykes, roads, shelters, and
generally all royal public projects. If they wish to be released from corvée,
they have only to pay the sum of sixteen ticals (baht) to their superiors, who
keep it or perhaps hire some other person in their place.

In the entire extent of the kingdom, a good portion of the people were not
subject to corvée but had to pay tribute annually, the value of which varied
from eight to sixteen ticals. There are those who pay in wooden beams,
bricks, tiles, lime, sand, bamboo, wax, honey, *bois d'aigle*, stick lac, oil,
resin, etc. This portion of the people is perhaps the happiest in that,
providing they pay their tribute in goods or silver, they are free the whole
year to do what they wish, except that in case of war they must enter
military service. [Pallegoix 1854, 1:296–297]

Had Tō, Thēp, and Chāēm remained in Bangkok, they would not
have escaped corvée or some other payment of tribute. The government of Rama IV continued building fortifications, temples, and
pleasure gardens, yet from 1855 onward, as the trade treaties began
to bring more goods from overseas, policy turned increasingly to
collecting taxes in currency and paying wages for the king's work.
Money was becoming as important as labor and produce along the
river front. Without his former monopoly on foreign trade, the king
sought income by tax farming and selling rights to collect taxes.
Before the end of the reign, cash revenue had more than doubled
(Thiphakarawong 1934a:336; Skinner 1957:119–125). So if the
fisherman brothers had remained in the capital they would have
spent fewer hours each year at forced labor but would have been
dunned or blackmailed by registration officials into paying the ex-
orbitant charges about which Dan Beach Bradley complained (see
Bangkok Calendar 1871:70–71).

Little or no mention of government occurs during these first
decades in Bang Chan, and this is the more surprising since the
advent of officials in the 1890s produced quite a stir. To be sure, the
presence of a Bunnag or even the existence of His Excellency's

residence exerted an influence, but not necessarily a protective one, over these squatters. We suspect that Bang Chan lay beyond the orbit of government, its inhabitants having "headed for the woods" (*paj pā*) as effectively as an escaped slave. Well-fed tax collectors on the outskirts of Bangkok chose not to squeeze these impecunious fisherfolk in a remote backwater. Had anyone followed their movements, he would see them turning in the side stream from the main canal like the tax-exempt retainers of His Excellency the Prime Minister. In the Bangkok market a fish dealer would do all he could to ensure smooth access of suppliers to his pier. A little tip to the local tax collector might help ensure this privilege, and perhaps he made up for this expense by paying less for the fish of certain people.

On each trip the fisherman brothers received some portion of the stated price for fish in Bangkok markets, 6.50 to 7.50 baht per picul (133.3 pounds) during the 1850s (Van der Heide 1906:84).[3] They returned home with no more cash than they came with, but each time with another purchased item that made living a little gentler. Of course, the labor-saving knives, mats, and baskets slowly accumulated as persons returned from the markets and women devoted more days to weaving. Hands to lighten the work increased, so that Tō, with two sons by his first wife, a third by his blind wife, and the adopted fourth child, could gradually turn more over to the new generation. Similarly Thēp, with two sons and three daughters, and Chaēm, with the six who survived, counted on the growing ones to gather firewood and grind in a mortar the seasoning for evening meals. By the age of fourteen they could handle a boat expertly and help enough to catch a portion of the needed fish. In the season of gardening, children helped weed the fields, drive birds from ripening crops, and carry sheaves of grain, each year doing a little more until at sixteen or eighteen they worked like adults. Chaēm's daughter and granddaughter recalled some of the scene:

We could not grow much rice because we could not drive the birds away. We grew only enough rice to eat, for no one wanted to buy rice in those days. We got some things like cloth by exchanging it for padi at Saēn Saēb canal. Every year my parents bought me a new cloth. After harvest people started fishing. Every family would fish. We use *jaū* and *khōb* [types of fishing gear] for catching *plā chaūn* and *plā salid* [types of fish]. If the husband fishes, the wife stays home and tends the house, and if the wife goes, the husband stays home. [*Did anyone get rich?*] No. One lives from hand to mouth [*tham mȳ, kin mȳ:* work by the hand, eat by the hand]. In the dry season Chāem had to live by digging earth. He earned one and a quarter baht for digging each cubic *wā* of earth [about four cubic meters and two days of work]. Before ordination all helped our parents to work; after that no one helped them anymore. [LMH 7/30/57; 8/6/57]

Before the grown children had departed, the households of the three brothers needed to summon each other and exchange labor less frequently. Each household could pound its own padi into rice and rethatch its own roof. So the three households tended to reserve their neighbors' help for harvest or special occasions such as the ordination of Tō's eldest son into the priesthood at the new temple called Bam Phen on Sāen Sāeb canal.[4] By the decade of the 1870s these first settlers were looking for house sites where some of their children might settle and still remain near enough to lend an occasional hand.

A New Hamlet

During this same decade of the 1870s a group of people, five or so households strong, suddenly appeared in the Bang Chan area. They chose to settle at a site downstream between the hamlet of the three brothers and the Moslem village at the neglected residence of Chao Phrayā Srīsurijawong. Word passed that these people had come from the village of former Laotian prisoners of war on Sāen Sāeb canal, and they could be seen building a large mound somewhat back from the rivulet, on the high ground. Thatched huts arose, and after a few rainy seasons the number of huts multiplied to twenty or so. They called their hamlet after the mound they had raised, Village of the Mound of Earthly Splendor (Bān Dāun Sī Phūm), and under this auspicious name seemed to look forward to a new and richer life (LMH 7/29/57; VIC 7/18/57).[5]

Unfortunately the tale of these Laotians has so decayed through their descendants' lack of interest in the past and through the turbulent jolts of subsequent events that many important features have disappeared. Clearly they were released from servitude, yet the royal order of Rama V in 1874 which "liberated" the slaves differed considerably from Lincoln's emancipation with a single stroke of the pen. The court in Bangkok and His Excellency Chao Phrayā Srīsurijawong in his capacity as regent for the young king were generally aware of the turmoil that followed liberation in the United States, even if they had not specifically heard of the thousands of former slaves who wandered the countryside singing hymns in search of Kingdom Come in the Land of the Blessed.[6] King Rama V sought to smooth the transition and phrased the emancipation order in such gradual terms that there was no need for any change to be evident for many years. Only children of slaves who had been born since the beginning of his reign in 1868 would be free, and then only on reaching maturity. Of course, they might redeem themselves a few years earlier by paying a price that diminished each year as they grew older, but all others would presumably remain slaves until the end of their days, unless they could buy their freedom. News of such an edict may have launched celebrations in many slave villages, but on the following day and for the years to come they would feel no automatic change. Only by 1889 would the first few emerge to taste life as freemen.

No sudden exodus from the Laotian villages on Saēn Saēb canal took place in the 1870s, yet the people were apparently free to move. One informant told of a grandfather who had lived in a Laotian village while serving as temple boy in nearby Bam Phen Temple (LMH 7/23/57). A cousin from Vientiane found him and proposed that he return to Vientiane. He replied that he was content to remain in Thailand. So the cousin left without him. It is unlikely that a slave boy would have entered a temple, even to carry the alms bowl of a priest, and certainly no slave was free to move where he wished. We suspect that some abolitionist nobleman ordered the liberation of these Laotians long before the royal edict took effect.

This prisoner-of-war village was somewhat less well off than the hamlet of Tō, Thēp, and Chaēm. The Laotians lived side by side in clusters of thatched huts, each household tilling for its own subsistence a strip of land amounting to a rai or two (a rai is 0.4 acres), as compared with Tō's three to five rai (LMH 7/23/57). A man could usually raise just enough rice for a family of four on one or two rai, and some years there might be enough surplus to distill some liquor or barter a little padi for market goods (Janlekha 1957:52–53). More persons in a household burdened the resources considerably; yet by borrowing a little from some neighboring kinsman, one could somehow get along. There were always fish and vegetables. With little or no cash in hand and with seldom any surplus to sell, they had even fewer tools and clothing than the fishing brothers. Freedom only added further strains. Each family had suddenly become a renter and had to pay, perhaps, a trifling rent to the proprietor. Taxes increased from four baht per year for slaves, which the master often had to pay from his own purse, to the freeman's sixteen baht.[7] These payments could be made in padi, but the old resources for growing no longer sufficed. Households had to look elsewhere to meet these demands.

The new hamlet of Laotians seems to have sprung from the effort of two households that moved and established themselves, accompanied by others who settled on separate but adjacent mounds. Sīlā and his wife Māum led a group to one mound. The two had come to the banks of Sāen Sāeb canal as children and subsequently married while still slaves. By the time they were freed, their household included seven children, so that keeping rice bowls full from a small patch of land was difficult. Yet a large family might become an advantage in the wilderness, where production is limited only by personal strength and will. There were always younger siblings, cousins, nephews, and nieces, restless young people eager to join a new venture.[8] The second group to move to the new hamlet on its own mound was led by a middle-aged couple with two grown children; Lī and his wife, Taw, came from Bangkok, where they had been serving in the palace of some nobleman. Their wealthy patron had evidently sent them away amply provided for, and they reached the older Laotian settlement equipped for farming with a buffalo and plow. People were eager to join a man of such substance, and he accepted five or six as clients.[9]

Probably Sīlā and Māum reached Bang Chan first, built a joint mound for themselves and three or four other households, and turned primarily to agriculture rather than fishing. A year or two later Lī and Taw arrived with their glistening plow and buffalo to build an adjacent mound. Land was abundant, the members of both groups were probably kinsmen; no grounds for competition arose except on one score. On Sīlā's mound differences of wealth were small, and work had to be done by exchange of labor. Lī, with his buffalo and plow, on the other hand, acted as patron to his clients and potentially was poised to draw the group from Sīlā's mound into his circle. This would have ended the separate venture. Whatever tensions may have arisen on this score, a granddaughter of Sīlā and Māum told of the resolution: "At the time when Sīlā and Māum were first here, they had no buffalo. They used a mattock [*chaub*] and sword [*phrahuad*] to cut weeds: then they burned them. After that

paring the rice field
oto by Lauriston Sharp

they worked the land over again with a mattock [and finally made holes for planting the padi]. They put one seed of rice in each hole. Later they bought a buffalo for twelve baht" (LMH 7/23/57). Sīlā and Maūm were anxious to increase the size of their fields by cultivating with buffalo and plow. Then they could grow padi on five or more rai of land, for these implements lightened the labor of weeding, and seeds could be broadcast without individual planting if one plowed a second time lightly. No less important, they could hold the labor force of one mound before it was tempted by the new equipment to join with Lī and Taw. So under two patrons the new hamlet grew to twenty households (LMH 7/29/57).

Despite the new equipment, the hamlet was a ragged sight for many years. Until protective cover grew to hold the soil, rains cut deep gashes into the slowly settling mound. Without trees to shade the roofs, the huts were oven-like at midday. For many seasons padi surplus was small and cash almost nonexistent, so that people wore their loincloths (phākhāwmā) to gray and tattered thinness, while inside the huts handy pots and knives were few. Boats as well as buffalo and plow had to be shared, but these circumstances unified the hamlet to a degree that could not be matched where resources were distributed more evenly. The two patrons could summon the work force to raise a common mound and later clear a small canal so that boats moved during high water from the hamlet to Bang Chan rivulet. After the harvest the whole work force could be mobilized to carry on shoulder poles the baskets of surplus padi for sale or barter on the banks of Sāen Sāeb canal. The new hamlet was beginning to realize the promise of its auspicious name.

The Moslems passed through the same years with fewer changes than the Laotians. During the period when Chao Phrayā Srīsurijawong served as regent and during his subsequent retirement at his country seat in Ratchaburī, their patron's visits stopped; but after the royal edict on slavery in 1874 his deputy came to address the assembled villagers. He offered them their freedom to move elsewhere but granted the privilege of continuing in the hamlet rent-free to anyone who wished to stay (LMH 7/18/57). We infer that when the imam and the elders of the hamlet met to consider this offer, they sensed a continuing obligation to serve the great man whose father before him had protected their community and who himself had shown equal love over the years and reaffirmed it with this generous offer. They thanked him, and no one moved from the hamlet. These elders were unlike Tō, who could influence no one but his brothers by his personal weight; they owned little if any more property than the poorer families, and so could withhold no favors from a willful client. Instead their village lay under the protection of Allah, who through holy writ directed the elders to command the good and punish the bad. A Moslem who acted contrary to the will of the elders risked both secular and divine punishment.[10] So life continued with little apparent change. Children were born, some young people married and moved to neighboring Moslem villages, elders died, and then in 1883 their patron died. He had not visited for many years, but had he come, many days would have been needed to replace the rotten planks and fallen shutters of his residence. Now his country clients visited him in Bangkok and paid their final respects at his cremation.

Disaster

So the hamlet might have continued indefinitely with all the gradual shifts of growing up and growing old. Toward the end of the 1880s, disaster struck just at the season when the new rice was yellowing, and all were looking to the harvest as soon as the flood-waters had receded a little more. From the wilderness came brown waves of squeaking, voracious rats drawn to the ripening grain in the fields. The alarm was shouted out in time for some to save a few baskets of padi from their stores. Others could only retreat up the house ladder and club the occasional stray rodent that dared climb a house post. When the hordes departed, only straw remained in the dry fields and a thin band of untouched grain which the flood had protected (LMH 8/18/57).

People have faced lean years with equanimity, and certainly the people of the Moslem hamlet might have expected aid from the family of their late patron. Yet within a few months only two households remained; the rest had moved east, deeper into the wilderness. The two households were those of the son and grand-daughter of their former leader. Even today some shadow of this leading man remains:

He was a brave and vigorous man. After the war in Saiburī, he came to Thonburī as prisoner of war with many of his younger kinsmen [lān]. While there in Thonburī, one day he could not bear to see his niece courting with the Thai people of Somdet Chao Phrayā Srīsurijawong the elder [presumably the father of Chao Phrayā Srīsurijawong]. He had special power and put his finger on the head of this girl and broke her head. When Somdet Chao Phrayā heard about this, he had our leader seized. The Somdet wondered why he did not defend himself and noticed that he did not seem afraid. When questioned, our leader said that he did not want to kill Thai people, even if he could. If the Somdet Chao Phrayā did not believe in his power, he would demonstrate it. So he put his finger on a piece of wood and split it in order to demonstrate his power. After that the Somdet Chao Phrayā released him and later gave him land for the Moslem people on his estate. [LMH 8/6/57]

Having excited the admiration of their patron's father as well as their patron himself, this unnamed man secured special treatment for his kinsmen, for they moved to Bang Chan to live next to His Excellency

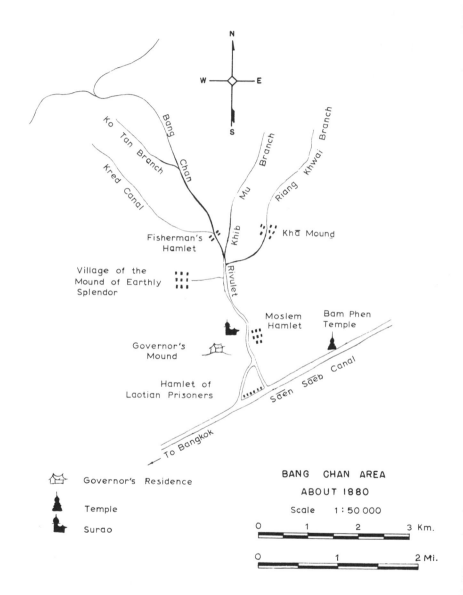

Governor's Residence

Temple

Surao

BANG   CHAN   AREA

ABOUT 1880

Scale   1 : 50 000

and with his help built their first surao. We can guess that at the meeting of the elders following the disaster of the rats some may have reminded the others that His Excellency had granted them freedom to move, and as he had not appeared for more than a decade, their obligations to him and his descendants had ended. The son of their former leader may have pointed to their continuing freedom from rent as evidence that the descendants of their patron still granted them benefits for which they owed services. Yet opportunities awaited those who would claim new lands, and many were clamoring to depart. Long debate only sharpened the differences among the elders, and no unitary sense of the meeting resulted. The hamlet could only divide, for the son of their former leader would not join in the error of the others, but remained alone to perform his duty.

About this same time the promising hamlet on the Mound of Earthly Splendor also disappeared. None of the descendants offered to explain why, nor did we press this question. Since the two hamlets lay within a few hundred yards of each other, the same wave of rats may have eaten their grain too. They had no patron in the city who might bring them rice in the emergency, and, with a lean year ahead when their own local patron could no longer help them, they may have decided to depart. Alternatively, after a few years of good crops, many may have been able to buy their own buffaloes and plows, so that they had no need of a patron's benefits. Maūm died, and Sīlā with his sons left for new lands. Lı and Taw also died, but not before marrying their son to the daughter of Sīlā and Maūm. This household with one other remained at the Mound of Earthly Splendor, lone remnants of the former hamlet.

In a generation of settlement the number of human inhabitants had decreased. Where fifty or more households had once stood, ten or a dozen remained. The two most populous hamlets had all but disappeared, and the wilderness weeds took over the fields that had been cleared. Only the unnamed hamlet of the three fishermen had begun to grow with the households of the children of Tō, Thēp, and Chaēm.

CHAPTER 4

Migration

Between 1885 and 1910 a new migration from Bangkok to Bang Chan ended the temporary triumph of the wilderness. This migration covered the countryside as the entire central plains filled with cultivators, but we are constrained to observe it mainly from the vantage point of Bang Chan. The one-hundred-odd new households that appeared there during this period, many of which moved on again after a few years, constituted certainly a surge of people, even if it resembled little that mass of wagons racing to stake out land claims in Oklahoma. This surge, in its character and speed, was more comparable with that seen in the settling of central and western New York from the 1790s on, after Iroquois hostilities had cooled. People spread here and there, taking up land like a puddle of slowly flowing water that extends an arm and swells to roundness before bursting out again in some new direction. As in New York, the movement consisted of small groups of kinsmen rather than of large organized parties, and each group tended to settle just beyond the remotest hamlet. All left their former homes in hopes of making a better living, yet few if any expected to strike it rich and return with their fortunes made. Like the Springfields and Burlingtons that sprouted across the American hills and plains, people from a given village tended to move to hamlets newly established by fellow villagers (Sharp et al. 1953:28). To follow the course of this migration with its particular characteristics we must look back a few years before its beginning.

Land and Its Meaning

The great capital, City of Heavenly Spirits (Krungthēp Mahānakhāun), was founded by Rama I during the 1780s. Geomancers helped select the site for a palace city while the military helped provide for its security, following in part lessons learned a century before from the ill-fated French military technical aid mission. During the succeeding years the encircling walls and moats were twice rebuilt in widening arcs to furnish a larger haven for the mounting population. Even in 1851 the chronicles tell us: "Every day villages and towns multiplied. People were more numerous than when the capital city was founded. It grew many feet. The capital extended its breadth again. So it was ordered that the Lord Minister of the heart, Chao Phrayā Srīsurijawong the prime minister, become director and in company with Chaomȳn Wajworanarod hire Chinese to dig a canal and moat the capital one stage farther . . ." (Thiphakarawong 1934a:70). Yet a few years after this second rebuilding, the population overflowed again into the surrounding padi fields. People from the provinces as well as from overseas were drawn toward the thriving city.

Presumably all who entered and established residence in the royal city or departed from it did so with permission of the king. At least in theory this was the case, and indirectly so in fact. Kings granted permission to various nobles to build palaces, designated sites for the construction of temples, and indicated to foreigners where they might locate their residences, businesses, and consulates. Yet large sections of the city were covered with a confusion of wooden houses, some facing canals, some on newly constructed streets, and some accessible only by a plank across a mud flat. Here most inhabitants had probably squeezed in without the direct authorization of the royal voice, though they had received permission from some superior in the towering hierarchy of rank. Each proprietor of a teahouse, master of a tinker's shop, or dweller in some dingy room paid a good rent in cash or services for his location, and those living aboard a boat on some canal did not escape dockage or mooring fees. Some renters knew very well the owners of the land where they lived: ". . . a long term lease was secured on a new site across the canal from the Bradley house, the rental sixty-five baht per month. They moved to this plot in 1838 after the owner, the Phra Klang, had erected two residences for Dr. Bradley and his colleagues" (Wells 1958:11). But the vast majority knew only the collector of rent; in turn these collectors paid rent to other collectors in a long trail that might eventually be traced back to some nobleman whose father or grandfather had received a grant of the land from the king.[1]

On the face of it, title to the land resembled fee simple in that the owner, like owners of property on Main Street or the Grand Canal, might sell, convey, or mortgage the land. An important difference lay in the king's right to condemn the land at any moment without having to justify his objective or even to compensate the owner. To the extent that this threat hovered over a piece of land, no one possessed land in our sense but rather used it and exploited it as long as he could (Dilock 1908:95–97; Wales 1934:122). We infer that lands within the city walls other than those retained by the crown were tightly held by a small number of people and that owners changed only at death or when His Majesty decided to appropriate a tract.

Outside the city walls there grew up a broken ring of nondescript buildings. There, where rents were low, some successful Chinese peddler with limited funds might open a snack shop. Perhaps he rented an upstairs room to a couple with children recently arrived from up-country. Through the window these people might look out on the open space where great storage pots and jars stood ready for sale near the maker's kiln. Not far away a Chinese gardener grew bean sprouts and fat cabbages on the mounds he had heaped up to keep the vegetables out of deep water during the rainy season. Beyond this fringe began the Thai farmer's padi fields, dotted with clumps of trees. Their huts stood in these groves, and such a zone extended a few miles out from the city's fringe to the edge of the wilderness.

Each extension of the city carried repercussions to the wilderness. As the population around the city walls expanded, new houses displaced small factories and gardens, which in turn moved farther out into padi fields. When at last room no longer sufficed to grow rice, the farmer sold out and started looking for new land in the wilderness. On reaching the area in which he wished to settle, a newcomer had to apply for permission to occupy land from the local commune headman (kamnan). As the government's local representative who collected taxes on land, this man knew the location of free land and was empowered to issue a certificate of preemption (*baj jiabjam*), which in the region of Minburī during the 1890s cost six baht for forty rai (LMH 5/25/53). In Bang Chan a man might claim up to fifty rai (twenty acres) and an extra fifty for each male child. After a year of occupation a certificate of possession (*trā chaūng*) might be obtained from the nearest office of the Department of Lands (Krom Nā). Thereafter the owner was expected to notify this government agency of any changes in title. If he abandoned the land, title was lost (Dilock 1908:72–73; Wales 1934:121–122).

Until late in the nineteenth century, when the urge to settle began, rural lands had so little value that almost no official attention was paid to them. A change began in the 1870s. In 1874 the purchase price of abandoned land was set by the Department of Lands at 0.25 baht per rai for uncleared land and 0.375 baht for cultivated land (Min. Ag. 1957:19). This was precisely the annual tax for these kinds of land. Moreover, as Wales states, people held small areas:

> In later times families seem to have gradually acquired estates up to 80 or 100 rai or even 200 rai. Princes and high officials could also buy land like other people and since, moreover, their large bodies of household retainers were considered as being members of their families, they were allowed to acquire extensive domains, up to as much as 10,000 rai. . . . The estates of the officials were comparatively small, the clients were attached to their patrons on a personal basis and could change them if the king gave permission; and moreover, the great landowners did not reside on their land but far away in the capital. [1934:122–123]'

We have already witnessed an instance of landholding of this kind, when Chao Phrayā Phraklāng and his son Chao Phrayā Srīsurijawong settled the Moslem prisoners of war who had become their retainers. It was useless to hold more land than could actually be used, for one had to pay taxes on it. Better to abandon unneeded land and acquire more later when one had the work force to exploit it. Land alone without men to create and maintain its usefulness was a very secondary consideration for anyone seeking to advance his reputation.[3]

During the 1870s symptoms of mounting tension over land claims appeared, perhaps for the first time on any noticeable scale. The main record of ownership until then had been the memory of the local commune headman who collected land taxes. Though the Department of Lands, after issuing its certificate of possession, was presumed to have received notice of abandonment or change in title, few owners seem to have troubled themselves about this formality. In 1874, when land disputes began to mount, the Department of Lands instructed its officials to issue specially signed receipts to each payer of land taxes. Litigants might then produce their receipts for an inquiring official to prove ownership (Min. Ag. 1957:15–16). A friendly commune headman was the chief guarantor of continued occupation of any particular bit of land, and until 1892 no boundaries were officially marked (Min. Ag. 1957:23). Only after 1900 were descriptions of real property recorded by the government. Then the snarl of conflicting claims could no longer be unraveled by judicial investigation. Arbitrary action offered the only remedy, and the Department of Lands replaced the old certificates with descriptive deeds (Min. Ag. 1957:63).

No *lares* or sacred ancestral shrines (*lāk bān*) exist in central Thailand to bind kinsmen to a particular plot of rural land and then protect them and their descendants from trespass. The Rice Mother (Māē Pōsob), who brings the padi to fruition, lives everywhere in central and southern Thailand. Mother Earth (Māē Thōranī), an elemental deity, has all land in her jurisdiction, just as the Goddess of Water (Mēkalā) reigns over the watery element. Many householders invite a guardian spirit (Phra Phūm) to protect them and their house and other possessions, but these guardians do not object to moving with the household. Only a few crusty supernaturals jealously inhabit a particular tree or cave and refuse to be moved; and they have no more interest in one kin group than in another. The Thai live anywhere. Landownership resembles the squares on a chess board, to be held and defended, but if one is forced to move or if a better position appears, no bonds of sentiment, symbol, or myth need first be broken. In cities people pay rent; in the country, taxes. When an occupant has received sufficient money to compensate for the pains of departing, another takes his place.

Ownership was reserved for the king, as implied by the title Lord of All the Earth (Phrachao Phāēndin). So too such vassals as the kings of Chiengmai and Luang Prabang owned land, but not in the sense of a bounded territory. They held the power to rule the people of regions that never had to be defined very precisely until late in the nineteenth century. Here "ownership" connotes not the sedentary oneness of the Middle English "our" and "being on one's own," but the defensive tenacity implied in "holding" and the German *Held*, today meaning "hero." When this idea of holding is divorced from land and attached to people, we approach the Thai concept of ownership. In 1901, when the new certificate of ownership was being issued by the Ministry of Agriculture, the announcement declared: "The land title granted an owner confers upon him the right of ownership [*kamsith*]. However, this does not authorize escape from responsibility or from the necessity of conforming to the law or paying taxes or obeying other official orders intended to promote public welfare" (Min. Ag. 1957:42). The Thai government was taking no chances that someone would consider himself a little king, witnessed by the word "ownership."[4]

Almost everyone occupied land rather than owned it. Only in the crowded sections of the city and its immediate surroundings did occupation of land carry authority. Such authority rested on the actual control over occupancy and the ability to impose rents.[5] Because of the resultant economic value, lands might be mortgaged; and we can imagine that moneylenders eagerly offered large sums to a nobleman fond of gambling, as long as the debts were secured by his lands within the city. Beyond the city walls lands acquired value to the extent that they might be rented, and as this urban-like rental value advanced into the countryside, land prices increased.

Royal Policy and the Social Order

Nations sometimes act as if they were phobic, and perhaps every society lives with an anguishing vision of its own demise. Both China and England seem to have been gnawed for centuries by fear of invasion. Of course, they had good grounds for those fears, yet the antidotes that each devised were excessive. Though the last invasion of England by an enemy occurred more than nine hundred years ago, the English have readily invaded Europe many times since then to oppose and subvert a growing continental power before an invasion could be mounted. China built, repaired, and extended its Great Wall at enormous cost in material and life in response to a similar threat. Some nations fear internal weaknesses. The Japanese have long been apprehensive about destruction by the uncontrolled passions of their own people, and among other defenses they have ardently cultivated the powers of the police. After revolution and long struggle to establish its own political unity, the United States seems to anticipate chaos from alternative political systems. Accordingly, officially and unofficially, it has long repressed "alien" political doctrines.[6]

Thailand sees its demise in the evaporation of its people. On that forlorn day a lone Thai will look across the Māe Nām to the spires of Bangkok, where only a few hungry dogs remain, howling among the deserted houses. The lone man has been abandoned by all his fellows. They did not shun him, nor had he offended them. They had just moved away because of circumstance, and he was helpless to prevent their going. Something like this happened after the fall of Ayutthayā in 1767. Those who had run away to hide during the seige returned to find everyone gone; those who had not been killed had been herded off as prisoners of war, like the Laotians and the Moslems. Then years followed when, without skilled people, living was difficult, and the small protective force could not cope with brigands along the waterways. But these and other foreseeable hardships of the aftermath were not the sensitive point. It was abandonment itself (*pliaw* is the Thai word).

Abandonment spells the end. Alone one is neither patron, client, nor partner. Without bonds to others, the individual as well as society perishes. There is no clientless patron, patronless client, or partnerless partner. Had Robinson Crusoe been a Thai, to survive his ordeal he would have had to meet his servant Friday on the beach after the storm. So each time a child leaves the household, a servant leaves his master, or an assistant leaves his chief in a government office, the specter of abandonment reappears. There is no way to hold one who has the right to change patrons. Anyone may run away, even beyond civilization to the forest (*paj pā*) if his patron offends him sufficiently, and of course a patron can send away or stop patronizing his obnoxious client. But by and large the weight of blame falls on the patron when a client leaves, and patrons considered themselves longsuffering. So when a patron has done all he can and still his client leaves, he has reached the depths of impotence.[7]

Hard times only throw the specter of abandonment into sharp relief. Then a patron rewards his clients less generously, and clients must work harder for less generous benefits. As sorry times reduce formerly affluent patrons to the same lower level, slight advantages suffice to draw clients from one patron to another. The end of the Village of the Mound of Earthly Splendor seems to have come about in this way. As soon as one of the Laotians could earn thirty baht, he could become an owner of plow and buffalo; his former patron's advantage in wealth was slight and so was the stability of his menage. Here was bankruptcy in the old economy of labor.[8]

The concern over abandonment is perhaps indicated by the zeal of each new king in reregistering the entire population (Wales 1934:97). The edict of Rama II, written shortly after his accession in 1809, described the following conditions as grounds for reregistration:

It has been the custom of kings from old time to preserve the Buddhist religion and to further its prosperity. The way of doing this was by keeping cohorts of good soldiers to form an army and by accumulation of weapons, with the royal power at the head. Thereby he vanquished all his enemies in warfare, and he prevented the Buddhist religion from being endangered by the enemy, as kings have always done.

In Bangkok, of the soldiers who have fought in former wars, some are old and unfit and some are dead. Those *brai hlvan* [*phraj luang*] who are fit have changed their patrons, and the latter have not reported this transference. Some of them have tried to get hold of old clients, while many cases are left unsettled until today. The lists have not been brought up to date, and so have not been correct for some time. Some of the clients have deserted and run away to hide in the jungle because the patrons overworked them, which they were unable to bear. Their patrons would not take any notice of their private affairs or happiness. Some ran away because they were afraid of punishment and some because they were afraid of their creditors. Some have run away because they were fined. They were afraid to return because they had done wrong, so they stayed on in the jungle for some time in spite of the discomfort. Some of these clients have gone to a governor and offered to work for him in return for protection and for his hiding the fact of their presence. In some cases a group of fourteen or fifteen persons have offered themselves as slaves to a prince of kram [krom] rank or a prince below kram rank or to officials, and have got documents to show they are under the protection of these important people. Then they have gone back to live as a band of outlaws in some district, saying that they were under a powerful master in the capital whose letters they have, and so would not work for their old patrons. Some of them became more daring and committed thefts, stealing elephants and buffaloes, and hiding them in their lairs. The owners of these animals knew about it so the thieves passed on the animals further away, and that caused fighting and sometimes killing. This resulted in much trouble during the last reign. [Wales 1934:132–133]

Registration of population is a normal course for governments seeking to collect taxes and apprehend criminals, but few governments seek to tattoo or brand anyone except a criminal, for whom special surveillance is necessary. Vagrancy is a misdemeanor in many countries; a vagrant without satisfactory identification may be arrested and investigated; but rarely is lack of proper identification per se a crime punishable by permanent attachment to the government as a royal slave (*thāt luang*) or to some official as a bondsman (*phraj som*) (Wales 1934:53; Rabibhadana 1969). Only under most unusual circumstances does a governor order soldiers to comb the backwoods and hill tracts for a harmless few who have decided to live apart from others. Most societies deem it a privilege for a person to live among its people and enforce exile or imprisonment on the delinquent few. But not Thailand. Exile was nonexistent and delinquents were killed.[9]

In the perfect Thai society every client was attached to a patron, but any participant knew very well that this ideal state depended on the freedom of clients to change patrons. If clients were too tightly bound to their patrons and exploited as drudges, they worked no better and were more likely to try to escape to the forests. If clients were too loosely bound, weavers might never finish their cloth and meals might go unprepared as people loitered in the marketplace. Somewhere between these extremes a sagacious king might find the optimal degree of limited freedom for a client to change patrons, and each sagacious king seems to have cinched the girth to a differing degree of tension.

Rama II believed in tightening control over the freedom to change patrons, for he sought out the strayed:

Let governors and officials give out orders to the district officers in order to make it known to those clients who have run away from their patrons, to *brai hlvan* [*phraj luang*] who are still fit, slaves who were originally prisoners of war, debt slaves who are hiding in the forest, to come back to their old chiefs willingly. They will be pardoned this time. . . .

If those clients who have run away still want to be under the protection of the jungle and refuse to come back willingly to their patrons, in whatever district they are, let the governor and officials send a force to capture them and their children and imprison them all. [Wales 1934:133–134]

These restrictive measures contrast with the views of Rama IV, who fifty years later urged that clients be turned loose to fend for themselves. He found his people too lazy and placid in their servility.

In 1855 King Mongkut made possible the continuous export of rice. Yet the people demonstrated a certain dissatisfaction about this measure because the rice, a chief food, became too expensive. Thereupon Mongkut declared in the year 1857 that peasants would have to strive for the possibility of receiving from their work the necessary wage to buy the more expensive rice, and this they had not yet accomplished. At the same time he indicated that the amount of uncleared but productive fields offered an opportunity to cultivate land, if anyone did not wish to pay the increased price. [Dilock 1908:81]

We recognize a familiar theme: a hungry client works better if he must feed himself.

How King Rama IV and his prime minister, Chao Phrayā Srīsurijawong, reached their views is not clear. Certainly by 1855 they seem to have settled on a fairly consistent social policy, for Bowring reports the following interview: "If the Kalahom [prime minister] be sincere, matters will end promisingly; if not, he is the most supereminent of hypocrites. He denounces the existing state of things with vehemence; says that bribery and misrule are often triumphant—that monopolies are the bane of the country, and the cause of the loss of trade and misery of the people. He told me I should be blessed if I put an end to them and encouraged me to persevere in a most vigorous persistence in my efforts for its over-throw" (Bowring 1857, 2:287).

Only five years earlier Sir James Brooke, with a similar mission to conclude a treaty of commerce with King Rama III, had been turned back at the mouth of the river. However the ideas may have been acquired, Adam Smith's doctrine of free enterprise had clearly caught the fancy of King Rama IV (who had seen the Brooke proposals) and of his minister, and seemed to them to offer a policy for righting the ills of the country. We further suspect that a Jeremy Bentham lurked somewhere in the offing when the prime minister addressed Bastian a few years later at the occasion of feeding several hundred priests in the palace. In the course of this act of piety by a Buddhist monarch, the prime minister whispered to the European visitor: "Instead of our feeding these beggars and day-light thieves, they ought to be made soldiers or turned to working; then they would be useful, but now they are just a burden to the country" (Bastian 1867:73). Such a statement was not intended to reach the ears of His Majesty, who had spent many years in the priesthood before mounting the throne. Nevertheless, this utilitarian critique of Buddhism represents more than a personal reaction of the prime minister; it recurs with a slightly more Marxian flavor in the writing of the young Prince Dilock from a German university (Dilock 1908:108–109).[10]

The underlying domestic reform was directed toward stimulating the will and initiative of thousands long accustomed to obediently awaiting their patrons' commands. More freedom would have to be given the clients, and along with it some stimulation to use it. Rama IV forgave taxes on uncleared lands for the first three years and encouraged people to become rice growers on their own (Dilock

1908:82–83). The holding of large acreages or plantations by absentee owners was not encouraged, however. He taxed many useful commodities, not only for the purpose of increasing revenue but also to encourage people to work harder in order to obtain what they needed. He may have succeeded in part, for according to a retrospective statement on revenues during this reign, completed in 1869, "the various things that remained were not taxed and so brought very little revenue. Food of every kind became more expensive; on this account the taxes began to rise; or because the number of people increased; or because the power of virtue made people force each other until they had to earn a living and so do something useful to make a profit. Until the time of the sinking of the world, there will still be people doing a variety of things in order to prosper" (Thiphakarawong 1934a:366). The chronicler's evidence shortly after the end of the reign showed that initiative did increase with prices.

During the next reign, in the 1870s and 1880s, Rama V seems to have continued on the course set by his father. Encouragement to settle new lands through tax abatement and digging of new canals in the wilderness continued. Perhaps the greatest single stimulus to individual initiative came from the series of measures that freed the slaves and removed the human being from among the commodities of the markets. Many private foreign companies secured permission to conduct business in the country, and in 1889 the royal favor shone upon a land development project under private capital, the so-called Khlaung Rangsit project under the Siam Canal and Irrigation Company (Borisad Khud Khlaung lae Khū Nā Sajām). This project made about 1.5 million rai of fertile land in the central plain available for persons able to pay the highest land prices in the country (Dilock 1908:99; Graham 1913:324–326).

In conjunction with this project a new turn of policy seems to have occurred. Rama V was no less fearful of abandonment by his subjects but continued to give them a free rein. He was troubled because with free rein they had moved little, and after nearly forty years enormous tracts of land remained without settlers. He resolved that a monarch must direct his subjects, set an example for them, and furnish them the means for doing their tasks. So from 1890 to the end of his reign in 1910 Rama V spent his major energies building the new machinery to help govern the people more effectively. Their transportation, education, welfare, and health required his attention. New branches of government had to be formed to carry on these new tasks and personnel trained to execute new duties effectively (Wyatt 1969). With this new machinery the king, as patron of patrons, granted greater benefits to more clients than anyone before him. Clients were freer to find new patrons on the lower levels of the social pyramid but were bound more tightly to their kings than Rama II would have dreamed possible. Rama V has been recognized ever since as King Chulalongkorn the Great.

Into Vacant Lands

Several accounts tell something of the circumstances during departures from the Bangkok region. One informant speaks of the decade of the 1890s: "My father and mother came from Bāngkapi, where the land was crowded. My father was persuaded to come to Bang Chan by Nāj Nēd, the man in charge. This man preferred not to be called *Nāj Kāung* and called himself 'royal deputy' [*chāng wāng*]. He hunted up places to move to. There were four households together, all relatives. He brought us to Kred canal, where we took up land we bought through him. Each household then held fifty rai" (LMH 8/26/57).[11] Population pressure drove these people away from their Bāngkapi lands, where they had lived for years and from which they journeyed to the palace for their annual three months of duty. Their superior evidently deputized a subordinate to assist the households seeking a new location, for a good patron must help his clients. Doubtless Nāj Nēd, the deputy, received some commissions along the way, thus making his duty less painful. In Bang Chan, necessarily continuing palace services, these people became known as the servants (*bāw*) or followers of the royal deputy (*chāngwāngchāb*).

Another woman told of her family's move to Bang Chan: "My maternal grandmother lived at Khlāung Tej but had land at Thā Phrachan near the royal cremation grounds. She sold her land but was cheated by an official who forced her to sell at a price below its real value. The father of my maternal grandfather had an orchard near Suanchid in Bangkok. He had a jar full of money. They called him 'Mr. Gold' (Khun Thāung). One of his sons gambled so much that he lost all the gardens, orchards, and rice fields. He became a beggar and smoked opium. So my maternal grandfather bought land here in Bang Chan while there was still some money left" (LMH 8/11/57). These sales occurred during the decade of the 1880s. Here we find an official who used his social position to force a sale of land at his own price, and an instance of the sacrifice of land to satisfy a gambling debt.

Of eight known cases in which people left the Bangkok region and moved to Bang Chan before 1910, six were clearly forced through circumstances to give up their land before moving. Whether the other two in fact chose to sell their lands and voluntarily move to the country is not clear from the record. The following account suggests a certain reluctance to move: "My husband's maternal grandmother was one of three sisters living in Khlāung Tej. They had equal plots of land there. This grandmother lost her land from gambling, but one of her older sisters, with no children, took the unlucky ones in with her and used her land. This sister bought land in Bang Chan. When she died, she gave the land in Bang Chan to her nieces and nephews. Among them were my father and mother. When the aunt died, they sold the land in Khlāung Tej to pay for the cremation, and then they moved to live in Bang Chan" (LMH 8/11/57). As long as a wealthier aunt could support the family, they remained in the Bangkok region. We suppose that if they had been able to sell the Bang Chan land for enough to meet the expenses of cremation, they would have sold it in preference to the Khlāung Tej land. Certainly the picture of Bang Chan was scarcely alluring: "To reach our place in Bang Chan from Sāen Saēb canal took a whole day, and you would have to spend the night before returning. The weeds were very thick, and the bottom of the boat often rested on weeds. Mosquitoes were thick, too" (LMH 3/1/54). Buffalo became sick "because of insect bites," and snakes "as big as your wrist" were frequently seen. Rats and weaverbirds always threatened rice crops. To have to move from the city was a misfortune, just as it had been a generation earlier when Tō, Thēp, and Chāem had moved.[12]

Circumstances during the 1880s and 1890s plucked away the umbrellas that had sheltered many city people. A man who earlier might easily have borrowed money on his services, and as debtor been sustained by his creditor, was now prevented from doing so by the abolition of slavery. The children of slaves born after 1868 could no longer become slaves again after they won freedom through maturity or purchase, and every year their numbers increased as an unattached and unattachable proletariat.

Some might offer their services for wages to former masters, who themselves were struggling to survive in an economy increasingly dependent on cash. ". . . Besides there is still a large number of lands returned to the state which lie at some distance from the market. Earlier, during the time of dependency on slavery, these areas could have been used productively because no wages were paid for this work. Now, however, it no longer pays to have it cultivated, and the costs of production are much too high in wages and workers. On this account the owners return this area back to the state, unless they want to pay taxes" (Dilock 1908:96–97). These landowners were attempting to retain their cheap labor, but in 1899 a law prohibited the payment of wages more than three years in advance, at the same time fixing the rate of repayment of such a debt at four baht per month (Duplatre 1933:119; Graham 1913:224). Thus a kind of minimum wage was set at forty-eight baht per year, or twice that amount if food were not provided. About the same time (1908), Dilock states, Laotians received eighty baht for nine months as agricultural workers.[13]

Despite relatively high wages in the city (Ingram 1955:56), employment possibilities were minimal. The developing commercial enterprises had long been organized on ethnic lines: "Western mercantile houses, faced initially with Chinese commercial dominance, had no choice but to employ Chinese compradores. While the operation of the system ensured predominantly Chinese employment in firms, the western merchants would not have had it otherwise, for they preferred Chinese industriousness and know-how to the easygoing work habits of the Thai" (Skinner 1957:103). Chinese guilds and associations had already organized many of the commercial tasks of the city.[14] Others who had secured a foothold in the city also remained. The *Siam Repository* (1870:335) described as slaves Laotian carpenters who worked on government buildings.[15] Three decades later Lunet de Lajonquière (1906:15, 62) stated that 15,000 Laotians, mainly carpenters, remained at work in Bangkok in the occupations of their fathers. Those who could find employment and were sufficiently organized to defend it might remain in the urban system. Those who lacked skills, organization, or entrée had to expect for a time haphazard shelter and scattered meals as occasional jobs came and went; theirs was a coolie existence.

The dream of Rama IV was being realized, but not by trade treaties or by making people buy necessities at increased prices.

Enterprise appeared, in fact, overnight as soon as slavery was abolished. Before that the improvident, the unfortunate, and the shiftless had been cared for as slaves by their creditors. Now those without wages to pay their rents had no place in the scheme. Thailand moved toward an approximation of the modern corporate society in the Western style, with production and trade carried on under government protection.[16] Once the wilderness had been a retreat for the disaffected few. In the new social order the many more without a place in the productive scheme had to fend for themselves, and the wilderness offered them a haven. There they were neither regarded as outcasts of the old style nor allowed to arrange their own ways of living altogether independently. Such a large group could not be permitted to run the risk of vanishing or of abandoning society. So they were carefully settled on virgin or other lands by newly appointed commune chiefs, registered at newly built district offices managed by officers newly trained in the recently established civil service, and supervised by newly organized police.

The spirit of free enterprise seemed occasionally to touch the migrants themselves to some degree, for a few said they hoped to become rich. But these were dreams or idle fantasies; not many really hoped to find the buried treasure of some forgotten temple, and any tale of gold mines and great new enterprises was only idle talk to amuse the paddlers along the way toward a hard life. Behind them in Bangkok remained the known models of the rich, the proprietor of a gambling house on the river, the government official in his teak house within a shaded garden. Anyone who aspired to one of these styles of living must have given up the dream long before settling into a boat bound for the wilderness. The riches that one might be able to count included a field along a broad canal not too far from a market, to which a man and his wife might bring the abundant crop raised with their own buffalo, plow, and helpful circle of kinsmen. They would return home with the tools and clothing that their household might need, and still find enough padi in the bin to give freely to the temple and to any neighbor who asked. If this good fortune continued, they might be able someday to build a house of dressed lumber protected by a great wooden naga, the protecting serpent, at each end of the roof peak. This house they would promise their youngest daughter if she and her husband remained and cared for them during their old age. Such a version of riches might be achieved, and if not at the first site of settlement, then they would try their luck elsewhere.

To Bang Chan and Beyond

Some moved from the Bangkok region by boat and some through the tall grasses overland on the backs of buffaloes. An old man recalled: "I was eleven years old when I came [ca. 1890]. My grandparents had come four years earlier and were living on Kred canal. They were my only kinsmen there. We came from Sāmsen. Here it was forest. The rice was not high because of many fish and birds that destroyed it. There were elephants too. Not far from my grandparents' house were others. Some houses were near the present surao. Near my grandparents were four houses belonging to Nāj Tō, Nāj Thēp, Nāj Chaēm, and Nāj Phan, the [adopted] son of Nāj Tō" (LMH 5/6/53). He, his parents, and his siblings, intending to fish for a living, had paddled up the Bang Chan rivulet past the few remaining households of the former Moslem and Laotian villages. Farther along lived the fisherman brothers, away from Sāmsen three decades or more but still able to attract "friends" from the old setting. The new households took up vacant land farther upstream.

Much untilled land also lay downstream from the fishermen's hamlet, and about the same year two other households, a man with grown children and his newly married son, appeared on the edge of the rivulet. They had come from Hualamphong, where the government had seized their lands to build a railway. Soon they were joined by others:

Our families came from Bāngkrabȳ and we were related to the Chanphed family from Hualamphong. Nāj Sī came because the railway condemned his land and did not pay him. Nāj Tō [his son-in-law] owned twenty-five rai of land near Wat Haekhwam. This was condemned for use by the army. Nāj Sī rented land in Bang Chan from Phrayjā Maekhlaung, who owned the land locally, but Nāj Tō bought the land he occupied. They came here because of the ease of living and the fish. They raised rice to eat and caught fish to sell in the market on Saēn Saēb canal. [LMH 8/3/57].

Thus new hamlets were beginning to form of groups of people known to each other from some association in the past or because they belonged to that amorphous cluster that people called kin.

Settlement extended first along the main canals and then branched up the rivulets and sloughs. From Saēn Saēb canal, up the rivulet of

Bang Chan, and then up the arm called Kred canal, well beyond the last household from Sāmsen, new people came. One Nāj Chek, of Chinese background, from the Bangkok suburb of Khlāung Tej, moved in with his Thai wife and her younger siblings to occupy land received from his wife's maternal aunt (see p. 266, n.7). A short distance away an attendant in the royal pharmacy bought land adjoining that of a group of Laotians, and erected a hut for himself, his wife, and his younger brother. A year or two later the deputy of another department settled four households on land purchased from Laotians. These Laotians said they had come from a Laotian village on Sāen Sāeb canal. They did not say whether they had spent a few years at the Village of the Mound of Earthly Splendor.

Those who sold their land to the newcomers pocketed the few baht and went on their way looking for new fields to clear. One of the Laotian descendants of Bang Chan related:

When I was young, my father set out for Canal Nineteen. The government dug the canal later, but then there was only a stream. We moved because my [maternal] grandmother had only sixty-six rai, and my mother did not receive any because there were many children.

At Canal Nineteen a man could take up as much land as he wanted, fifty or one hundred rai. There were no temples or hamlet headmen [phū jaj bān]. If someone died, he would be cremated in the fields or sometimes buried without the blessings of a priest, but people seldom died. We drove away the elephants at night and the birds by day. Wild pigs would come and eat the rice. I went out to tend the buffalo. During the first three years we could not raise a crop, because the water flowed off the fields before the rice was ripe. At that time there were no barriers around the edges of the field to hold the water. When we lost our crop, we borrowed rice from a rich neighbor, but finally after three years we let the rich man take our field. Then we came back to Bang Chan. Many had the same trouble but my brother did not sell. He waited for improvements. Now he is rich. [LMH 7/16/57]

So they went from Bang Chan to build other hamlets and slowly learned to look more cautiously at the terrain where they would settle. It had to be neither so high that the floods of the rainy season would recede before the crop was ripe nor so low that the rice plants would be drowned. They looked to see that the land had not already been claimed by another who silently waited a year until the heavy clearing was finished before asserting his claim.[17] They tried to judge soil fertility before paying some agent for land on which no crop would grow. They called in the kamnan to measure their plot lest a later comer infringe upon holdings, and fortified their claim with a new-style title deed.

The protecting branches of government were at first no better equipped than those of any newly opened territory to keep the brigands at bay and to cope with the claims and counterclaims of litigants over land. Though Prince Damrong (Somdet Krom Phrayā Damrong Rāchānuphāb) began in 1892 to reform the Department of the Interior (Krom Mahād Thai), his new district officers, village headmen, and police force would have needed the wisdom of Solomon to untangle the snarls over land claims alone (Graham 1913:254–257; Min. Ag. 1957:33). In 1898 the new minister of agriculture (Chao Phrayā Thewetwonwiwan) rushed a land survey and prepared to issue new title deeds recorded in each district, but a decade later the job had been finished in only a few areas (Graham 1913:288–289; Min. Ag. 1957:59–63). The system of water gates to hold water on the fields until the padi was ready for harvest was probably the most effective single measure of all in protecting farm crops (Min. Ag. 1957:70). In 1899 education sponsored by the government at village temples began, primarily through the efforts of Prince Wachirayan, with some sixty elementary schools in villages of four provinces adjacent to Bangkok (Thai National Archives, 5 S. 26/12). Two decades later government was able to protect its people on almost all new lands, and the last thickets in Bang Chan had been cleared for planting. So the last weaverbirds moved onward to join their cousins and build their nests in thickets nearer the edge of the wilderness.

CHAPTER 5

The New Life

Were it possible today to locate a follower of Achilles who happened to have a retentive memory and could tell us about the fall of Troy, we would probably find him an unsatisfactory witness for our present interest. He might have helped his hero strap on the breastplate each morning, even ridden in the chariot beside him through many a battle. After eagerly describing combat in exhaustive detail, he might turn to the ritual wooing of the gods, who determined, according to him, the battle's outcome. We should listen patiently for a time to his tales but at last seek to introduce topics more pertinent to our interests: How did the various leaders finance their expeditions? How did they obtain the requisite supply of food and material? What supplies had to be kept on hand? Even if such questions, fit for stewards and victualers, did not affront our veteran, he would probably not remember many points vital to our inquiry.

We face comparable problems in reconstructing a history of the Thai past. Our canons of explanation require search among the natural antecedents of an event for "sufficient" causes, but to the Thai the "sufficient" causes fit another cosmic order. Events grow like vines, ensnaring certain people in their tendrils. A Buddhist priest once told of having his eye caught by a lottery ticket under a vendor's stand. He was moved to buy it, and it turned out not to have been the winning number. As such events have meanings that perceptive people may be able to understand, the priest drew from his experience the straightforward moral that people, and he in particular, were foolish to gamble.[1] Behind events lie moral forces that teach lessons to those who examine them. These moral forces have been set in motion by conduct in past existences, and the outcome of an event in which a person has become entangled depends on his virtue or sin in past lives. The balance of these virtues and sins is usually referred to as the individual's store of merit (*bun*). Those with sufficient stores of merit fare well; those with insufficient merit are punished. The old capital of Ayutthayā fell because the Burmans enjoyed sufficient merit, while the Thai were being punished for their sin. In this supremely just world, all follows the moral law (*tham*): good deeds bring happiness to the doer; evil deeds bring misfortune. According to this Buddhist view, the men, material, and morale that we emphasize as causes of a battle's outcome contribute only incidentally. The major determinant is the moral law.

Because of this predisposition, our Thai informants tended to disregard the natural antecedents of events. Their causes lay concealed from human view. No one hoped to explain in advance why one soldier was brutally slain while his companion was spared. People felt satisfied merely to note the outcomes of events that demonstrated the merit or sinfulness of the persons involved.[2] The epic poet of Bang Chan would depict actors and events like shadow puppets on an illuminated screen rather than full-bodied Hectors and Achilleses. In our tale we have had to fashion the natural antecedents as best we could from inference, not from the solid testimony of our witnesses.

The Trader and the Temple

We were fortunate that the death of a certain trader named Sin had occurred less than sixty years earlier. Otherwise he might have been completely forgotten, for the past fades quickly in Bang Chan. He was said to have been the son of a Chinese gardener, to have resided in Khlāung Tej, and to have made his living by paddling a sampan between producers and markets (LMH 8/4/57). By the late 1800s, perhaps earlier, Sin had discovered the hamlet of the three fisherman brothers, Chāem, Tō, and Thēp, where now eight or ten households had fish for sale. Sin, who dealt directly with Bangkok vendors, could at least save them a trip to Sāen Sāeb canal and perhaps offer them a higher price for their catches than the trader there usually offered. Ordinarily he could find somewhere in his boat a few lengths of rope or pieces of crockery to sell in the countryside, and he offered to bring on the following week any item short of an elephant that a customer might wish. He even had a few medicines with him and was known to have cured sick people.[3]

Sin had a further valuable asset, the result of his many years along the rivulets off Sāen Sāeb canal. In his trading he had talked with many people and could see how some prospered while others failed. As he accepted padi, fish, and rice in payment for his wares, he came to know where the best fields and ponds were located. So persons seeking to move from Bangkok into the countryside did well to consult him. He seems to have advised a certain Kong and his wife, of Sāmsen, to establish themselves near the hamlet of fishermen, already peopled with their cousins. His influence, however, was more extensive with kinsmen in Khlāung Tej, whom he advised to take up lands along Kred canal. There he sent his niece and her husband when they had to move (LMH 8/11/57). Probably the royal deputy consulted Sin before settling his clients on Kred canal near Sin's own kin. A few years later Sin followed his own advice and moved also to live on Kred canal.

This trader, curer, and knowledgeable man came to believe his death lay not far in the future. Like many at this point in life, he began to ponder his station in the coming existence. He had not done sufficient evil to be reborn a dog or a buffalo, yet neither had he done sufficient good to be reborn a rich merchant or a government official. In many small ways he had done good for people, yet more direct and active merit making would be desirable. No one told how he reached the decision to build a temple in Bang Chan, but certainly making merit this way built on the solid precedent of many a king, noble, and man of means.[4]

Bang Chan had no temple. Persons wishing to make merit went to festivals at the Bam Phen temple on Sāen Sāeb canal. The sons of Tō, and perhaps of Chāem and Thēp, had been ordained and resided there as priests. But the journey took two hours of paddling, and people welcomed the idea of a priest in residence at a nearer temple, if only for the easier making of merit. The presence of a temple would benefit the nearby residents, and more young men from Bang Chan could begin their adult lives instructed in the consequences of evil.[5] Within each hamlet disputes and crime would consequently dwindle. These priests could conduct the final rites for the dead properly, and the ghosts of the deceased would be less likely to harass the living.

A village temple resembles in certain ways rural churches in North America. The gilded tail of the naga over the glazed orange roof tiles is as much an architectural focus for the surrounding Thai hamlets as the white church spire in a New England valley. At the temple people from various localities greet each other on holidays, much as churchgoers chat after Sunday services. Both groups have committees of laymen to oversee the buildings in conjunction with resident clerics, and these committees organize secular festivities to raise funds. Though birth and marriage call for no temple rites in Thailand, followers of both Christianity and Buddhism bring their dead for final blessing before burial or cremation.

Beyond these similarities a fundamental difference in their relations with their communities distinguishes the church from the Buddhist temple. Here we refer to the concept of membership in Christian churches, which survives from the Judaic tribal past, for in theory Christians, as well as Jews and Moslems, live their lives within religious communities. Their children are formally introduced to the participants, ideally maintain regular periodic contact with them, grow up to take marital vows within the religious community, and finally are dispatched to the hereafter with the special prerogatives of membership in the community of believers. Though battered by secular currents, the church community remains a living influence in many sections of the West.

In contrast, a function of the Buddhist temple is to provide certain services to a secular community. The Lord Buddha was a teacher who showed the effects of good and evil deeds, hence guided the way to improvement of one's lot in this and coming existences. Not all people are ready to listen to his teachings; those who are not will suffer for their shortcomings. The community is unconcerned, for sin ultimately affects only the individual perpetrator. So when yellow-robed priests appear in their boats collecting alms along the canal, they do not thank those who fill their begging bowls with food; they receive their donations in silence, for they are enabling members of the community to make merit. The almsgiver thanks the priest for accepting his offering.

The rest of the priests' roles in the community are incidental to offering the chance to make merit. We do not know when or how priests came to perform the tonsure ceremony for a growing child, to sing blessings for a new house or a bridal pair, and to dispatch the soul of a dead person, but we can surmise that many of these services were accretions during the two and a half millennia of Buddhism. To

Rice to the priests, merit to the people
Photo by Lauriston Sharp

the Thai the words of priests at these times have auspicious power, coming as they do through the long line of teachers from the Lord Buddha himself. The temple houses a monastic community into which men enter for life or a few months by taking vows of abstinence and poverty. Withdrawn from secular life, nourished and

shown the highest forms of respect by a supporting laity, each
member of the order is expected to devote himself to study of the
doctrine and disciplined contemplation, learning thus to improve his
understanding of the Lord Buddha's teachings and his ability to
follow these precepts. This he does primarily for his own personal
benefit, accruing merit for himself and only incidentally adding to
the merit of his close kin and, to a lesser degree, of the surrounding
community that serves him.

But he also stands ready to serve the lay community more directly
when it calls upon him to do so. He may expound doctrine to laymen
when several gather together at the temple and formally request that
he preach a sermon. His preaching helps each individual enmeshed
in profane affairs to renew his understanding or to enhance it, and
thus to lead a better life in which more merit will be acquired. The
physical presence of a priest or several of the brotherhood of priests
permits and stimulates a lay community to make merit by supporting the temple and its clerical occupants and by celebrating religious
festivals there with them. Furthermore, through the years temples
may become centers of learning, in which priests who are specialists
may teach their brothers in the order such arts as the curing of
disease, clairvoyance, the casting of spells, tattooing, and the reading
of the stars. To these priests with special skills rice growers may
come to ascertain the auspicious day for a first plowing or planting.
Similarly a parent arranging the marriage of his child might determine from a priestly astrologer whether the temperaments of the
prospective pair would be compatible.

At first Sin sought to locate the temple in the vicinity of his
kinsmen's hamlet on Kred canal, but no one would sell him the land
he needed. He turned then to his friends at the hamlet of the
fishermen, and a man named Phlym, the son of Tō by his second
wife, the blind woman, sold him twelve rai of land for twelve baht.
During the slack season after harvest in 1891 or 1892, Sin summoned
the strength of many households eager to make merit to heap up a
mound for the temple pavilion (sālā) and make a terrace around its
doors. Local people also assisted a skilled carpenter from Khlaūng
Tej to erect this single building. Because Thai architectural space
must be subdivided into odd numbers of parts, they fashioned an
audience hall, a room for a resident priest with his temple boys, and a
portico. Various local people contributed during that dry season to a

fund that reached 100 baht, in order to buy a Buddha image and, finances permitting, a preaching chair where the priest would sit to chant his sermons. A group of elders then made their way to the Bam Phen temple, where, over tea in a priest's quarters, they invited one Phra Samut to come and live at the new temple. After sanctifying the new pavilion with its grounds, he took up residence. Two households sent their adolescent sons to serve him.

Here were the modest beginnings: land bought and a pavilion erected at a cost of probably less than 200 baht. Sin had been able to accumulate this much and more through his years of paddling the canals, a few satangs' profit here and a salyng there. A year or two later found him settled on Kred canal with wife and daughter, half an hour by skiff from devotions. When he passed, people affectionately called him Uncle Sin.

The New Hamlet on Kred Canal

In appearance the new hamlet on Kred canal was almost indistinguishable from a hundred other settlements in central Thailand. Its plan, the plan that grows when people build their dwellings on their own plots and each of those plots runs to the water's edge, accorded with that of almost every other hamlet in the vicinity.[6] The common thatched huts on raw earthen mounds provided no architectural novelty. People were farmers, and their returns from their crops differed so little that no central hamlet authority based on economic power or prestige could grow. Neighbors exchanged help at weeding and harvest time. People borrowed padi freely when supplies ran short, and sold as much as they could spare to buy their own tools, crockery, and cloth. Skilled work required the summoning of the few specialists. By experience one man knew enough more about carpentry or mechanics to be in demand if a plow broke. Another had learned from a teacher the mixing of concoctions that would restore the body's balance of the element of fire when fever struck. An old aunt could be called for barbering, if she were not too busy tending her daughter's children. Except for the better soil and the presence of his own kinsmen on Kred canal, Uncle Sin might have settled as happily almost anywhere else in the wide central plain.

This new hamlet, however, was not altogether a Thai Middletown. Unlike most places, this one contained four clusters of kinsmen who lived in close proximity to each other. There might have been four hamlets. Except for the common occupation of growing rice, nothing brought these people together. The first settlers were Laotians from Sāen Sāeb canal who probably reached there before 1890. Two of these households remained long enough to be remembered by our informants (LMH 8/13/57). Most inhabitants could say they had come from Khlāung Tej in one of two groups of kinsmen: Uncle Sin with his children, nephews, nieces, and grandchildren—four households altogether—made up one group. The second was a cluster of brothers and sisters with cousins, who formed six households within a few years. Finally five households came from Bāngkapi district. Altogether there were eighteen households in the hamlet, possibly ninety people.[7]

From its beginning this hamlet was larger and certainly richer than the largest hamlet before this time, the Village of the Mound of Earthly Splendor. It outshone the two hamlets of fishermen on Bang Chan's rivulet. The four or five other Khlāung Tej migrants who had settled upstream on the main rivulet were completely overshadowed. In the new hamlet, except possibly for the Laotians, all had come with buffalo and plow ready to grow rice, as if they had merely moved the location of their livelihood. Uncle Sin, who founded the temple, was a good deal better off than most of those who sold him fish. His nephews and nieces were able, a few years later, to exploit their connections with influential people in Bangkok so as to send their sons to school in the city. Aside from the Laotians, men in the other groups of kinsmen were still obliged to work three months of the year in the king's service. In 1949 it was still possible to meet one of these elders:

Iam is a man of seventy-two years and one of the living pioneers. He was born in Phrapadāeng near Bangkok and came with a first group of settlers at the age of thirteen. At the age of thirty he went to work in the Royal Palace in the position of *nāj wen* (man in waiting) during the reign of King Chulalongkorn and King Vajiravudh. He served for thirteen years in the royal household and achieved the rank of *khun praves vetha*. He retired at the age of forty-three and started working in the padi fields, as he felt that farming was a more peaceful and freer life.

His house is a tall wooden structure with a corrugated iron roof. One of his dogs is so fierce that his wife has to use a long stick to manage it. People around do not dare go to his house. He has three or four pictures of kings of the Chakkri dynasty hanging on his wall, a very old Buddha image on a shelf, and some religious books written on palm leaves. [SM 1/27/49]

But for some, such work for the king was a burden rather than a privilege. It required a day's journey along the canal to the city, often at times when labor was needed for farming. Four from Bang Chan worked in the Medical Department (Krom Mau) of the palace, mixing complex prescriptions; one served as guard in a prison (*phathammarong*); another served in the Fine Arts Department (Krom Sinlapākaun), painting murals and refurbishing the royal temples. Later some of these men transferred to the Fireworks Department (Krom Daukmaiphloeng) and became responsible for displays at royal fetes and cremations. These workers earned no pay from their corvée service but might be sheltered in special quarters during their period of duty. Though they were exempt from head tax, a greater advantage lay in their connection with a protecting government official in the capital. At home they moved about with greater immunity from squeezes by local officials than ordinary fishermen and farmers enjoyed.

Because of its agricultural emphasis, this new hamlet developed a rhythm and spirit that further distinguished it from the others. The two fishing hamlets on Bang Chan's rivulet may have had a week or a month of poor catches in addition to the slow period during the dry season, but the periods of tension and release were irregular, like the fall of the winning number in a dice game: if today's catch were not good, tomorrow's might be better. The stores near the Bam Phen temple on Saen Saeb canal also alternated between dull and lively days of trade, affected by the weather, the season, and the calendar of holidays. In the nearby market town of Minburi the same rhythm prevailed, but less strongly because of the even flow of official affairs in the new provincial offices.[8] The agricultural year, on the contrary, offered great sweeps of tense gloom followed by exuberance or despair.

In May, when the rains were due, rice growers everywhere worried. Everyone waited uneasily as the great monsoon clouds towered higher each day. Would the rains come too late, so that the rice would dry up and wither? When showers arrived—some years not until June—householders rejoiced at the croaking of frogs and the little fish swimming in the puddles. The joy of this release soon gave way to new tensions as the rains increased and water rose in the rivulets. Would the rains come too fast and drown the shoots? For five months, until November, a brooding anxiety enveloped the hamlet, putting an edge on most conversations. Unless birds and rodents were greater nuisances than usual, there was little one could do for the rice once weeding was completed. The festivals of Buddhist Lent (Phansā) were not carefree holidays but opportunities advisably seized for merit making, in case this little increment might balance the difference between a good crop and a poor one.[9] Fevers set in with the dankness of the rainy season, and wet winds poured through breaks in the thatching. Not even when the Rice Mother (Mae Pōsob) became "pregnant," that day when the germinal grain first appeared on the stalks, could a farmer breathe easily. He sent his wife with a tray of sweetmeats and perfumes to try to secure the spirit's favor. As the grain swelled, the children, too, were enlisted in the final battle to shoot mud pellets at marauding birds and rats.

Only when the first household raised a flag in the morning mists to call the workers to harvest the crop was the spell broken. From each household, one or two came singing through the fields to the dooryard of their host. Each brought a finger knife (kae) the size of a small clam shell, wielded by the index finger against the thumb, for cutting the stalks individually before binding them into sheaves. After the owner had given simple thanks to the spiritual lord of the place (chao thī), the Rice Mother, and the various other deities who made the crop possible, each worker moved to his designated section of the field, a quarter of a rai for each, to be finished in time for a meal late in the morning. Large-wheeled wagons drawn by ambling buffalo moved each grower's sheaves into a single great pile in the fields (JRH 12/14/53). As a worker finished his allotted plot, he retired to the grower's house for the hearty feast.

Perhaps on the same evening threshing began: "We put a post at the center of the pile of grain and tied the buffalo to it. Each neighbor brought a buffalo. Sometimes there would be twenty animals tied in a line and circling the pole. They would be whipped and made to run. If a buffalo could work well, was fast and could go ahead of the others, they would move him away from the center. It was like gambling: the man who had the fastest buffalo at the farthest end of the circle would be given a colored cloth. Oh, it was fun in the old days!" (JRH 12/14/53).

As soon as possible the boys of the neighborhood carried off the

The harvest
Photo by Lauriston Sharp

padi, singing as they heaped it in the owner's dooryard. As the last measure was poured, they planted a flag on top of the pile. A man with a good crop liked to leave it there a few days for the admiration of his neighbors. Then some evening the winnowing began: "The young people went to any household where a flag was raised in the evening. Before they winnowed and put the padi in the bin, a man who knew the ceremony called the spirit of the rice [*riak khwan khāw*]. Then they began winnowing. They had to start at an auspicious time, and the owner himself had to begin by winnowing a certain amount. People came to help; each house sent a person for the night. The owner provided drink for everyone" (LMH 8/15/57).

Then followed the dry season. A woman described her youth in the new hamlet:

Whenever we went to the temple or to visit a house, we wore a red silk scarf over our shoulder. Then we knew that the person was going out for a good time or for merit. On ordinary days it was just a red cloth. At a visit we'd chat or make cakes and arrange the betel trays for the priests at an ordination. Before I was married, I liked to dance the sword dance (*kabīkabāung*). My father taught me. We kept time to a drum with one or two swords; it was like fighting. We practiced at home morning and evening. Then we did it at every tonsure or ordination ceremony. The host gave us a piece of cloth for this. [JRH 12/12/53]

In addition to these household rites, an annual fair was held at the temple to gather funds for its maintenance. With materials bought from the proceeds, people gathered to replace broken roof tiles or repair a floor in a priest's quarters. Sometimes neighbors made rice liquor; then they would gather for a gay evening of talk, song, and laughter before gradually drifting home to sleep if off.[10] In April came the three days of New Year, when all gaily poured water on each other as they approached and left the temple.[11] Later in the day some household raised a flag to invite people for gambling.[12] In the evenings young people sat in a circle and sang, inviting Mother Splendor (Mac̄ Sī) to possess a girl so that she would dance for them.[13]

From this New Year until the time of rains and of work returned, the dry, hot season served mainly for ceremonies of pious merit making: the ordination of a young man entering the brotherhood for the season of "Lent," or of an older man returning to it; the cremation of a respected older person whose body had been preserved until his scattered kindred could gather for the rite; the day of the Lord Buddha's birth, enlightenment, and death; and regular visits to the temple. The people strove for a calm mood in expectation of coming anxieties. The Thai year had no robust beginning or final withering, but grew toward maturity like the rice, through delicate uncertainty.

The joys of the harvest did not come every year, even though extensions of the recently constructed Rangsit canal system for irrigation and the final building of water gates in 1908 (Min. Ag. 1957:83) increased the likelihood of a good crop. A woman related: "For three years after my marriage [ca. 1903–1906] we lost the rice in the fields because of the mice. My oldest son was still small, and I had to buy and sell things in the market to support my father and children. Life was hard; my shoulder hurt under the carrying pole. I sold the rice that remained so that I could buy things to trade" (LMI I

8/15/57). When the crop failed, men remained at home to guard and tend the property. The women went to places where certain items were readily available, bought them cheaply, and took them for sale to places where they were scarce. With the proceeds the women bought inexpensive items of that locality and moved on. These trading expeditions often took them from their homes for many weeks. Eventually they returned home with rice and cloth for the family. Such hungry years increased the jubilation in years of bounty.

The festivities of the abundant years helped weld the diverse elements of the new hamlet together. As the youths passed each other carrying baskets of rice, a young man could whisper an invitation for a rendezvous after dark with a girl and receive a reply by the raising of an eyebrow a few minutes later. Parents had no difficulty forgiving and welcoming into their house a young man who had eloped with their daughter, if he were known in the hamlet for his industry. Within a few years the hamlet coalesced into a group of cousins joined by marriage.[14]

Perhaps as many as half a dozen young men from outside the hamlet appeared on the scene each year with some kind of introduction to a household: an acquaintance from a store on Saēn Saēb canal, or, after 1906, a fellow soldier or policeman who had served his two years in company with a local youth. As hired men, such newcomers might stay from a few weeks to a year or more. An elderly man described his coming to Bang Chan about 1903: "My father moved from Bam Phen because there was no land there for him, and went to Nakāun Nāyok Province. The land was wilderness and could be cleared fairly easily. We had lived there for twelve years when my father and mother died. Then I traveled to many provinces and finally stayed in Bang Chan because my wife lived there. This is a good place to grow rice, and I have stayed here ever since. Then when I came I was twenty, and now I am seventy" (LMH 6/9/53).

A footloose youth found it advantageous to marry the boss's daughter; he might come into land and house. He had first to demonstrate his industry and run the gauntlet of his wife's brothers, sisters, and uncles, any one of whom might wish to block his hopes. Poor young women of good repute from other hamlets also moved in as the brides of young men of substance, the arrangements sometimes being made through intermediaries (LMH 8/13/57).

Certainly not all migrants into the community were single.

Household groups appeared each year in search of land to buy or rent. Usually they identified themselves as cousins and expected a cordial greeting because of their family connections. But among them also appeared households with no claim to a kinsman's favor. An owner of fifty rai might welcome one or more such families. Ordinarily he could not cultivate more than ten or twenty rai of padi and a few more in a garden, and the rest stood in brush for the buffalo to graze. The uncultivated portion might be rented:

My father was poor and loved to roam [paj thiaw]. He had relatives here in Bang Chan, and his cousins asked him to come with his wife and children [when they heard he was homeless] so that he might live beside them. There were not many houses at the time; this was before the temple was built. So he came but worked for himself. He had no rent to pay because he used the land to grow a crop by clearing some each year. If he had used cleared land he would have had to pay one baht per year for each rai that he rented. After three years he moved to clear lands for another kinsman. Two years later he rented from another household at three baht per rai. [LMH 8/19/57]

Though this particular household, which arrived about 1895, remained to become a part of the community, many moved on after a year or two in search of land to preempt.

Despite its lack of formal authority, the hamlet had ways of turning away the less welcome. Within a household it was easy enough for the head to send away an unsatisfactory hired man no longer wanted as a client. Similarly, the owner of property might intimate that his tenant need not remain for the coming season. But what of an undesirable household that owned property? A woman told of three that came with her parents:

There was Kong and his wife, Thim; Chum and his wife, also named Thim; Ploj and Chaj. Each owned fifty rai by clearing it. When it was cleared, they received title. All were relatives, but not brothers and sisters of the same parents. Thim who married Kong was my maternal grandmother. Both of them died here, and their daughter sold the land to my mother. Chum and Thim were cousins of my father and mortgaged the land to him. They were poor, gambled and drank a lot. Chum liked fun of this kind but went into debt and then moved away. Ploj and Chaj were also cousins of my father. They became poor, sold their land, and went back to Hua Māk to live with her parents. [LMH 8/26/57]

We are not told why the daughter of the first household sold her land to her half sister, but poverty was clearly a factor in the second two cases. This was no prudish community that frowned on gambling or drinking per se. Rather, the question of desirability hinged on the degree of a household's independence and its ability to participate in hamlet interchange. Friendly neighbors exchanged all manner of goods and services without reckoning the balance, but a neighboring household with an indifferent harvest, a passion for gambling, and an appetite for liquor could not hold up its end of the exchange. These people came too often with an empty basket for padi. Even the most compassionate helper had eventually to choose between cutting the benefits to his own household members and aiding an improvident cousin. All began to reckon what they had given and what had not been returned. Poor cousins might postpone privation by acting as comparative strangers and offering their land as security for an interest-bearing loan, but if then they again could not participate in the interchange, they covered their embarrassment by departing.[15]

In the face of more threatening characters, a community first showed its disfavor by withholding neighborly help. Though a person in disfavor might get along alone without hamlet interchange and invitations to festivities, it was awkward for him to harvest, thresh, and winnow his crop without help. Were a person too thick-skinned to take these hints, rumors of alleged crimes and plans to appeal to the police usually sufficed. A man who was said to have committed murder took up residence in a hamlet outside Bang Chan: "Some things were stolen, and the headman blamed my father. So we moved to Prathūmtani. Father worked there to raise buffalo and had twelve head. They proved to be a nuisance because they strayed in the padi fields and ate the grain. So we had to move again" (LMH 12/29/53). In only one instance did a member of a Bang Chan hamlet kill a kinsman, and this killing was thought to have been committed by mistake. Once hamlet members ganged up and killed an offending outsider, but this was an unusual occurrence.[16] More frequently we heard of assault at night by some unseen assailant, but generally people seem to have tolerated abuse for some time rather than risk an open breech of the convention of smiles and small talk.

Because of this difficulty in making an open rupture, the new hamlet acquired another special characteristic. A man appeared bearing the reputation for a dangerous temper, the courage that anger brings, and such skill with a sword that few dared cross him. His daughter told about his life before he came to the new hamlet.

My father, Chyn, lived at Khlaūng Tej. He did not work at any occupation because he was a rogue or hoodlum [naklēng]. He did not really live anywhere because he might happen to quarrel or beat someone and so had to move about frequently. So he went away with his wife and children to Governor's Canal [Khlāung Kud Chao Myang] to escape his pursuers. At that time my father owed money to Khun Bunsag, a government officer who called him to live with him and farm rice. Chyn lived there three years, but one day when he was going to get grass for the buffalo, a group of people came to arrest him, claiming he had stolen a boat. They took the case to the court at Pāk Lad and the judge ruled that the boat belonged to Khun Bunsag. So father won, but he was always a rogue and so apt to be accused. One day Khun Bunsag said, "If you can go elsewhere, please go. I will forget the money you owe me." He always helped my father, until the day when his patience was gone. [LMH 8/19/57][17]

Chyn, free of bondage as a debt slave, then moved with his household to the new hamlet on Kred canal at the invitation of a cousin. From his kinsmen he rented lands. If his reputation did not precede him, he soon acquired a similar one. People said that he was not a friendly neighbor. The officially appointed headman of the area lost three fingers in a sword fight with him (LMH 2/8/54). His daughter told of an incident that occurred a few years later: "My sister Chim married Thaen as his second wife, and all lived together in the same house nearby in our hamlet. When she married, my father gave her a buffalo. Later Chim had two children, but Thaen did not care for them. When my father saw that Chim got nothing from her husband, he took the buffalo back and his daughter, too. So her children grew up at my father's house" (LMH 8/10/57). Such interference was unheard of. A father does not snatch his married daughter home, especially if she has already lived a number of years in another household.

Chyn's talismans protected him against knife and bullet wounds, so that the more outrageous his behavior, the greater his reputation for invulnerability and the more willing his neighbors to let him have his way.[18] His skill with a sword interested young men of the hamlet, some of whom had returned as veterans from the Ngiaw or Shan uprising of 1902. By teaching them some new tricks of sword-play, Chyn gathered a group of followers and thus further fortified his position.

No one said just when or how, but this gang of ruffians became the unofficial police for the hamlet. They began by convoying groups of hamlet residents to temple fairs and other events. Under Chyn's order all moved docilely and safely together at the appointed time to their destination and back. He tolerated neither delay nor insubordination. He once beat his younger brother, who, drunk at some festival, addressed him improperly. When another belligerent gang of young men from Minburi appeared at a Bang Chan temple fair and issued a challenge, Chyn and his group sent them back bleeding. Under his protection, few buffalo were stolen from the new hamlet (LMH 12/29/53).

About 1905 an energetic priest by the name of Phra Samutmo came from Khlaūng Tej to Bang Chan, urging local residents to build a more handsome temple. Though there were a pavilion and residences for a few priests, the essential core of any temple, a sanctuary (bōt), was still lacking.[19] To erect this and other desired architectural features, the priest asked for contributions. Some could build their stores of merit by giving in kind, while the poor could give their labor. Phra Samutmo advocated the traditional brick construction covered with stucco and decorated with floral patterns of tile and porcelain, in the style of the towering Temple of the Dawn (Wat Arun) on the Thonburī shore opposite Bangkok. After two hundred people turned out at his bidding to create a suitable foundation mound, craftsmen from Bangkok carried on the more delicate facets of the building. Phra Samutmo further secured the help of a man employed by the Fine Arts Department to come from his home in the new hamlet on Kred canal and paint the interior with scenes from the life of Lord Buddha.

Chyn also had become part of this project, as his daughter explained:

When Phra Samutmo was looking for help to build the sanctuary, he called on Tuan, the hamlet headman at Canal Eight, and there met my father one day. They had not known each other before this. He told Phra Mo he wanted to see a sanctuary at the temple in Bang Chan, and then Phra Mo wanted to build it. My father was always leader of the group because he was a martinet [naklēng tō]. People obeyed him. When the workmen who were loading boats to bring the materials for the sanctuary quarreled, all trouble stopped as soon as my father raised his hand. Phra Mo needed help. When the sanctuary was finished, Phra Mo wanted to give my father a certificate to show that he was official guardian of the temple [makanājok] because he had been acting like one for a long time. But my father never received it. [LMH 8/19/57]

On the day for the dedication of the new building, Chyn imperiously supervised the landing of the visiting boats, the feeding of the scores of priests, and the preparations for the ceremonies at the auspicious hour.

One glory leads to another, and Bang Chan's temple became further embellished. Since His Majesty Rama V delighted in fireworks, his servitors in the Royal Fireworks Department were instructed to prepare some for competition. Workers from the new hamlet on Kred canal rolled paper cylinders of powder and fastened in fuses. Following a glorious evening of ingenious rocketry and fountains of sparks, it was announced that His Majesty had preferred the display from Bang Chan. He presented the group of winning workers with the customary little gold cups; but having learned of the new temple near their hamlet, he was also moved to give it a name: Temple of the People's Faith in the Moral Law (Wat Rādsadthātham). Phra Samutmo seized on the resulting enthusiasm and built a porcelain-studded reliquary (*wihān*) to match the new sanctuary. Again Chyn supervised the workers until its completion about 1909.

From then until his death (ca. 1918), Chyn's influence maintained order not only in his own hamlet and at the new temple but in many parts of the surrounding area. Once a husband and wife complained to him that a man living near Bam Phen temple had tried to seduce their daughter at night by entering the house, and asked Chyn to judge the case. He directed the defendant to ask the girl's parents for their consent in the proper manner, and the two were subsequently married. Another time he trussed up a noisy drunk at a temple fair and left him struggling in his bonds until he was sober. When people of his hamlet invited the priests in order to make merit, or celebrated the New Year, they always invited Chyn to be present and saw that he was served with honors in keeping with his respected position (LMH 12/29/53).

So the new hamlet on Kred canal grew with a certain distinction beyond any bestowed by its original medley of kin groups, its few well-to-do people like Uncle Sin, or its people with special duties in the royal departments. Its unity came not only from the common celebrations after successful harvests, associations at a new temple, and a degree of homogeneity achieved through the selection of its more permanent members by pressures of local opinion; for a few years Chyn supplied it with an informal government of sorts which brought people together in close security. Even under Chyn's authority, the hamlet continued to act as an assemblage of cooperating autonomous households; yet all households welcomed his demon-like protection against theft and assault by outsiders. People ascribed his rise from humble beginnings to his merit from past lives, and his appointment as guardian of the temple was proof.[20]

The Squire of Bang Chan

Late in the 1890s or early in the new century, an unpredictable event took place in the hamlet of the fishermen that quickened and altered the easy rhythm of fishing and growing subsistence crops. If we must seek a human agent for this change, the protagonist was undoubtedly Phlym, son of Tō by his blind second wife. He was the one who lay in his mother's womb when she was frightened by the sound of some creature crawling over the roof and falling into the water below. We have also encountered Phlym as the seller of land for the new temple to Uncle Sin.

We can offer little more than Phlym's store of merit from past lives to explain his rise from anonymous fisherman to local eminence. It was in a distant Bangkok palace that Prince Damrong formed an indispensable base for Phlym's rise by providing the law for reorganization of local government which his royal brother promulgated in 1896. (Laws 1935a). A second condition for Phlym's rise was subsequently set when provincial headquarters were established in Minburī, only three kilometers away from Phlym's hamlet as the crow flies. Certainly the new provincial governor (*phū wā rātchakān myang*) did not deign to consult a fisherman in defining the districts or communes of the new province, nor had any attribute that Phlym possessed up to that time drawn the population necessary to form a new administrative unit.[21] Yet he was chosen above all other local people to become kamnan, chief of the new commune in which Bang Chan lay.

Because of the absence of old maps and the many shifts of administrative boundaries as population rose, the area of the new commune cannot be fixed with any precision. To the east it probably extended to the area known as Khā Mound (Khōk Khā), where the descendants of these tribal peoples had turned from subsistence to market living, if not yet from animism to Buddhism. Down Bang Chan's rivulet past the new temple pavilion the commune included a scattering of eight or ten households. There a son of Lī and Tau had settled with the daughter of Maūm and Sīlā in one of two remaining households from the Mound of Earthly Splendor. This son was

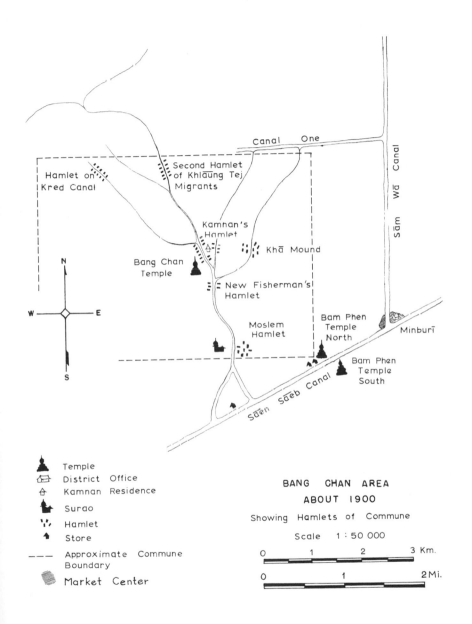

Temple
District Office
Kamnan Residence
Surao
Hamlet
Store
Approximate Commune
Boundary
Market Center

BANG CHAN AREA
ABOUT 1900
Showing Hamlets of Commune
Scale   1 : 50 000

0   1   2   3 Km.

0   1   2 Mi.

appointed headman over these households. Among them were the two stout Moslem homes whose determined men were continuing religious services as best they could at the all but empty surao. Nearby lived four households of newcomers from the Bangkok region. Upstream past the temple the commune covered not only the new hamlet on Kred canal but the smaller second hamlet of Khlaung Tej people on Bang Chan's rivulet, where one of the newcomers served as headman. At least these five hamlets seem to have fallen under the jurisdiction of the new commune.

The new district officer had to select some local resident who knew the lands that were vacant and the lands already taken up, and who claimed them. This new kamnan had to meet the new settlers, issue them preemption certificates, and later collect the land tax from them. He had to have courage to meet such high dignitaries as the governor, perhaps even a minister, as well as such lesser officials as the district officer. He had to demonstrate personal authority by relaying orders to the hamlet headmen and the people themselves. Until a police force was organized in 1906, he enforced the law; and even with the police, it was he that was responsible for keeping the peace among local people. A respected person of energy was required to enact such a role with success.

We guess some reasons for the elimination of many available candidates. No newcomers from Bangkok were familiar enough with the bushy terrain behind the clearings or sure enough of the limits of unmarked lands to direct people where to settle. So such figures as Uncle Sin and Chyn the martinet could not be considered. The choice fell among the older settlers. No Khā or poor descendant of Laotians could easily draw the respect of Bangkok emigrants, proud of their urban connections and disdainful of country bumpkins. The two Moslem households offered persons with capacity for leadership, yet to introduce a Moslem to supervise the predominantly Buddhist population would be to risk conflict needlessly.[22] We are left with the hamlet of the three fisherman brothers.

Not all segments of this hamlet prospered. Neither Thēp nor Chaēm could persuade more than a single child to remain at home to aid his toil, and this may serve as a rough measure of their wealth: the number of people they could lure to live with them. Thēp's daughter married a neighbor's oafish son who gulped down several bridal cakes during his procession to the bride's house. When the referee announced a shortage of three cakes from the number specified in the contract, a moment of panic occurred, but all broke into forgiving laughter when the bridegroom admitted the theft (LMH 8/7/57). The groom subsequently melted into obscurity. Chaēm's children also vanished from the scene, becoming small fishermen on the banks of Saēn Saēb canal. One returned briefly to occupy a portion of his father's lands after the latter's death but was soon in debt and moved away again. The youngest daughter, who looked after the old man in his declining years, remembered that she was "very poor" (JRH 2/18/54). She married a Chinese peddler who made and sold liquor from surplus rice (LMH 8/4/57). These residents of the hamlet could not claim sufficient stature to fill the new job.

The choice narrowed to the sons of Tō, all but one of whom lived in the hamlet. The missing son had moved away to Bangkok, where he died before marrying. Phan, the adopted son, had adequate land for his household needs. At one time he began an orchard but he let it run down. Mainly he fished. His children seem not to have married in Bang Chan. Kham, the eldest son of Tō, had a sizable holding of 120 rai, fished for a living, and no doubt prospered from his rents. His children remained with him. Of Phan and Kham, the latter was the more energetic and the better manager. Phlym had in his youth spent a few months as priest at Bam Phen temple before marrying the daughter of a Saēn Saēb fisherman. Their first surviving child was born in 1876 and a second one about 1886. Between these two years Phlym returned to live with his father, possibly when his stepmother died, in order to look after the old man. From this time the signs of prosperity began to accumulate. Bang Chan people who knew him observed, "He was not considered rich at first. Only when his children grew up was he well off" (JRH 2/18/54). When Tō preempted and cleared more land than he needed, an extra hundred rai, both father and son may have grasped the coming significance of landholding. By 1892 Phlym had already acquired land enough to sell off twelve rai for a temple. A year or two later, when Tō had passed the age for hard labor, a section of land near the house site was converted into an orchard, presumably by Phlym. About 1898 he took a second wife, who bore him two children. We judge that at the time the new kamnan was to be selected, Phlym with his wives and larger household was the most prosperous and most aggressive person of his hamlet, hence the most widely known. Though he was the less favored son of a lesser wife, he had developed his own as well as his father's holdings. Local people would say that he succeeded because of his merit.

If questions arose concerning hamlet leadership before Phlym's appointment as kamnan, there were no ambiguities afterward. Along with his title he received a new name, as was customary at the time of appointment to any royal office; he was addressed no longer as Phlym but as Aphiban, meaning protector. His income rose immediately. From tax receipts he gained three or four hundred baht per year, an amount that reached six hundred or more as the commune grew (LMH 10/5/57). Kham was distinctly second, and whether or not hard feelings arose between them, he sold his local holdings to a neighbor rather than to his half brother, taking his own household and those of his married children to the developing lands at Canal 21 (LMH 8/6/57).[23] The adopted brother, Phan, stayed on until after the death of his wife; then he and his children also departed (LMH 8/17/57).

Phlym's mounting wealth drew new people to the hamlet. Forgotten cousins began to appear. His father's younger sister, years before, had married a rich Chinese and borne a child who as a grown man came to settle (LMH 8/4/57). A daughter of Phlym told of the relatives of her father's second wife: "Chaēng and Pāw came when I was seven years old. They came from Sāmsen but had little land there. Pāw's mother was my mother's sister. At first they settled on the land of Phan, who wished to leave, and they rented lands from my father. Eventually they moved to live on the lands they rented" (LMH 8/6/57). A granddaughter of Phlym's mother's sister arrived with her Chinese husband. The parents-in-law of Phlym's eldest daughter sought harbor (LMH 7/22/57). Some years later one of the children of Phlym's paternal uncle (Thēp) returned with her husband: "Sem's husband was ordained in Bangkok. She was living in Bang Sȳ at the time. After marrying, they moved to Bang Chan because they were kinsmen [phak phuak]. They had to buy land from the kamnan, about twenty rai at three to four chang [240–320 baht]" (LMH 8/7/57). As these and other relatives moved in, the new official prospered by renting or selling land to those who would join him and later grew richer still by collecting their taxes. We estimate that the hamlet increased from 15 households in 1892 to 50 or more by 1910, from 75 people to roughly 250.[24]

Not only the hamlet grew; Phlym's household grew as well. Though his second wife ran away with another man, the two children of the brief marriage remained with their father. A more constant third wife subsequently moved in and over the years bore Phlym six more children. She was the daughter of a poor woman, a cousin of his first wife, who arrived one day to take up residence. She was fifteen years old. "She was not beautiful then, because when she came, she was sick and very thin. Phlym was able to cure her. He was rich, and so she did not object to marrying him. Her parents pushed her into it. He gave her parents a thousand baht as milk money. They lived across the canal in a little house and rented lands from someone [other than Phlym] until Phlym's death" (JRH 2/19/ 54). She became his favorite wife and lived in the same house with him. Sometimes the two made trips to visit the temple fairs in Bangkok (LMH 1/31/53). Phlym also increased his holdings by marrying wealthy widows and helping them to manage their property:

Pāw was a sister of my mother, the kamnan's second wife. At first she settled on the land where Phan, the adopted brother of my father, lived. She and her husband rented lands across the rivulet. They had a big household with seven children. Her husband was a drunkard and cruel. He tried one night to shoot Pāw, but she ran away and hid. Later someone in the dark cut him across the face with a sword, but he did not die of the wound. Separation followed: he went away and remarried. Pāw continued living in the same house. At first she rented land but later bought two pieces. Then she married my father, who married her in order to be her guardian. He had one child by her, but the child died in infancy. [LMH 7/ 26/57]

This lone woman, who could manage to buy as well as cultivate land, remained Phlym's wife until her death. In all there were seven wives over the years.

Phlym settled each wife in her own house in one compound as long as there was space, with the exception of Pāw, who remained in her own house. Later he moved his seventh wife in with Pāw. Each wife had her own kitchen and cooked for the children who lived with her. Phlym occupied a separate house of his own at the former compound, into which he brought his favorite. His two eldest daughters with their husbands occupied their own houses in this compound. Every household appears to have worked an assigned section of the kamnan's lands. The favorite wife described the ordering of the day:

In the morning I fed the buffalo and cleaned the dung away. Then I sometimes cooked and did housework, sometimes looked for feed for the buffalo. All day I worked. In the compound about thirty people lived together, and each house cooked separately. Each house had three to five buffalo. All houses joined together for harvesting and plowing. Each household pounded its own padi [to make rice]. When the kamnan had special work, he called all together. Sometimes he asked all to roast green rice [*khāw mao*]. This he sent as a gift to the district officer or the governor of the province. Sometimes he gave a *kwian* [a "cartful," or about one ton] of new rice to these people. . . . [LMH 11/30/53]

Assisting these wives in running the compound were two or more families of servants: "Chan and $\overline{Y}$, Dī and Nuan were two families of servants. They owed one hundred and twenty baht to a man named Rian at Canal Twenty, and the families asked Phlym to pay off their debts. This he did. They were never called slaves [*bāw*] but everyone knew they were. Phlym paid them sixty baht each year for their work, but they did not want to repay him; so they always owed him money. They worked in the fields, built houses, and ate the same food as everyone else" (LMH 7/24/57).[25] Even after these people had their freedom because of the final abolition of slavery in 1905, they continued to live with the kamnan as hired hands. They were essential to the running of his enterprises. About 1917, when labor was difficult to secure, Phlym rented out some of his acreage (LMH 8/6/57).

A daughter described the scene when the kamnan was home: "Every night I could count sixty or seventy people who gathered under the house. Children, grandchildren, their wives and husbands, no one else came. The kamnan wanted to meet them every day to prevent quarreling. If anyone did not appear, he ordered someone to call the missing person. If anyone had quarreled, he would order the younger to call the elder to come; he asked them why they quarreled and made them be good to each other again" (LMH 7/30/57). He held a tight reign over his compound. Holidays were less carefree than in other hamlets, for he discouraged young men from coming, lest his daughters or wives be tempted to leave, as at least one had already done. So at New Year's the inhabitants of his compound took offerings to the temple but raised no flag in the afternoon for gambling, nor did young people gather in the evening to invite Mother Splendor (Māe Sī) to possess one of them. Visitors tended to be officials, who were courteously invited to a meal and then sent on their way when their business was finished.

Phlym's wealth and official power enabled him to organize any enterprise he deemed needed. Like Chyn the martinet, he wore an array of amulets about his neck to make him invulnerable. His authority, too, rested in part on occult powers: "The kamnan learned from many teachers to make holy water, expel spirits, and many other things. He could stop quarrels and prevent people from accusing each other in court. He knew love magic, too . . ." (LMH 7/6/57).[26] One young priest moved to Bang Chan in order to learn from him.

When thieves menaced his hamlet, Phlym could organize a defense against them, one that became somewhat more automatic than Chyn's: "Phlym had to have his sons [and sons-in-law] on duty every night, each taking a three-hour watch. Later he thought of another way of preventing robbery by collecting all the neighboring buffalo into one place. There were between three and four hundred. Neighbors asked Phlym to care for them, and each brought two or three. Phlym then asked his servants to look after them, and each owner paid the watchers" (LMH 7/30/57).

He could command the hamlet's work force far better than Chyn. Once when the water in the fields was low, he directed his men to raise a dam to hold back the water in Bang Chan's rivulet, to hasten the flooding of the fields of his hamlet. Those below the dam had to wait for their water, and some thought Phlym selfish but did not dare speak out against him (JRH 2/18/54). But when the dam broke a year or two later, it was not repaired. He gained further by being able to distribute government benefits; after the flood of 1919, for example, he handed out rice provided by the government to families with lost crops and drowned buffaloes (LMH 8/6/57). But probably his main authority rested on his ability to grant or withhold favors: "When Kong died in 1920, his eldest son, Pring, wanted to sell his father's land in order to divide the residue among his brothers and sisters and to pay the costs of cremation. There were about fifty rai of land. Pring went to Phlym, who at first advised him to keep the land or divide it among the children. Pring said no one wanted land and that he himself had enough to work. Phlym agreed to buy if for ten chang [eight hundred baht]" (LMH 8/17/57). The number and splendor of benefits that Phlym could offer far exceeded those that Chyn could propose.

Hamlet and commune life were far from austere under Phlym. Though he discouraged ordinary celebration in his compound, he did not seek to prevent gambling or drinking in other hamlet house-holds. He staged magnificent celebrations whenever he chose. For an ordinary feeding of the priests and reading of a sermon to make merit, he could call on the ten households of his own compound for food. Were an important dignitary coming as guest, all households of the hamlet might be called upon to contribute. For the most magnificent occasions he could invite the entire commune to come with eggs, ducks, and chickens, or, in the case of the Moslem households, with beef. At the tonsure ceremony of one of his daughters he presented her with 128 rai of land. At a famous ceremony of homage to his teachers (*waj khrū*) for the annual renewal of his occult powers, a theatrical troupe played a new drama every night for a week. All were glad to come with food for such celebrations. Chyn, in contrast, could threaten but not reward.

During Phlym's life his hamlet differed considerably from the ordinary type, in which households of similar resources reciprocate like services. Exchange of labor and produce necessarily took place in his hamlet, but his compound dominated all local exchanges. If services had to be rendered, Phlym's needs came first; if a buffalo were sick, Phlym was first to be asked to lend one. There were also greater variations in wealth here than in most hamlets. There was no need to send the poor away as encumbrances, for they could be hired to serve Phlym's well-fed ménage; and even the most self-sufficient householder could celebrate the ordination of a son with a little more style because of the kamnan's generous contributions.

As patrons, both Phlym and Chyn were limited. Both may oc-casionally have directed spouses outside their own compounds to stop fighting or to take better care of their children, but Chyn's risk in doing so was greater than Phlym's. Chyn's fewer resources could never hold so many people with the prospects of immediate and tangible aid; and fewer people granted him license to impose. Phlym's kindness and wrath showered over a wider area and were more deeply felt, yet with all his influence he never developed a hamlet organization that went beyond the familiar kind, based on reciprocation of benefits. The corral for buffalo, his major commu-nal effort, lasted only as long as the peril of theft.

About 1920, on his sixtieth birthday—after five cycles of twelve years—Phlym expressed the wish to retire from his duties as kamnan, but neither his superior nor the lesser hamlet headmen

...d for a temple fair
...to by Lauriston Sharp

would grant him the freedom from responsibility ordinarily allowed an elderly man (LMH 7/30/57). So he continued to gather the taxes and receive officials. He sent the bodies of two lesser wives to the temple to await cremation, and a few years later he had his will secretly written in the presence of witnesses at the district office. In 1928 his own coffin was borne to the temple, where the priests chanted the verses reminding people of the transience of all living things.

Phlym may have hoped to keep some part of his entourage together, for in his will he left his homestead and nine rai of shady orchard for the joint use of his children and grandchildren. Perhaps he selected his masterful second daughter to receive half of his lands in the hope that she might hold much of the group together, but the favoring of the second daughter over her sulky older sister caused a rift to develop that obliged the more able manager to leave the area. He settled two large timbered houses and abundant lands (some said also "a bucket of gold ornaments") on his favorite wife, the former young waif whom he rescued from poverty; but she sold the land to help pay for a "better" site in Minburī, then lost that during the Depression, and even had to sell the house timbers to the woman who had foreclosed her mortgage and who gained much merit by giving them to Bam Phen North temple for dormitories (LS 3/29/49). Phlym deemed that Pāw, another surviving spouse, had enough already and dismissed her without further notice. A third received the support of her five children, each favored with a few rai. In the course of time they lost their pittances and moved away (JRH 8/27/ 53, 10/21/53).

The populous hamlet also dwindled. Those who had some freedom of choice tended to move in search of better opportunities. The new owners loosened ties with tenants of former owners and drew in new ones of their own choice.

Thian and Pian, grandchildren of Phlym, lived here, but after Pian's death the children moved with their father to Canal Four.
The husband of Phlym's oldest daughter left her when she became poor, and married at Canal One.
Ned and Im had twenty rai of land and a house near Phlym. They pawned the land to Id and Lēg before Ned died. After his death, Rūn wanted to buy the house, but the creditors did not agree to sell. Rūn, with the help of Ned's daughter, Khem, took the dispute to court, and they awarded the land to Khem, who sold it to Rūn. [LMH 8/26/57]

Households drifted away, leaving some mounds to other people and some vacant. The hamlet, after nearly three decades of focused activity, dissolved to something like the former federation of equal autonomous households. Prosperity continued, though at a less heady level, because the hamlet lay on good land with controlled water; besides, the price of padi was rising. Yet the magnet that attracted people was weak, differing little from those of other hamlets. Those who remained remembered an earlier, better day.

CHAPTER 6

Patrons and Their Work

As Buddhists the Thai assume a cosmos of nearly perfect justice. Those who break its moral laws are punished; those who contribute toward its scheme of justice are rewarded. The legal process moves steadily without benefit of published grievance, rules of evidence, or right of appeal. Sometimes impersonal nature is said to reach out and execute judgment by allowing one man to find a treasure while afflicting another with disease. More often judgment is said to be carried out by one of the countless beings that inhabit the cosmos. These beings, humans among them, stand somewhere in a hierarchy of power and impersonal wisdom. The higher ones in this hierarchy, having overcome selfishness, have risen through successive rebirths to positions where they may wield power over those below them. Low beings, such as animals, are relatively powerless and can be controlled by humans, who with their knowledge of traps, nets, and weapons can subdue even ferocious tigers. In turn humans are controlled by other humans, higher spiritual beings, and gods, who because of merit have achieved positions of power. Misuse of power and wisdom will inevitably result in their diminution or loss, either in this life or in another, after rebirth at a lower level. As beings strive upward or fall back, through their own actions increasing or decreasing their store of merit, there is merit mobility for all except those few who have escaped by achieving Nirvana.

Control of others suggests force or threat, but higher beings rarely work in such a manner. Because of their selflessness, they act compassionately toward beings beneath them, as a mother soothes her injured child without thought of her own wound. The child, in turn, is free to accept or reject its mother's attentions, but in rejecting them, it must accept the consequences, perhaps that help will not come so readily on another occasion. The Lord Buddha gave man knowledge of the moral law of the universe. Man stands free to reject it and be reborn as man or animal, or to accept the knowledge and decrease his suffering by rebirth as a superior being. So higher beings, with their greater selflessness, compassion, and wisdom, aid lower beings.

The familiar patrons and their clients of this world are segments of this cosmic hierarchy. They extend from slave to king, each entrusted to perform his duty as client to those above him, and in turn as patron to those below him. As patron a man compassionately gives benefits to his clients in return for their gratefully rendered services. Should he fail to give them their benefits, he stands in danger of losing them; should his benefits be great, he will never want for aid. As client, each must reciprocate, but if duties are performed in a slovenly manner, these benefits disappear. The lonely beggar with outstretched hand has alienated some patron and is suffering the consequences. The dutiful client, on the other hand, is richly rewarded (Hanks 1962).

History recounts the work of patrons. According to the Chronicles of the North, settlement of Thai people began in the northern part of present Thailand when the patron god Indra desired to instruct the people in the precepts of Buddhism. He sent Visu Kamma, disguised as what may be a kind of deer, to the kingdom of his client Phrayā Korani, whose men pursued it through many adventures until they founded a city (Notton 1926, 1:1–10). Similarly, by looking to the patrons of Bang Chan we may observe the benefits they brought to this area. Some of these lesser human patrons we have already met: Uncle Sin, who gave the temple; Chyn the martinet, who protected his fellow hamlet residents and the temple; and Kamnan Phlym, benefactor of his hamlet and commune. Bang Chan's patrons include human, demihuman, and spiritual beings.

Human Patrons

Mari was helped by his patrons to raise himself from trader to landlord. He could trace his father's and his father's father's line back to Pattani, where they were captured by a general of Rama III and brought as spoils of war to Bangkok. Like the slaves of the Bunnags, these people were settled on Sāen Sāeb canal under a patron (LMH 12/9/53). Born after 1868, the date set by Rama V for the children of slaves to be born free, Mari was never a slave. We know nothing of his life until he asked for a particular woman in marriage; her father had remained in the Bang Chan area dauntlessly guarding the property of the Bunnags and the surao of Allah. Mari took the henna-stained hand of his bride and moved to live conveniently near his work in Minburī. There he purchased fish and garden produce for sale in the Bangkok markets. When padi became the important produce of the region, he bought a larger boat, the better to handle the bigger cargoes. In 1914, at about the age of forty, he bought land in Bang Chan and profited from the increased prices by growing some padi himself as well as transporting it. The profits were converted into farmlands worked by renters or by his grown children. He became imam of the local surao congregation (LMH 8/3/57). By the time of his wife's death, about 1925, he had made a pilgrimage to Mecca and become owner of 500 rai of rice-producing land, with holdings scattered over several communes. These lands he gave to his children when he moved from Bang Chan to marry for a second time (JRH 6/25/53).

Rama IV, who advocated free enterprise for his kingdom, would have been delighted to hear the tale of Mari's initiative. Despite his resemblance to self-made capitalists of the West, it can scarcely be argued that individual enterprise took place in any Western sense. We have seen that the important jobs in Bangkok had been cornered by Chinese artisans or skilled workers of other ethnic groups. The city's retail outlets were similarly controlled. In principle, the control operated like the land concessions of the nineteenth century. The owner of a market granted concessions to retailers eager for access to the buying public. Each retailer in turn granted concessions to a limited number of suppliers, such as Mari, who scoured the canals for chickens, betel, or whatever the countryside was producing. The supplier received a somewhat lower price than he might have obtained if he had peddled his wares from house to house. Yet in terms of the volume and stability of business, he was better off to spend his time hunting up wares for the insatiable market. Besides, a supplier considered himself a notch or two higher on the social scale than a peddler.

Access to these closed groups was gained through a series of introductions by one or more patrons. A young man fresh from the home of his parents might be lent a boat to begin operations. A supplier patron might allocate to this new client some of the farms where produce had customarily been bought. The rest he had to find for himself. Once arrived with his wares at a Bangkok market, he had to be introduced to the retailer by a patron. Instead of a market with free access, we find guildlike monopolies at each step. Self-made men are all but inconceivable in this scene.[1]

In the more glorious ascents to higher social levels the patrons appear distinctly in the foreground. Three grandnephews of Uncle Sin were growing up in the no-longer-new hamlet on Kred canal, the year about 1908.[2] Their father had prospered and become the owner of 120 rai of land, more than double his initial holdings. A widow of one of these grandnephews told the story she had heard:

My husband's father and mother knew an old Laotian priest named Āchan Thā at Chakra temple in Bangkok. When they wanted my husband's older brother to go to school, they sent him to live with this priest at the temple and go to school. At first he was a temple boy but later he became a novice and still later a priest at this same temple. He became well known as a preacher and used to be invited to give sermons in the palace. While he was still a novice at the temple, my husband was sent to join him. My husband became sick; so his mother brought him back in less than one year. He never continued his education, because their father died, and he had to help his mother raise rice. The next time he went away he went to join the cavalry for his two years of military service. Then he fell from his horse and injured his liver. This became a permanent injury all his life. [About 1915] my husband's younger brother was also sent for his education to Chakra temple, where he lived with his eldest brother. He stayed there many years but was a priest for only two years. This eldest brother, before his death, recommended him to the naval school and was able to support him while he was there. He became an officer in the Royal Navy, now has a place to live in Bangkok, and plenty of money. [LMH 9/22/53]

Of these three brothers, the eldest died a promising young priest. The second in effect never left Bang Chan, though he became a prosperous farmer. The third rose to high position as a naval officer. Though Buddhists would certainly comment on the varying store of merit enjoyed by these brothers, here we must underscore the patron's task.[3] The old Laotian priest first made it possible for these brothers to enter the temple and secure their education; without aid of this kind, entry would have been very difficult if not impossible.[4] In effect the parents transferred their children to the priest. They gave up the services rendered by all but one of their children in return for the priest's help in educating the others. Then when the eldest son was established, he became the patron for his youngest brother and could introduce him to the naval school. From the temple he moved to other patrons in the navy, who guided him further.

The Lord of Life

Besides these lesser patrons, Bang Chan experienced the benefits of a new patron during the first decades of the twentieth century. This was the king. To be sure, this figure with his awesome titles— Lord of Life (Chao Chīwit), Lord of All the Earth (Phrachao Phāendin), and many others—had long been present on the scene. Yet he did not rule the people. Instead he was the benefactor of a few chosen people of the realm. From the king these royal clients received a monopoly of power over the people of certain provinces and a provincial city as seat of government. In gratitude they returned annual tribute, appeared at the capital to the royal summons, drank in ceremony the water of fidelity, and supplied the royal army with troops. They in turn farmed out monopolies of power to favorites who were the traditional equivalents of modern district officers. Each received from this patron an opportunity to grow rich from the wealth of food and labor at his disposal and forwarded a share to the patron. For his part the king provided for the defense of the realm, built temples to ensure its preservation, raised some of the resources he needed through trade or his special monopoly over the port of Bangkok, and dealt with foreigners. Only when the common people served at one or more of these tasks did he rule them. At best he ruled the people indirectly.

In theory a king could withhold these patents of power. Rama IV took over directly the care of his palace city. His famous edict commanding the people to cease throwing refuse in the canals was but one example of his personal interest in making Bangkok agreeable for foreign residents (Moffat 1961:30–31). He had simply decided to exercise the monopoly of power over the city himself.[5]

In the next reign, Rama V began to take upon himself, bit by bit, the direct rule of his realm. Instead of granting his clients monopolies of power, they were to become his official arms, reaching to the farthest hamlet in the kingdom. Instead of granting his governors the right to live from the revenues they could collect, he paid them salaries to carry out his will. The transition to the new organizational form came to take greater time than its authors had hoped. Nevertheless, people such as the residents of Bang Chan, whose temple Rama V had named, did encounter the royal presence directly for the first time.

Like most of the Chakri sovereigns of the past, Rama V and his successor, Rama VI (1910–1925), had canals dug extensively. It had been discovered that waterways were not just avenues by which clients could escape into the wilderness, but access routes for new settlers. In the adjoining provinces beyond Bang Chan, royal engineers laid out and supervised the digging of canals through the plains. Some people left Bang Chan to take up these newly opened lands. In 1902 Rama V granted to a certain well-known Nāj Loet a charter for passenger service by steam launch to help move people and their goods to these remote spots.[6] The extending of canals, however, involved complex hydraulic problems of level, volume, and flow. Nāj Loet's launches could not pass through parts of Sāen Sāeb canal during the dry season because it had become filled with silt. In 1902 the royal engineers went to work dredging out a new channel (Min. Ag. 1957:69). Then farmers complained that the water level in the new canals was not high enough to flood their fields; they lost their rice crops (LMH 7/14/57). The royal patron responded by erecting a series of locks and gates to regulate the water level (Min. Ag. 1957:93; Ingram 1955:79–87).

Bang Chan farmers were grateful for the water controls provided by their patron. One of the residents of the new hamlet on Kred canal remembered: "The water gates helped make the water stay longer in the field. Before the water gates we plowed and planted in dry land, and when it rained, the rice would sprout. After this we could plow in wet soil and the rice sprouted right away. We could no longer thresh in the fields because the land was under water. So we moved to thresh on the house mound" (LMH 8/12/57). Traders such as Mari were also grateful for the water gates, for now the canals held enough water during the dry months to enable them to take their boatloads of padi to market.

The royal patron further assumed the task of maintaining order within the country. He withdrew this whole slice of sovereignty from the royal governors and turned over to them the narrower duty of enforcing his decrees. Graham, who witnessed the transition, commented:

A matter of scarcely less importance than the organization of the general administration was the provision of an adequate police force. With the time honored custom of collusion between officials and professional criminals strong in the land, from which indeed many of the old chiefs [royal governors] derived considerable profit, it was scarcely to be expected that any genuine effort to suppress crime entirely would be made by the country justices of the old regime, even at the urgent command of the king. By creating a monopoly of this form of industry the chiefs no doubt exercised a sort of check, and restricted evil-doing to the ranks of their own dependents, for it was very noticeable that with the recognition of rural officialdom and the removal from the chiefs of their powers and authority, violent crime of every description increased to an alarming extent and very soon passed altogether beyond the control of the authorities. [Graham 1913:255–256]

These new salaried officials, some trained by European advisers, eschewed the granting of monopolies in crime. Their only recourse was force, but the assistant district officer (palad amphōē) plus a few kamnans and hamlet headmen formed a pathetic group to cope with the problem. Accordingly, a countrywide police force was organized in 1906. Two years later police stations were erected in the provincial center at Minburī and in the district office of Bāngkapi. Yet for a while brigands continued to flourish in the area. A nearby resident described the scene: "Saēn Saēb canal was without many houses. At Bam Phen temple robbers were frequent. They fastened a rope high up across the canal to prevent the rice boats [with their tall masts and sails] from passing. The boatmen caught in the rope would have to come ashore, where the robbers threatened to kill them if they did not give up their money. The police were only at Bāngkapi and Minburī" (LMH 8/18/57). At Bang Chan the need for vigilance continued for a decade or more, and hamlets organized their own protection.

As the new police organization began to work, residents of Bang Chan sensed its effect first in the efforts to enforce the edict of Rama VI in the year of 1912 against gambling. Gambling had long been a holiday pleasure during the New Year celebrations, and even a monarch's voice was not powerful enough to stop it immediately (Lumbini 1925:180). A woman said:

We have always played cards in this part of Bang Chan, even though we are nearer the police station [than those living farther north on Bang Chan's rivulet]. If the police came to arrest people, we would pay them or give them food and drink. . . . Some police wanted to play cards and made good money gambling. When such a policeman came along, he took off his hat and held it high on a pole to warn us he was coming, then we could see over the tall grass. People would stop and invite him to come in. Now police thirst less for money. They are trained well. They listen to sermons on every Priest's Day [Wan Phra]. If one of them thinks of money too much, he has to resign. [JRH 12/3/53]

Gradually the king's servants learned to keep his peace more effectively, and farmers of Bang Chan were grateful for another benefit from their patron.

Rama V had long espoused the value of education for his clients. A formal palace school for princes and selected children of officials was organized during the first years of his reign. He personally founded schools in Bangkok, dispatched many of his sons to European schools and universities, and with the aid of Prince Damrong made the first step toward universal education (Jumsai 1951:19–23). In 1899 the Buddhist priests throughout the kingdom were ordered to begin giving instruction to the young in the vicinity of their temples. Any man or boy who wished might join the classes and learn to read sacred scriptures in the vernacular.

Under the system administered by Prince Wachirayan the central government appointed priests as education and religious directors of the various administrative circles (*monthon*) or groups of provinces throughout the country; and these, province by province, established subelementary (*mūnlasyksā*) and elementary (*prathom*) schools in those village temples where one or more priests were willing and able to serve as teachers. The director for Bangkok Circle (Monthon Krungthēp), which covered the lower Chao Phrayā river area, including Bang Chan, moved briskly and in the first year established, he says, some 59 schools with 69 teachers and 1,544 pupils in four of the rural provinces. A Bang Chan Canal Temple School (Rongrian Wat Khlaūng Bang Chan) is specifically reported to have been in operation in 1901, with one priest-teacher giving instruction at the mūnlasyksā level to thirty-six pupils. The new school is mentioned in 1902 but thereafter becomes lost in more general district and provincial statistics. This brief glimpse in old official reports suggests that Bang Chan promptly heeded the government order to establish a temple school and that it recruited a larger than average class of students (Thai National Archives, 5 S, 26/12, "Reports on [Ecclesiastical Affairs in] Monthon Krungthēp," Phra Thammatrailōkāchān, R.S. 119, R.S. 121, 1899/1900, 1902/03). Perhaps we can see here the energetic hands of leader Chyn, the new kamnan Phlym, or Uncle Sin.

The government provided encouragement but no financial support and little supervision for the new school in Bang Chan, which must have been conducted in an amateur, informal, and irregular manner, and probably sometimes not at all. An older man recalled:

When I was about eight, my parents sent me to the temple as a temple boy when my mother's younger brother was ordained. I was a lazy boy and did not want to learn. I just wanted to run away and stay home. Once I ran away but hid in the bushes near my parents' house because I was afraid they would punish me. When it was dark, my parents cried because they were afraid I was in trouble. Then I came out of the weeds and met them. They did not punish me but sent me back to the temple the next day. My parents wanted me to learn to read, but I liked to play around and have fun. I liked tattooing and also to work as a blacksmith, hammering out knives for sale. After living at the temple for four years I returned home. [LMH 3/1/54]

Only the more prosperous farmers could spare their children for any regular or extended schooling; the poor needed them to tend the buffalo and work in the padi fields.[7] All would have sent their sons, if they could, to study sacred texts and thereby learn life's moral principles.[8] By itself, literacy offered little of value to the farmer, who supported priests in part to provide literary services for him. But because sacred texts were important and contact with them was of value, the new schooling was considered an asset, and parents in Bang Chan were pleased with this benefit provided by their royal patron (Hanks 1959).

Bang Chan clients were also pleased with the new system of recorded land deeds, since it helped reduce friction between neighbors: "Once I had an argument with my neighbor. She was plowing in my land. We sent for Kamnan Phlym. He settled it by putting up land markers. He knew because of the title deed showing where the boundary lay" (JRH 6/25/53). The clients of the royal patron were released from corvée but were expected to pay somewhat higher taxes in return. The poll tax inaugurated in 1896 varied between 1.5 and 6 baht according to the prosperity of the region (Ingram 1955:59). Land taxes increased and were calculated according to the yield of the field as well as whether or not the land was under cultivation (ibid.:77). Few found their tax burdens heavy at 1.25 baht per rai or less.[9] The former palace workers alone still owed corvée service; they were ordered to be ready for summons at any time. Rama VI called infrequently on their services, and then permitted them to hire substitutes (LMH 2/6/54).

The days of freedom from public service were limited, for in 1904 a new edict called for national conscription for military service. The district offices were soon calling upon young men for examination and selection. In Bang Chan many young men resumed farm work on the day following their interviews.[10] A few from each commune boarded one of Nāj Loet's steam launches for the army or police barracks. One man recalled, "At twenty-two [1920] I was drafted to be a policeman and worked at the police department in Bangkok for one year. I got top grade in the examination and so was moved to the station near the Jause bridge. When I got top grade on another examination, I got twenty baht a month as salary. After two years I left the service because my time was up. I came back to Bang Chan to work with my mother" (JRH 10/23/53).

Some six of Bang Chan's young men were taken into the Royal Guards, that regiment where all received slightly higher pay and special uniforms for their part in state ceremonies (LMH 8/3/57). Despite urgings to remain in service as the date of severance approached, no one from Bang Chan remained beyond the minimum term. Severance was an anticipated relief; it was said in Bang Chan, "Soldiers are treated like slaves" (JRH 10/1/53). Tales by returning conscripts did not dispel local apprehension; but even so, when they had a choice, village young men tended to choose the army rather than the despised police (LS 10/5/48).

In 1913 Rama VI publicly observed that he had reduced his clients' liability to corvée in order to afford them time to devote themselves "diligently to the pursuits of livelihood." Thus he felt justified in restricting access to firearms and drugs, and prohibited gambling on holidays "in order to avoid the propensity of people to waste their money" (Lumbini 1925:180). Besides urging industry on his clients, in 1918 he further declared, "In connection with the work of prospering the condition of the Siamese nation as befits a civilized people, I have ordered the Decree relating to the use of family names to come into force during this year . . ." (ibid.:218).

Most of these edicts drifted over the heads of the country people, who took little notice. Bang Chan hardly honored the prohibition on gambling, as we have seen. Few owned firearms or used drugs. The farmers had never had family names but were willing enough to adopt them, if this would please their patron. District officials rendered aid to those who had difficulty thinking of one. Brothers usually honored their parents by taking the same name, but sometimes husbands took the names of their wives. Soon almost everyone had complied, yet for many years neighbors had to shout around to get the family name of the people next door.[11] The more significant promulgations of the reign (the new laws and court procedures, the augmented postal system, the extension of the railway, even the Wild Tiger Corps) affected little these law-abiding illiterate paddlers of boats a few miles outside the capital.

The Spirit Patrons

Agriculture is a mechanical process, the stirring of soil, dropping of seeds, and gathering of the resulting crop. Yet more than this is needed to assure a Bang Chan farmer that he will have his crop in December or January. Fish, rats, and birds may spoil the harvest. A sudden November storm may flatten the grain. A buffalo may die the night before plowing. Any one of these events affects the harvest, and farmers are keenly aware of multiple contingencies beyond their control. This knowledge does not incline a man to select his seed less carefully or to decide that weeding is unimportant. Equally important, however, are the spirit patrons to whom he turns for help.

The king too once made offerings to the guardians of the realm through the royal plowing and other ceremonies that ensured good crops within the country (Wales 1931:228–237, 256–264). Farmers in Bang Chan still observe comparable rites on a smaller scale. The first plowing must be done on an auspicious day in May or June. A man brings flowers, incense, and candles, perhaps sweets, and places them in a corner of the field. Facing the direction of the naga, the serpent on whose back the cosmos rests, but who also, as a rainbow, provides the rain from heaven, he recites the following address:

> Lord of the Place, Lord of the Land,
> Please protect the rice from insects.
> Please make the rice grow well.
> Mother Earth, Mother of Rivers,
> Please protect the rice from all attacks.
> [JRH 3/2/54]

Then he prods the buffalo and plows three concentric furrows in a direction that smoothes the scales of the cosmic serpent (LS 11/4/48). A few weeks later, at the first sowing of rice, he again offers incense and petitions his spiritual patrons:

> Lord of the Place, Lord of the Land,
> Mother Earth, Mother of Rivers,
> May you protect the Rice Mother from harm.
> [JRH 3/2/54]

Those who uproot the padi shoots from the seed bed and transplant them into the fields also call upon these spirit protectors to guard the crop.

In November, as the padi kernels begin to form, a woman goes into the fields with offerings for the Rice Mother. This deity is so beautiful in her pregnancy that a man, carried away by her charm, would frighten her with his advances. Consequently it must be a woman who brings the sour-tasting fruits that pregnant women prefer and invokes her, saying:

> Mother Rice, mother of splendor,
> Mother with the beauteous hair,
> Mother with starlike eyes,
> Mother on a level with gods,
> Mother of most feminine beauty,
>
> Hail spirit of rice, come!
> Stay wherever you wish in the fields.
> Come and help the kernels grow,
> Come into the granary in abundance, come.
> [JRH 12/18/54]

As the first stalks of the new crop are cut, a farmer lights an incense stick and gives thanks. Once the crop is on the threshing floor, a woman for the last time goes out to the field. With a few gleanings and rice stalks she makes a little doll and invites the soul of the Rice Mother to enter the doll and be transported to the house. The doll ceremonially enters its special abode, the granary, as the first padi is moved from the threshing floor for storage. Again the Rice Mother's permission must be obtained before padi is removed from the granary, and then it must be taken out only on special days during the months with even numbers of days. When the crop is sold, the boatman, after loading his boat with padi, pauses and returns the spirit of rice to the house with wishes for an abundant harvest in the coming year.[12]

The work of spirit patrons extends far beyond these few concerned with agriculture. The Earth Guardian (Phra Phūm) watches over each house from his own little house in the northeast corner of the compound. He should be notified when the Rice Mother is coming to the house, just as he is notified of any other newcomer, be it an overnight guest or a newborn baby. The ancestral spirits (phī pūjātājāj) customarily receive offerings when a daughter of the house is married.[13] When offended, they sometimes cause illness (Textor 1960:223–235). There are guardian spirits of various places, such as Lord Father Saēn Saēb (Chao Phau Saēn Saēb), who may accept some special petition for help. These spirit patrons are numerous, their jurisdictions rather vaguely specified; when properly addressed (bon), they render unusual aid.[14]

In 1917, the year of the Little Snake, the waters rose and flooded the fields for a great distance. Farmers first brought their buffalo to higher ground on the house mounds. As the waters rose still higher, they moved the beasts to the house platforms. Fodder was gone. People scurried to rescue the store of last year's padi and shared it with the buffalo. Children fished from windows in their houses. A man made his fastest boat trip to Bangkok, right over the fields where the rice plants had drowned. When the waters receded, people counted their dead buffalo and looked into empty granaries. Women set off to earn money. The price of rice, already swollen by the demands of hungry people in war-torn Europe, rose to unprecedented heights. The royal patron rushed to help his clients, forsaken by their spirit patrons. In his birthday address Rama VI stated:

The government authorities have rendered every possible assistance within their power. They have helped to convey cattle to places of refuge on high ground, carried out various protective measures, attended to the farm animals afflicted with disease, and provided remunerative employment for destitute inhabitants. The Buddhist clergy has assisted by allowing the monasteries situated on high ground to be used as refuges for cattle, and the temples and other buildings therein as places for temporarily storing the grain belonging to the people affected by the floods. . . . [Lumbini 1925:208]

Through relief funds, grain was bought for distribution as food among the destitute and for seed among the farmers. They planted it, but almost everywhere it withered in the drought of the follow-ing season. Influenza and plague struck the nation (Lumbini 1925:220–221). The king sent his doctors to instruct the people in the prevention of disease and took steps to regulate the price of rice (ibid.:224).

If angered spirit guardians caused the damage, the particular protectors of Bang Chan were soothed enough to grant their clients special favors after the flood. The crop of 1918 was locally good; prices were high. Those who ordinarily fished for a living left their gear under their houses and rented land to grow rice. Prosperity reached this spot in the countryside: "I made money and got rich after the flood year. In the old days one kwian brought forty baht. The year after the flood one kwian brought one hundred sixty baht. Many Chinese came to buy the padi. The government was sending rice to foreign countries and was buying as much as it could. That year I was twenty years old, and everyone in the family was rich" (LMH 8/11/54).[15]

Farmers suddenly became heavy buyers. They had long bought their plowshares, yoking chains, and mattocks in the market. Sugar, coconuts, chili, and garlic had been luxuries to be bought only occasionally. Whenever floods had washed away the home gardens and orchards in other years, people had done without. But now with money jingling in their little bags they could buy salt fish and coconuts from the south and even have enough left over to replace worn clothing and implements. Up the side canals came a host of vendors eager to sell cupboards, tables, and teapots to these pros-pering ones (LMH 5/20/53, 2/22/54). In two or three years the old thatch and bamboo seemed less in keeping with their new wealth. Houses of sawed teak, the eaves capped with naga-like finials, rose along the canals to match the one of Kamnan Phlym.

Some farmers, fearful of losing their grain another year, sought to conserve their earnings:

When the children were grown and my brother and I could work in the fields, mother changed to buying and selling things. She did not want to use up the money we were earning and so kept buying more things to sell. She bought pots for cooking, coconuts, betel nut, and bananas. At that time people used sugar in a pot which cost one salyng. She bought these things in the stores along Saēn Saēb canal in order to sell them later in Bang Chan. In the dry season the children would go with her to help carry things home. When the water in the canals was low, she could not go very far to sell. In this way the money from the crop was not used up; we could live from the profits of trade. [LMH 8/4/57]

In the wake of this prosperity the last bits of brush were cleared away. Owners, eager to gather in the profits for themselves, sent away their tenants. All hands turned to the fields. With an extra team of buffalo, a small household could work twenty or thirty rai, a large one as much as fifty. Those with still larger holdings invested in hired labor. Men from the northeast who a few years later would become pedicab drivers in Bangkok hired themselves out for the growing season at eighty to one hundred baht (JRH 12/3/53). Poor relatives also came to join their wealthier kinsmen: "My parents lived on Sām Wā canal near Minburī. There were many of us, and we were very poor. We rented lands there. My father's younger sister and her husband asked my father to come and rent a field of fifty rai. I was seventeen or eighteen years old at the time, and we moved here two years after the flood of 1917" (LMH 9/22/53).

Pleased with such demonstrations of compassion toward those below them in the hierarchy, the spirit patrons lightened the work of the farmers. For several seasons Bang Chan watched as a tall tower began to grow across the fields near Minburī. One day in the year 1920 smoke began to ooze from its top. A steam mill had been built on the bank of Saen Saeb canal to grind the padi into rice. Curious farmers paddled past the dusty wharf to watch grain boats loading and unloading. In a few more years many from Bang Chan brought their boats alongside these docks to have their own padi milled.

Bang Chan prospered for at least a decade. Its patrons had drawn people to settle on the land and extinguish the last claims of the wilderness. The weaverbirds disappeared; weeds and mosquitoes thinned out. A new Bang Chan was born.

The Fruit of Their Work

Bang Chan was hardly identifiable until the 1920s. The rivulet that acquired that name had drained the plains for centuries. The temple with the same name had been built on its banks a generation earlier. Perhaps the commune of Kamnan Phlym bore that name in the registry at the district office. Where the name came from no one knew. Most names of locations on the central plain suggest a landmark or some activity that occurred there, such as Marketville (Bāng Sȳ) or Bottleville (Bāng Khuad). Bang Chan means Village of the

Rise, or the Steep Place, yet no resident ever pointed to any feature of the monotonous plain that would justify the name.

Before the 1920s local people saw as hamlets only the distant places where others dwelt. Like watching the blue of a lake melt at close range into green and gray, they regarded themselves as household dwellers. A woman described the scene: "From Sāen Sāeb canal I would go up Bang Chan canal to the mosque. Beyond this were some houses where the road bridge now stands. Then came the Tō Imam's house. Beyond were no more houses until the temple. Near the temple was my father's mound. Up Kred canal lived Sud; on Bang Chan canal was grandmother Faeng. Farther along was Nāng Pan. At the far end of Kred canal was Waud Kred [the local name for the hamlet on Kred canal, never used by its residents]" (LMH 8/3/57). Only in the more distant places did this observer begin to see the collective; nearby were just dwellings where known people lived. The Laotians alone had seen a collective identity when they named their hamlet Village of the Mound of Earthly Splendor. The rest were too unconcerned with any collective identity to wish to search out a collective name.[16]

As new settlers came and built their houses on the land they intended to plow, even the isolation that made hamlets identifiable until the 1920s disappeared. Boatmen passed no long, solitary stretches of brush along the banks. Houses formerly clustered now spread out as owners decided to work the whole of their lands by themselves. A uniformity of dwellings and fields emerged in the Bang Chan area.

The social communities bound together by the exchange of labor and services had begun to decline a dozen years before 1920. No one called all his neighbors to thresh the crop in the fields after 1908 because the water level was too high. Having cut the crop, the workers went home, and the owner's houseboat brought the sheaves of padi to the house mound by boat. There two or three buffalo barely had room to tread out the grain between stacks of straw and mounds of padi. Two or three people did the work formerly done by the hamlet. Machines for winnowing the threshed padi began to appear; one person cranked the blower while his helper fed the machine (LMH 8/18/57). As for milling, those who took their padi to the mill in Minburi and brought rice home no longer needed to call out the young people. The more enduring high water and the disappearance of tall grasses thinned the vegetation so that weeding too became a task for only a few people. A hamlet had no occasion to meet except on the days of harvest.

Since all sought to grow more padi, such labor-saving arrangements were heartily welcomed. All households worked to the limits of their capacity for their own advancement. They exchanged labor grudgingly, when possible hiring labor to speed the extra tilling and to process a larger crop (LMH 8/18/57). Grown children at home were counted as blessings, and a family was reckoned as poor or wealthy according to its available working children (LS 12/31/48). Lacking these resources, a man ventured to exchange labor for a few of the more arduous tasks "only with special people" (LMH 2/8/54).[17] A transformation was taking place in the padi field:

Formerly if we had no food, we could go to a neighbor's house to eat with them. It was easy to ask them for help. We could stay two or three days with them and eat chicken. We could borrow a buffalo for planting. Since there were fewer people, we could plant rice in another man's field without his paying attention. Now we must work every day to earn money. Even a banana leaf has value for sale. [LMH 11/31/53]

Like most people of Bang Chan when discussing the past, this old man spoke in a matter-of-fact tone.

Households turned to emphasizing their independence, self-sufficiency, and achievements:

My son's life is like mine. My son and daughter-in-law lived with me. I too lived with my parents after marriage [1915–1920]. Then when my other children were big enough to help he moved out. I gave my son a few rai of land to work and sell for himself. I also gave him a buffalo and plow; these are the instruments of his occupation. All the rice money came to me, just as it went to my father; and if I asked for money, my father gave it to me. When the money first came in, you could buy anything you liked: a house, food, or anything. I too was living in a thatch house next to my father's and built a big house which cost five hundred to six hundred baht. My son's house cost three thousand to four thousand baht. [JRH 1/29/54]

Fewer children chose to set off for new lands on the edge of the wilderness. Parents could hold them at home in the big teak houses built by Chinese carpenters (LMH 2/8/54). No longer busy at work bees, people staged tonsure ceremonies for their eleven- and thirteen-year-olds.[18] A woman who grew up in the hamlet at Kred canal recalled the ordination of her son in the early 1920s: "We had a

The harvest returns to the farmhouse
Photo by Lauriston Sharp

theatrical troupe playing for a day and a night. Altogether we paid nine hundred baht.[19] It was not like today. People brought food, not money. When it was all over, there was food enough for another celebration" (LMH 8/13/57). Such celebrations demonstrated parental love for a child as well as a household's capacity for ostentatious spending and for attracting people from far and near.

Yet the younger generation had outgrown its tiny hamlets and roamed over the countryside. Young men were free to move about in the slack season: "When I was seventeen or eighteen [about 1920], I wanted to go to the gambling place on Sāen Sāeb canal which was open every Priest's Day [Wan Phra]. It was the day before priest's day [Wan Kon]. I was working at home with my parents but did not have any money. I decided to steal some padi. So I told my mother I

threshing
to by Lauriston Sharp

wanted to go back to the house from the fields. I stole two thang of padi and sent it with Cham to be sold. So I got baht for gambling the next day" (LMH 3/1/54).

About the same period six young men from five scattered locations within Bang Chan formed themselves into a gang of rogues (na-klēng). They met as friends for drinking and attended ordination ceremonies as a group. One of these young men decided a few years later to organize a theatrical troupe (likē):

After getting married I decided to learn acting. I went to Bangkok after harvest to learn because I had some relatives who were actors. When I came back, I became head of a theatrical group. There were thirteen people in all. We played "Khun Chang Khun Phaen," and "Phrām Kae Saun" or "Laksanawong." My neighbor's boy Chom was a child announcer who had to speak like an Indian. We played in many places as far away as Chachoengsao and Nakāun Nāyok. The most we made was eighty baht for playing all day and all night long. The least we earned was thirty-five baht. [LMH 11/31/53][20]

A broad field of movement had burst upon the young.

While hamlets dissolved into households or neighborhoods and youth moved into a larger world, Bang Chan was born. It lacked geographical boundaries, for farmers had settled in the interstices between it and its neighbors, just as they had settled between the hamlets. Administrative lines crisscrossed here and there. People knew they lived in the administrative hamlet (mūbān) of headman Liam or Tuj in the commune of Kamnan Saung or Suk in the district of Bāngkapi or Minburī. For all the effect these boundaries had in making a social community, residents might as well have been told their latitude and longitude.

Bang Chan had a center, the temple. Aside from its religious functions, it served at first as no more than a landmark for directing strangers. The tower of the reliquary built by Phra Samutmo loomed across the padi fields like a beacon. Subsequent merit makers embellished the temple grounds with memorials (chēdī), boatlanding shelters, bridges, and sacred images. People of the area came with food for the priests, and brought their sons for ordination and their dead for cremation. Just as the market square with its fountain served as a pivot for many a European village, so Bang Chan's temple came to be thought of as the community's center. There the people came for boat races; there the temple fair was held, and the annual round of rites.

It offered only the barest political focus. The head priest, with his lay manager and corps of assistants, was scarcely a patron comparable to Kamnan Phlym. He might summon the strength of the surrounding householders to dig a pond for the priests, but only those pious ones who felt that they must gain merit came to dig for a few days; the less concerned occupied themselves elsewhere and sensed no loss of benefits. Some head priests demanded greater piety by refusing to permit fishing near the temple, so as to prevent the taking of life. Others left with the people the initiative in making merit. Still the head priest was a patron of sorts. Certainly everyone respected him, for he was learned and must have had more than the average store of merit to have achieved such a position. He could attract the services of the most important men of the area. And the destitute came and received a portion of the food given to the priests. During a flood the temple mound offered haven for buffalo and kept stores of grain dry. One had but to ask the head priest when to begin plowing and in what direction, and he looked it up in his book. Each year the priests chanted for an abundant, but not too abundant, rain (Wells 1960:89–95). Priests from the temple blessed new houses, placated the ghosts of the recently dead, and offered their medicine and rituals for curing the sick. They could not loan money on a parcel of land or prevent theft of buffalo, but still, here were constant patrons for all afflicted by existence. One magnificent kamnan appeared but then disappeared; the temple continued, its organized chapter of priests the only perdurable corporate entity in the social life of the community.

Gradually Bang Chan became something of an identity around this center. Bang Chan was a presence, but one did nothing in its name. A group of men might cut the weeds in the canal to make passage easier for boats, but this they did at the request of the temple manager or the head priest for the temple fair. A man built a wooden house for his wife and children but never to beautify Bang Chan. The young man on his way to a rendezvous spoke of leaving and returning to Bang Chan, but no known point precisely marked the place of his departure or return. The community became most tangible when he was away from it, perhaps in talking with farmers from other localities while waiting at the dock of the rice mill. He lived in Bang Chan while others lived on Sām Wā canal or at Lōlae. In speaking to them he sometimes referred to "Bang Chan people" (chāw Bang Chan).

We have but to contrast this shadowy identity with the concreteness of the former hamlets under a patron. The hamlet's existence depended on the benefits given by the lord, even in his absence, and the services returned by the inhabitants. They, slaves and freemen, lived there at his bidding; by following his wishes they could live. When needs arose, he satisfied them. Kamnan Phlym also gave his hamlet firm identity. When clients disputed the ownership of land or sought money, they came to him. Indeed, they had moved to or remained at his hamlet because of him.

Without such a patron a community was shapeless. To be sure, the king was Bang Chan's patron, but the patron of all the people is the patron of none. His officials were only remote figures. Their impersonal duties—suppression of crimes, organization of work on canals, land surveys—were appreciated benefits, but they brought the officials little nearer to the farmers. Loaning money to a client, paying his debt, or speaking to a landlord on his behalf exceeded their office. Besides, as salaried officials, they often lacked the resources necessary for an office of this kind.[21] On the local scene the salaryless hamlet headman without private wealth could serve no more competently. Kamnan Phlym was an anachronism from the past who resembled the old rural leaders, the chao myang (see Graham 1913:251–254). As long as he collected taxes, received his share of them, and lived in the community, he could minister to popular needs in a personal fashion, and serve as a local rallying point. His successor, shorn of these powers, perhaps lacking wealth and receiving only a salary, could not replace him. Without the patron there was no community, no collective existence that was recognizable.[22]

Bang Chan had never enjoyed so many patrons. The benefits proffered were greater than had ever been received. Household heads had never cared more lavishly for their clients. Rice buyers from the mill had never offered higher prices. Public peace had never been so well kept as by the district officer with his aides in the police. The king tended to the souls of his subjects more effectively by providing schools for their sons. The Rice Mother and Lords of the Place and Land had filled the granaries to unprecedented fullness. Each desire was met by some one of these many patrons; as an assemblage with shadowy identity Bang Chan flourished. The day was coming, however, when distress would force Bang Chan to seek other patrons for help.

CHAPTER 7

Years of Austerity

In one of the more popular Jataka tales it is related that King Wessantara gave away his wealth, his kingdom, and finally his children (Alabaster 1871:184). Thereby he gained such merit that in his next existence he became the Lord Buddha. Similarly parents, by giving their sons to the temple, make greater merit than by any other single act of devotion.[1] They give up their valuable helpers at a time when they are most competent. Indeed, a son's obligation to his parents ends at this point, and if parents wish his help after his resignation from the monastic order, they must bargain for his services almost as in the open market.[2]

At ordination parents may simply accompany the young man to the temple on the appointed day. There the candidate, with head and eyebrows shaved, sits astride the shoulders of a companion and is borne clockwise in the direction of life three times around the sanctuary and left at the doorway. With his begging bowl and yellow robes beside him, he makes obeisance before the assembled chapter of priests and requests admission to the order.

A wealthy parent, however, may arrange a day or two of ceremonies and celebration at home to invest the son with the soul of the naga (*tham khwan nāg*) before accompanying him to the temple. Once a member of this serpent race transformed himself into a human being in order to be ordained a Buddhist priest and so acquire human virtue (Wells 1960:135). The rites in the home include an exhortation by an old and respected man, who brings tears to the eyes of the son and others with a discourse that dwells in detail on the pain the boy has caused his parents since before his birth; only now will he begin to make up for it as he earns merit for them in the temple. Then the candidate, elaborately arrayed, sets off with the princely procession of umbrella bearers and musicians who conduct him to the temple. There, in emulation of the Lord Buddha, who put aside his princely trappings, he is stripped of his finery and abandoned by his parents. Reduced to anonymity, he enters the sanctuary on a par with any poor boy. Both reply to the same questions, take the same vows, and receive nearly identical robes and meager utensils.

Understanding the precepts of Buddhism requires the rigors of monastic discipline. He who would learn must move apart from the world for at least the three months of Buddhist Lent. Only then can he grasp clearly that the world is an illusion. Through asceticism the newly ordained priest becomes transformed. When he suffers hunger, he must focus his mind in order to resist the illusion of this reality. He must come to understand that the body, made of hair, nails, flesh, bone, teeth, and skin, has no reality and is transient.[3] By practice a priest can learn to act in opposition to his first impulses and come to lead a life free from sin. A Bang Chan grandfather observed, "First you must suffer; then you will have happiness" (LMH 2/23/54).

If we observe temple life, the two hundred–odd rules of the monastic order appear gentle enough. There are no whips or hair shirts in the Buddhist temple, no vows of silence, no total deprivations. Yet in subtle ways the gentler practices chafe on just those sensitivities that Thai society employs to hold itself together. Each new priest has voluntarily cut himself off from the parent guardians who looked after him. When a kind mother sends the best food to her son at the temple, he is reminded the more acutely of the benefits that he has forgone. The new world is foreign, and its strange language of Pali for the moment separates him from the reassurance that the clear rules of the order and a superior can provide. When he walks in his robes through the familiar world beyond the temple, it has turned upside down; those to whom he once deferred now address him in deferential language. A man recalled something of his experience during the first few days: "I felt troubled. If one knows the rules well there is no trouble. If one does not know them well, he feels troubled. Sometimes I went to see the head priest when I did something wrong. Those who do not know the rules well do not know how to talk with a senior priest. When I was invited to visit a house and sat on a mat, I felt troubled. I had to thank the host in Pali. This is done before eating and before returning to the temple. Even when staying at the temple a priest must give thanks. I felt troubled because I knew little Pali" (LMH 2/23/54). Here is the chaotic helplessness of abandonment. The priest stands alone. Beyond the hours spent in religious observances his time is unfilled. Some priests lie sleeping in their rooms. Others busy themselves at making boat paddles, repairing skiffs, or learning such rites as those for blessing a new house and for exorcising demons. New skills may be developed or old ones enhanced, as by studying to build up a stock of elaborate magical tattooing designs or to improve a knowledge of electricity gained during army service. Each man is thrown upon his own resources to find and develop his priestly skills or to neglect them. It depends upon the individual.

Should a priest seriously break a rule of the order, his isolation is increased. He must go alone at night into the forest and undergo special ceremonies (*puriwad*) to strengthen right conduct. A Bang Chan man described his experience: "It trains the mind to be in a lonely place. It helps concentration. One night I slept close to a village and heard people singing. When I listened to the words of the song, my emotions followed them. Then the effects of my errors struck me. Many ants came and bit me. The following night ants came again, because I had doubts in my mind. In the morning I followed the ceremony of expiation [*plong ābat*]. Then the ants disappeared. There can be no doubt that my sins had caused the ants to come" (LMH 8/31/53). Though Europeans would be tempted to phrase this "expiation" as discipline in resisting temptation, Phillips (1965:61) astutely observes that the Thai experience few conflicts between obligations and personal desires. Instead, this priest was exploring the consequences of sin, as if he had to convince himself that the consequences of sin are truly painful. When he left the order, he was strengthened to do right.[4] People said that he was no longer "raw" (*dip*) but "cooked" (*sug*) and addressed him as illustrious or learned, a pandit (*thid*). He was ready for adult responsibility and hence eligible for marriage.

From 1930 to 1945 Bang Chan underwent fifteen years of travail. The decade of easy living had ended. A new period began as prices for padi sagged and dropped. The king, the Rice Mother, the Lord of the Place, and even the gods of the Chinese merchants were unable to restore the former prices. People might petition with offers of pigs' heads and dramatic performances, but few of these petitions were answered.

Depression

The sixty baht per kwian that rice buyers had offered in 1929 became a mere forty baht in 1930 (Ingram 1955:38). To some this simply meant that grandfather's cremation would have to be post-poned in hope of a higher price in the following year. Others had to bypass repairs of the roof or the purchase of new clothing. In the following year padi prices moved even lower. Then the pinch began in earnest. Sacrifices had to be made. The cremation was postponed again; the roof leaked in new places, the clothing became tattered. More women became more active in buying and selling, just as they had always done in emergencies:

In those days we could not live on what we made from ten rai of land. When we were short of money, I and my husband made drink for sale. When we had time, we secretly distilled whiskey in order to sell it. We sold it secretly in the fields. We had to buy and sell secretly. Oh, it was cheap, only forty satang a bottle. . . . When I went out selling, I ate plenty. I ate so much that the people who came with me used to look at my eyes, and they could tell that I ate a lot. I didn't sleep, rowing to Pratū Nām [in Bangkok]. I was dying for sleep. On our way back we had to row against the current. It was difficult. We bought this and that, such as betel leaves, chilies, limes, sugar cane, eatable things, oranges, anything that we happened to find cheap; we bought them to be sold in Bang Chan. Then we collected vegetables from Bang Chan to sell in Bangkok. But we could manage to live. [HPP 10/4/57]

Others hoped to continue the good life a little less painfully and asked a kinsman for a small loan to tide them over. The wealthy kinsmen, however, could not spare any very helpful sums. Many, like certain heirs of Kamnan Phlym, pawned their lands and sub-sequently lost them: "I finally sold the lands that father left me long ago. I had been sick, and my children were small. I pawned the lands and expected to get them back when I had enough money. When I had enough, the man I owed refused to give them back. He wanted to have the title changed at the district office. I said, 'If you don't give me three rai for living, I won't change the title.' So now I have three rai where the house is and never have bought any more land since" (JRH 2/19/54). With the decline in padi prices, land values had decreased, and this woman was seeking to retain some of her lands at the lower price. By bargaining a little she was able to salvage three of the thirty rai from her legacy. Most had even less to show of their legacies, as if the years of walking under the kamnan's umbrella had ill equipped them to travel with only their hats to shield them.

Owners became renters and renters became hired laborers. They told their stories succinctly: "My father moved here in 1930. He owned thirty-eight rai of land. The land was mortgaged, and father lost it since he could not raise ten thousand baht" (LMH 2/23/54); "I lived eight years in Canal One and then moved back to Bang Chan. Prices were low for rice, and the owner sold the farm I was renting. On returning here, I began to work full time as a carpenter" (LMH 8/31/53). While the former lost his land and became a renter, the latter lost his plow and buffalo on smaller loans. Without the tools of farming, he could only turn to wage work, sometimes at building, more dependably as a hired hand during the agricultural season. The head priest gave him permission to build a bamboo shelter for his wife and children at Bang Chan's temple, where he needed to pay no rent. When he earned nothing, his family could at least share some of the food left over by the priests.[5]

As the destitute gave up and sought shelter from such persons as the head priest, those who could remain under the guardian spirits of the land and of the crop ate well enough. Despite tattered clothing and worn mattocks, their fields still provided rice. The canals offered fish and water plants. Some even managed to take advantage of falling prices: "Daeng owed her cousin two hundred and forty baht. She had mortgaged the land to this cousin, and when this cousin wanted her money, Daeng could not do anything. So her son and daughter paid their mother's debt and got the land. It was ten rai of land, and the price of rice fell to twenty-five baht per kwian. That was in the depression time" (JRH 6/26/53).[6] Land that had been worth as much as three hundred baht per rai was selling for as little as twenty-four baht. Daeng's children acquired land at an even lower price.

A farmer's most obvious reply to low prices is to increase his yield, provided it costs him little more. Some Bang Chan farmers began to move in this direction by changing from the broadcast method of planting to transplanting, which multiplied labor costs but doubled the yield (KJ 2/3/49). Instead of seeding an entire field and allowing it to grow, the transplanter starts his seed in a well-diked and watered bed near his house. After six weeks he uproots the thickly growing plants and replants them evenly spaced in well-prepared outlying fields. In this way every foot of growing surface is used, and no bald patches of water break the even texture of the growing grain. In this way the crop may be doubled and the harvesting made easier and more efficient (LS 11/10/48). Some farmers had previously tried this method in limited areas (LMH 8/2/57). At that time labor was so scarce that the method found little favor. In the 1930s households were teeming with grown children unable to find a haven elsewhere. Household heads had many hands to put to work. A man recalled making the change:

At first we could not make the change because there were many weeds. This made it difficult to transplant, but broadcasting yielded only about ten thang per rai of padi. No one transplanted at first. Then various farmers tried it. I tried it first on one rai. I tried moving the plants that I had sown from around the edge to the middle of the field, where formerly the rice did not grow well. [*What about the weeds?*] There were more when we broadcast. Farmers now pull them out, but they used to let them grow in with the rice. The best crop by broadcasting was one year when I got fifteen thang per rai. [LMH 6/9/53]

With this method the field had to be diked, the seedbed flooded, the weeds carefully removed, the seedlings uprooted and transplanted. A bigger harvest than ever was then processed into clean mounds of padi.[7]

One could not be just a rice grower during these years when many hands were available in the household. Extra industries were developed to earn a little more cash. More ducks and chickens were raised for their meat and eggs. Pigs appeared under more houses, and even Buddhists helped their neighbors at butchering time, taking home a piece of cooked pork as they departed (LMH 8/13/57).[8] Home gardens all but abandoned in the prosperous 1920s flourished again. People dug deeper fish ponds to be emptied when the flood had receded. There they collected hundreds of fish, some of which were dried and stored.[9]

At the same time people also turned to ways of making their tasks more efficient. The old suspended water shovel (*chōng lōng*) was replaced by a treadmill apparatus that turned a wheel (*chak*). Children could splash water up through a trough into the seedbeds by working the treads. A woman recalled her childhood:

I turned the treadmill for pumping water into the fields. By working all day at it, we could barely get water enough to cover one rai of land. I began this work when I was old enough to reach the pole that steadied us while we pushed the treadles. I did not go to school at all and worked all the time. At thirteen I had to care for my younger brothers and sister. I also cooked. If the rice was too raw or too wet, I was punished. I did not dare run away lest my parents beat me. We were poor and kept no rice at the house, but mother would bring in enough for the meal. After a day's work in the field, mother was tired and would punish me if things were not right. [LMH 7/21/57]

The labor exchange was revived to uproot the rice sprouts from the seedbed. Groups of men made the rounds to jerk up the seedlings, flail away the excess mud from the roots with a resounding slap against the thigh, and firm the clean plants into neat bundles that could be moved by shoulder pole from the seedbeds to the surrounding fields. Then the household took over, setting out the plants in the muddy waters of freshly harrowed fields. All should be finished in a week or less so that the seedlings would not wither before replanting. At harvest time the labor group reappeared, this time equipped with small sickles (*khiaw*) that cut more quickly than the old finger knives, even at the risk of insulting Māe Pōsob (LMH 8/4/57). Though the market for padi was glutted, prices fell no lower through the decade.

His Majesty's Affairs and the National Government

Back when the price of rice began to drop, Rama VII (1925–1935) was concerned over the mounting deficits in the treasury. In his 1931 address from the throne to the Supreme Council (Phraborom Wongsānuwong) he declared:

The most serious matter during this present year is the financial situation, concerning which I spoke last year, but the distress has not diminished. . . . This year the finances of the realm are more critical than last year because of poor economic conditions. This depression is taking place all over the world and is not a difficulty for just one country. . . . Consider the total quantity of rice being consumed by the world and the continuously diminishing share of this total being supplied by Siam! Here is the problem that confronts Siam at this time" [Min. Ag. 1956:177–179]

The king confessed his powerlessness to influence world rice prices, yet he sought to alleviate the country's plight. A survey of rural economic conditions had been ordered by the Ministry of Commerce (see Zimmerman 1931). A new department of agricultural research was established to study the domestic production of rice as well as its marketing abroad. Government departments were pared of personnel; Minburī was reduced to a district (amphǒe) of Phranakhǎun, or Bangkok Province (Laws 1936:443–445); experimental farms founded in the previous reign were closed (Thompson 1941:381–382).[10]

In June of 1932, revolution effectively separated the king from his charges. New guardians rose in his place to wield authority. All was accomplished before any voice could rise either to protest or to hail the change from the "affairs of the king" (rātchakān) to the "government of the nation" (ratabān). Rumors of the revolution must have spread quickly to the countryside, but country people had no part in these lofty matters. Not even Kamnan Phlym would have raised his voice.

Bang Chan doubtless applauded the new government's abolition of taxes on fruit trees and gardens (Thompson 1941:66). An unknown number heeded the announcement of an election and went to vote in 1933 (Phillips 1958). This handful of farmers quietly returned, after casting their ballots, to face anew their plaguing debts. Change of patrons seemed to have produced few immediate discernible benefits.

Three years after the revolution, however, a first direct benefit did come to Bang Chan from the government on high. The district officer and his educational assistant announced that a government school would be built. The late kamnan's wealthy daughter, the widow of a schoolteacher (see above), gave three rai of land as a school site, appropriately located near the temple, the traditional center of learning (SM 2/35/49). Local people might earn some cash by digging a mound for the building and later by assisting the skilled carpenters in building the structure. Girls as well as boys between eight and fifteen years of age were expected to attend, at least until they completed the four-grade curriculum.[11] Priests at the temple were released from secular pedagogic duties.

When classes began with teachers imported from other communities, secular education was not entirely a novelty in the area. In 1932 a hamlet headman had invited a priest from nearby Khū temple to teach reading and writing in his hamlet at three baht per pupil per year. Though that priest declined the offer, another did accept and held school for thirty boys until the government school opened (SM 3/25/49; JRH 10/20/53; LMH 1/24/54). The parents of these children doubtless welcomed the new opportunities in local education. Others, however, complained that they needed their children at home for chores, even if the school arranged its vacations to correspond with the heaviest work demands during the growing season. They doubted that a child who was going to be a farmer needed an education (Hanks 1959). For the first year the new head teacher did not press his demands for attendance, but "from the year 1936 to 1939 children came to school more often. The head teacher was strict about the rules. Every teacher had to come to school and teach. If a child were absent seven days in one month, the head teacher had the power to call parents to explain. If the absences continued, parents had to pay a fine at the district office" (LMH 12/29/53).

Opposition to the school on grounds that girls should not be required to attend never developed seriously. All ready arguments—the loss of labor, the uselessness of education for farmers—applied equally to both sexes. Some objected to the secular character of the education: a person should learn to read sacred texts and not just to read in general. Yet these people would not deny knowledge of the moral law to women. Only the occasional irate parent of a freshly eloped daughter blamed the school for teaching her to write love letters. Within a few days the new couple was home forgiven, and the question of her literacy never rose again.

Whether the monarchy was absolute or constitutional, the problems of low prices in a slumping world market continued. In addition to making international deals to absorb portions of the crop, the government directed its Department of Agriculture and Fisheries to select high-quality rice seed and distribute it among the farmers (Min. Ag. 1951:209–213). One of the Bang Chan headmen remembered: "The government had a contest and we sent in the best rice varieties as a sample. Rice should be long and thin; a big nose in rice is bad. In the old days we had many varieties because we planted what we liked, but now the government is the manager who tells the district officer, the kamnan, and the hamlet headman to plant good varieties. Rice was studied by the government; so it told farmers to take care to maintain the quality of rice and not let it get wet. The government loves the people as a mother loves its child" (JRH 12/17/53). Not everyone immediately followed this mother's advice. They preferred to wait and see with their own eyes how well the new government varieties grew. So a few of the wealthier farmers tried them out, and after seeing their success, others followed who could less afford to gamble.

Respite

Their karma saved a few Bang Chan farmers from the full lash of insolvency. The grandnephew of Uncle Sin, instead of joining his more honored brothers in Bangkok, worked the land that his father had cleared and came to acquire several hundred additional rai of ricelands. One of the nine daughters of Kamnan Phlym also fared well. Both were sober persons of thrifty habit, both worked steadily, neither gambled or drank. In these virtues they still looked like a hundred other household heads who had to labor for the district officer just to pay their taxes. What did their karma provide that saved these two?

Since we are better acquainted with the kamnan's daughter, let us follow her course. Jum was Phlym's second daughter, born in the days when her father was still seeking to make a living. Both sisters grew up like any fisherman's daughters, learning to paddle a boat, to wade about in knee-deep muck trapping fish, and to drive the birds away from the padi field. Jum was a little taller, more slender, more comely and dutiful than her older sister. Perhaps she was also a little shrewder. By the time their father had married a second wife and become kamnan, they had become young women. Their father, ever conscious of his assets, sought to marry them well, but the older daughter eloped with one of the young men hired to work around the place. Though the kamnan was disappointed, he forgave the new couple and moved them into his compound with his own two wives.

According to her own account, Jum married more advantageously: "My husband came from Prapadaeng, which then was a province. He was a teacher at the school in Bam Phen temple, where the head priest was a friend of my father. So my husband and I met many times before marriage. His older brother acted as go-between and arranged the marriage for a price between three and five hundred baht" (JRH 7/10/53). The young teacher, with his older brother's help, staged a handsome formal procession to the kamnan's compound, into which he moved to live. From this union two daughters were born during the 1910s. Through her husband's instruction Jum became the first literate woman in Bang Chan. But her young husband, who was being groomed to carry on when the kamnan resigned, suddenly died.[12] After her husband's cremation the bereaved widow devoted herself to her aging father. In gratitude he seized the opportunity made possible by the revision of the civil code in 1926 (Thompson 1941:684) to draw up a will. Instead of bequeathing his property to his heirs in equal shares, as was customary, he bequeathed to his oldest daughter 40 rai of land and to Jum 500 (JRH 8/27/53). Earlier each had received 100 rai as a gift from the father.[13] The elder daughter's husband soon left her in search of a richer spouse. The inheritance caused a feud between the two sisters which lasted until the elder's death.

As already noted, most of the recipients of the kamnan's land quickly lost their legacies. Jum was an exception, though she had to earn extra money like everyone else. She told of her difficulties: "More than twenty-five years ago I used to take my rents in rice, but the price went down as low as twenty five baht per kwian. Rice was not valuable then, and I had to ask the merchant to buy it. I paid one baht tax for each rai of land. Then I had difficulty paying the tax of six hundred baht. I took as rent one thang for each rai, and one thang sold at thirty satang [0.30 baht]" (LMH 8/17/57). At 30 baht per kwian (100 thang), this woman's rents in no way covered her taxes, so that to remain solvent she had to act shrewdly. As she was one of the larger landholders in Bang Chan, in fact the daughter of the kamnan, people turned to her for loans:

Thung received twenty-five rai of land from his father but became hard up. So he pawned the land for eighteen and a half chang [1,480 baht]. He had a wife and child, but they ran away from him. He was slightly mad. When he got the money, he loaned it out expecting to collect interest, but he could not get the money back. So he came asking me to buy the land. I did not have cash on hand but promised to give him a little from time to time. When Thung died a few months later, he still had credit for a thousand baht. One of his nephews came after his death to claim the land. He said that since I had not paid the full price, the land was not mine. In the contract it was written that in a certain number of months the land would belong to me. The nephew wanted to take it to court, but later we settled out of court by paying money." [LMH 8/6/57]

All Jum's assets had to be employed to meet these shortages, and collecting debts from cash-short farmers was difficult. Still it was well within her power to help her older sister during those days of distress, had she wished to. According to one witness, "Jum's older sister pawned forty rai of land and had no money to redeem it. So Jum bought the land from the moneylender. She ought to have held the land for her older sister and told her to find some money to redeem it. Instead she changed title and rented it" (JRH 2/4/54).

Jum gave no quarter in her feud. In addition, she turned to her other assets, two daughters ready for marriage. The recently arrived head teacher at the new school, a bachelor, became the most eligible young man in the area. The eldest daughter took advantage of the fact that she lived near the school and within a year became his bride. With the milk money and her son-in-law's contribution to the household from his small but constant salary, Jum could relax a little. A few years later the younger daughter married a promising clerk in the district office. Thus Jum emerged from the decade with more land and assets than when she began. Some people called her a tight-fisted, sharp dealer with little generosity, but her own household considered her a very competent manager.

That education could be a springboard to a salaried position became clear to a son of the kamnan by a minor wife. His wife told of the experience during the 1930s:

When Kamnan Phlym died, we were robbed of many things. One of the children stole an engine. So my husband and I moved out. We took the old house down and set it up on the seventy rai of land we owned. As we were very poor, we got into debt with my husband's maternal uncle. When my husband got more money, he wanted to pay off the debt, but this uncle wanted the land and not the money. The uncle wanted my husband to work the land and to change the title to his name. When all was ready, he did not give my husband the money and rented the land to someone else. So my husband was angry and would not attend his uncle's cremation. Then with no land to work, he went to Minburī and became a teacher of carpentry in the vocational school. [JRH 8/7/53]

This son had attended only the ordinary temple school in Bang Chan and had become a priest, yet for all his rustic background he was somehow undaunted at dealing with literate matters. The attraction of teacher's pay to a dispossessed renter was clear enough, even if it could not have exceeded forty baht per month (Thompson 1941:776). At deflated prices he could maintain a respectable if modest household in keeping with his status.

What made teaching a thinkable step for this son of the kamnan? Special attitudes were creeping into the minds of the residents of the kamnan's compound which had subtly begun to separate its members from the rice farmers around. A daughter-in-law described the raising of her children during the 1920s: "My children wanted an education because they did not like farming. They were raised in Bang Chan. Their parents worked in the fields, but they never did. My oldest daughter went to school and became a teacher. She teaches home economics. She could save money and give it to her younger brother for his education" (JRH 7/31/53). Bang Chan describes such children as "chickens" because they dislike getting their feet wet (Sharp et al. 1953:31). "Ducks," children of rice farmers content with their condition, do not mind splashing in the water and mud at their work.[14] Though even the kamnan's wealthy daughter waded in the fields like any other farm child, her own children never weeded, carried sheaves from the field, or did any other heavy work. Official status had brought new tastes to the kamnan's compound and reduced old fears of rebuff by persons in high position. Some of these descendants were eager to step out of the padi fields. Two sons and at least six grandchildren became teachers. Others acquired the tastes for a better standard of living but not the skills to achieve it.

Thus her karma brought Jum new sources of cash to tide her through the lean years. Similarly Uncle Sin's nephew on the land could call on his salaried brother in Bangkok when a little extra cash would add to his landholdings. Those who passed these times intact greeted the slight increase of padi price in the late 1930s as if it were a pot of well-spiced cobra curry. With higher rentals from the more abundant crop and low prices for commodities, they were "rich." These farmers might add some of the new devices that made farming easier. Among them was the *noria* or "dragon" pump promoted by the government for lifting water through an inclined trough by an endless belt of little paddles (*rahad*) (Min. Ag. 1957:213-214). It could be operated tediously by hand or foot power; then three brothers famous in the vicinity fashioned a windmill that, hitched to one of these new devices, could flood a field in a few day or night hours when the reliably steady monsoon winds were blowing at just the time such work was needed. Others bought portable gasoline en-

gines that could bail out a fish pond in the calms of the dry season
(Janlekha 1957:93).[15] By renting these devices to a neighbor or
tenant, the owner could add to his rice or cash income.

Agony Renewed

In Bangkok the new guardians in the ministries and the National
Assembly were learning to oversee their charges more efficiently
than the monarchs they had superseded. They were able to cultivate
sentiments of fervent nationalism more effectively than could Rama
VI with his Wild Tiger Corps and anti-Chinese propaganda. Instead
of giving moral lectures from the throne on gambling and waiting
months for the order to percolate through ministries via monthons,
provinces, and districts to the villages, the new government could
address the people directly over the few battery radios scattered
about Bang Chan. In a few hours passing boatmen brought the word
to the remotest backwaters. While former guardians were interested
in modernizing and beautifying the capital architecturally, the new
patrons turned to beautifying the inhabitants as well by ordering all
people to wear hats and shoes in addition to their ordinary costumes
when working or visiting in government offices and to stop chewing
betel nut altogether. With the additional cosmetic of a new ballroom
round dance (*ramwong*) popularized and disseminated by radio to all
sections of the country, the new guardians faced the world of nations
more confidently because of the fullness of their Thai heritage (Vella
1955:385).

So Bang Chan women rented hats at the outskirts of the city from
entrepreneurs ever alert to new possibilities of earning a living. If
their husbands came too, these same costumers fitted a not-too-
uncomfortable pair of shoes to their callused feet. Then the boatload
might proceed to the marketplace without fear of being stopped by
the police. The wife of a village physician recalled how her husband
helped popularize the new dance during his annual ceremony of
paying respect to his teachers: "When my husband celebrated his
annual ceremony of thanks to his teachers of medicine, he sent for
professional dancers to dance the new ramwong. Lots of boys from
the neighborhood came but only a few girls. Parents do not like their
daughters to go to a dance like this. Daughters do not like to go
because they feel shy" (JRH 11/5/53). The new dance was too
daring for Bang Chan.

Suddenly the music over the radio became martial; sober statements on Thailand's international position were proclaimed. People listened and rumors flew as fast as a skiff on the canal could be paddled. In 1940 Paris had crumpled and retired into a helpless Vichy. Defenses were weak in French Indochina when Bangkok directed its army into Laos and Cambodia to recover territory lost to the French during the nineteenth century. Young men were drafted into the army, and at least one from Bang Chan died in battle before the Japanese arbitrated the dispute in favor of Thailand (SM 1/26/49). Then at the end of the year of the Snake, 1941, the Thai opposed but briefly the landing of Japanese soldiers along the coast of Thailand. Directives quickly issued out of Bangkok to welcome these armies in transit. So in the following year Bang Chan saw Japanese planes in the sky and heard that Japanese soldiers were at Don Myang airport and were walking the streets of Bangkok. Many Thai were apprehensive: "We were afraid the Japanese would reign over Thailand. We feared they would come and settle down" (JRH 10/28/53). The Thai recruits, instead of being sent home, received orders to guard the railways, the bridges, and the camps of interned enemy aliens. Fewer hands were ready to plow the fields and transplant the padi: "My second son was never ordained a priest, and now he has four children. He was a soldier for seven years during the war. He served in the military police. He liked it but he also wanted to help his parents with the farming. His younger brother and sister were still small and could not help very much" (JRH 2/19/54). The very old and very young were pressed into tending the crop, while the youth mounted guard in the city.

In 1942 few extra hands were needed for the crop. The spirit guardians failed to protect the rice: deep brown water surged over the fields, ruining the crop.[16] The poor had too little to carry them through that gaunt year:

We were short of food during the flood. There was not enough left over to last us through the year, but we ate normal amounts until it was gone. The government sold milled rice cheap at the district office, only two baht a thang. But the rice was not good. Whoever had enough of his own rice left over did not give it away; he kept it for his own household. Some people got a crop of sorts but most often the rice sank into the water. People did not know where to turn. My son went to buy padi, milled it at home, and sold it to the police station. He wasted money selling rice because some people did not pay him. [JRH 1/28/54]

Those weighed down with debts dropped like overripe fruit from the trees. Owners again handed their title deeds to creditors; renters again sold their plows and buffalo and looked for work at digging a fish pond or mounding a garden. Thus had flood and drought always treated the people, but this flood aggravated a variety of shortages. Some articles could not be found at black-market prices even by the rich. A mother described her household: "I borrowed money to buy food because my son's poultry raising was not enough to support the family. There was enough fish and vegetables but not rice. There was enough rice for seed in our granary but not enough for eating. . . . People ate the same amount of rice as usual, but it was troublesome buying things for the family. I could not buy clothes, and because I hadn't enough clothing to wear, I could not travel around for buying and selling. Some families had to wear rice bags" (LMH 12/29/53).

Not all turned abject. Some households passed the one neat loincloth to whoever was going to market (LS 1/27/49). Then people began trading previously unmarketable items. One man sold atap leaves to the Japanese camps for building, while his partner stole them back at night for resale the next day (JRH 10/28/53). Another, an army private, collaborated with his colonel in stealing Japanese army equipment, thus acquiring new buffalo, thatch, farm tools, and other valuables (LS 2/2/49). Another developed an inland trade, bringing rice from the Bangkok region to the south of Thailand and returning with fruits; his profits at a sideline in smuggling were good until the police caught him (JRH 7/9/53). A few began to manufacture mills for grinding rice at home, and they sold as fast as anyone could make them (LMH 3/1/54).

As the new crop grew into a somewhat better harvest, bombing began in Bangkok. New households of frightened city people appeared along the canals leading from the city. Sales for peddlers increased, and some were not just busy making a few satang to keep themselves alive: "I was a trader, and everything sold easily because the other traders were afraid of the bombs. I went to visit my son at his regiment. Once, while there, a plane came over and dropped bombs. I was frightened and sat praying under a bamboo tree. . . . All the money I received from trading went for my husband's cremation. I thought maybe the merit from this cremation would keep my son safe during the war" (JRH 1/22/54). City folk gladly exchanged old clothes for help in building a house, and farmers plied the new residents with rice, bananas, and pork.

Then the war's shape began to change. Allied resistance mounted toward defeat of the invaders in Burma. Free Thai were landed at Don Myang airfield and even roamed the streets of Bangkok. American bombings increased and a stray bomb fell in Bang Chan, killing a pig. Not long after, the war was over.

Victory and Defeat

No one in Bang Chan said whether or not people rejoiced when the war ended. Though all were happy to have escaped the bombing, no victory parade was announced, no day of national mourning. The new government entered, but no one knew whether it was a government of enslavement or liberation. Some Bang Chan farmers snatched up a boat and went to see the bombed docks and railway station in Bangkok, then returned to tend the crop. They felt no great change, just as a true ascetic senses no relief when his chastisement ends. The suffering was not pointless or arbitrary; it was as necessary as the pains of a mother bringing forth a child. As long as the child was born, the pain was unimportant. So after its years of pain Bang Chan was "cooked" (sug), and was no longer "raw" (dip).

He who has been cooked in the priesthood and so may be addressed as thid (learned and wise) knows that suffering is the product of an individual's past sins. Thus suffering, however incomprehensible, may be welcomed as an expiation of those sins. When the suffering ends, such a man may rejoice that his merit has increased proportionately. This was one of the meanings of the grandfather who told his grandson: "First you must suffer; then you will have happiness."

The old man may also have meant that suffering is a necessary ingredient for perfecting oneself. Without the suffering that sin produces, man could not move toward his saintly potential. To rise above illusions and perceive the world as sham, one must have suffered. A priest told of trying to clarify his mind and relieve himself of oppressive thoughts: "About six years ago, I became able to concentrate [kamathān] when I went to the wilds. For a long time I practiced. Sometimes I did not feel hungry any more. Sometimes I felt a wind blowing out of my ears. It took ten years. Now I can gaze at something and keep my mind concentrated. I can interpret tales

for their underlying meaning and find lost articles by clairvoyance"
(LMH 2/15/54). Without years of suffering he would never have
developed such powers.

Being cooked carries a further resonance that echoes up from a
pre-Buddhist past. Not only men but women are cooked. After
giving birth to a child, Bang Chan women lie for an uneven but
varying number of days beside a slow fire (*jū faj*). All mothers have
suffered in bearing children and suffer again while, as they say, the
heat dries the excess water element within the body (J. R. Hanks
1963). This practice is shared by many peoples across Southeast Asia
and into the Pacific.[17] Today its meaning varies from place to place,
but many agree to the broad theme of coming of age, of achieving a
culturally mature status.

If Bang Chan people were cooked by the fifteen years of suffering,
how had they matured in the experience? It affected little their
relations with their spiritual and temporal guardians. These superiors were not bound by any covenant that required them to make the
people prosper. Nor was suffering to be construed as punishment for
some lapse in obligations. Farmers petitioned the Rice Mother each
year with offerings, but only when the crop was bountiful did they
return abundant thanks. The Lord of the Place, like the district
officer, might freely grant the wish of a petitioner today and deny
him the same tomorrow. No farmer hoped to fathom his whimsical
conduct. A guardian's love for his charges alone guaranteed de-
pendability, but how could affection be known except by the bounty
it produced (see Phillips 1965:160)?

Nor did being cooked mean simply that Bang Chan had learned to
operate in a cash economy. Thailand had used lozenge- or bullet-
shaped coins and cowrie shells as currency for centuries. Farmers
never handled many of the more valuable denominations, but for at
least fifty years they had been accustomed to receiving cash for their
crops and paying cash for taxes and many goods. Both women and
men understood how to invest savings in commodities in order to
save capital and live from the profits. Interest, known as the cowrie
blossom (*dāuk bia*), was familiar enough from the days of debt
slavery.

Until the 1920s the cash economy had been a marginal affair. Most
dealings within Bang Chan were in padi. Rents, temple offerings,
even many trade obligations at the nearby stores on Sāen Sāeb canal

were paid in measured rice. If a farmer needed currency, he took a cash-paying job or asked his wife for some of her trading profits. When he paid his cash obligation he went back to padi dealings.

During the 1920s cash dealings became increasingly important. Farmers, long able to estimate how much rice a household would consume until the next harvest, found themselves in trouble applying the same formula to cash consumption. The appetite for padi could be satisfied, but the appetite for cash was insatiable. People learned to calculate income and expenses, but to play the game of a cash economy skillfully required some new habits. The lad from the government school had to calculate the price of padi per thang for his parents. They always had sold the crop for whatever one or another of the mill agents would give. It did not take the lad many years to learn to sell a little and wait for the seasonal rise before selling the rest (Janlekha 1957:131). Similarly he knew where money could be borrowed at the least cost because he could calculate the interest rates. These skills helped to make him cooked.

The importance of abundant rice of uniform high quality became clear to all who were dealing in the world market, however remote that market was to farmers who had never smelled the sea. They employed any new device that produced this abundance with the least pain. They began to consider the heap of padi after harvest less as a glorious end in itself than as a symbol of the cash it might bring. Perhaps this explains why the young felt less urge to sing the triumphant songs of harvest and discarded them during the 1930s when the old people died. They further learned that even a banana leaf may have value in money. What they could manufacture under their houses with their own lands might well have value.

Bang Chan's industriousness in the face of suffering would have pleased Rama IV, with his panacea from Adam Smith. Yet no rice farmer was so seduced by his successes in trade or manufacture as to wish to become an entrepreneur of this kind. Wealth in money lured no one except those women traders who had to deal in fear of their families' starvation (LMH 8/13/57). A carpenter, who doubtless prospered by building little houses along the canals for refugees from Bangkok, declared, "Farming is better than carpentry because farming is rich in things to eat. A carpenter suffers because he depends on wages alone. If sick, he earns nothing. A carpenter's equipment wears out quickly, but a farmer's equipment wears out slowly"

(LMH 9/1/53). Working for cash alone exposed one to uncertainties. Only one man turned voluntarily away from farming during those years. He decided in 1942 to contract for small jobs of carpentry and digging, using the sons of his neighbors as the work crew. He remained, however, a landowner. This new venture only supplemented his rents from the land he had turned over to tenants. At any time he could repossess his lands, and all the while his bins bulged with padi for the household (LMH 8/13/57).

Bang Chan clung to padi. It had a deep significance, for which metal and paper, even when they bore the king's likeness, could not easily substitute. Within the brown husk of padi lies the rice.[18] Unlike bread, rice is not just the staff of life: it is life itself. From rice comes flesh and blood. The rice that a mother eats becomes the baby within her body (J. R. Hanks 1961). Rice is food, food is rice (khāw); the vegetables or meat that people eat at meals simply adorn the rice with special flavors (kab khāw). As food, rice is the vital essence of the social order. Food and shelter form the basis for the services a patron anticipates from his clients. To preserve the life of a household as long as possible, the patron serves a full dish of rice, even in famine days when his bins are ebbing. Serving less than abundantly implies a lessening of the patron's esteem for his clients. He offers food to the priests to make merit. To solicit the assistance of a spirit guardian, he promises food, though the guardians prefer the sweet odors of cooked pork or the essence of rice liquor to plain rice.

The bond to rice and padi runs even deeper. Bang Chan lies at the heart of an abundant land. Thai pride themselves on this abundance: "In the water, fish; in the fields, rice" (Naj nām mī plā, naj nā mī khāw) runs a familiar proverb going back centuries to King Rāma Kamheng. Yet all worry over going hungry. Coffeehouses and food peddlers invariably sell out their wares in this population of snack eaters. The pilgrim away from his farm home must still his fear of starving, though he can find something to eat at almost every turn. The householder dares not ration his dwindling supply of food, while hosts of a celebration would feel boundless shame were the food insufficient, which it never is. The young man anticipating ordination is filled with apprehension by his vow to fast between noon and the following dawn. People regard themselves as sick when they have lost their appetites (Sharp et al. 1953:260). Only persons with such an abundance of merit that they have all but metamorphosed into noncorporeality can overcome their feelings of hunger. Loss of appetite signifies either sickness or sanctity.

This concern for food is clearly related to fear of abandonment, that phobia shared by high and low. Without food one stands alone, unprotected, isolated, clientless or patronless, abandoned and helpless. Through suffering Bang Chan has learned many things and proved again that those who try to stand alone are foolhardy.[19]

CHAPTER 8

Transformation Scene

The Festivities

In Thai the word *ngān* means both festival and work. It is also a measure of land area equal to one-fourth of a rai, and in this context it represents the amount a man harvests in half a day. In the Bang Chan scene, having a ngān also implies the summoning of strength (khāū raeng) to carry out a chore. A farmer holds a ngān to drain a fish pond, to build a house, or to harvest the crop. The host, known as the receiver (*phū rab rāung*), announces the day, lays out the work to be done, and at the end feeds the workers (see Tirabutana 1958:31). Life-cycle rites have the same form, be they for topknot cutting, ordination, cremation, or even marriage, a ceremony that has only recently become important for Bang Chan. Guests come bringing food or money to the host and stay to prepare food or assist with the ceremonial. Similarly in calendric rites at the temple, those of the Buddhist "Lenten" season, New Year's, and half a year later at Sād, a harvest festival, householders help the priests accomplish a cosmic transformation. So ngān means work, but not necessarily arduous work. It has the sociable gaiety of a husking or quilting bee, often combined with the lavishness of a festival or fiesta. We have no equivalent in English, so we shall speak simply of festivities.

The most important festivity for any person is his cremation, as distinct from his death. Except for special emergencies, the two are ordinarily separated by a time span varying from one hundred days to several years.[1] While cremation always takes place at a temple, death rites occur anywhere, though preferably at the home of the deceased. By tying the hands and feet of the corpse, providing it with money, covering the face with a wax mask, and nailing up the coffin, the survivors seek to protect the living from a potentially hostile spirit.[2] The removal of the body through the wall of the house and its delivery to the temple further underscore protection. When the priests read sermons at the household of the deceased, not only does the spirit gain merit for a future life but the inhabitants of the household are fortified against the spirit, should it return to its former home. Thus death rites are prophylactic against petulant ghosts, while cremation rites dispatch the spirit from this world.

A cremation festivity (ngān phao sob), particularly one of some pretension, requires months of advance preparation.[3] Large sums of money must be collected from affluent relatives just to begin to buy food for a thousand meals, robes for fifty priests, and presents for five hundred guests. During the 1940s and 1950s Bang Chan hosts sent out invitations printed in Bangkok. Nowadays, also in the Bangkok mode, the occasional host in the countryside may reprint, as a favor for his guests, a book of Buddhist precepts with a brief biography of the deceased. Frequently he hires from Bangkok a handsome bier complete with gilded angels and a generator to power fluorescent lights. An undertaker prepares the body and manages the pyre; a carver of banana stalks ornaments the cremation platform; flower arrangers deck the bier and make bouquets to give away; an orchestra plays throughout the day and night. A theatrical performance, and possibly also a shadow play or movie, will entertain the guests. If people have been invited from the capital, it is necessary to arrange transportation, perhaps even build a special road to help the buses come near the temple. So 15,000 baht is not an unusual initial outlay (Janlekha 1957:149).

This period of preparation necessarily overlaps the time for welcoming guests. The first to arrive, the near kinsmen, are set to work grating coconuts or pressing eggs through a sieve to make golden-thread sweets. Someone must fetch the priests from the more distant temples. Others escort the arriving priests to their prearranged cushions in the pavilion. As lay guests enter, the host personally receives their contributions and ensures that they are fed.[4] Finally when the temple, filled with people clad in their best, vibrates with the music of gongs, drums, and oboes, the gods and demigods are invited to descend from the heavens to protect the assemblage from danger.

Already the rites have begun. Holding the sacred cotton cord that leads inside the bier to the bones, the corps of priests chants sutras for the deceased; the emanations following the sacred cord invigorate his soul. Sermons add to the merit. Now and then the orchestra proclaims to the heavens via loudspeakers that another soul is about to arrive from the earth. During the last night on earth the deceased is diverted by dramatic performances. Next morning he gains further merit through feeding the priests and hearing other sermons.

About four o'clock in the afternoon the undertaker removes from the bier a small tinseled box containing the bones of the deceased. A procession headed by chanting priests moves from the pavilion, leading the box by the sacred cord. Kinsmen fall into line behind the priests. The way is short, for the cremation platform, resplendent with carved banana stalks and garlands of flowers, lies nearby in the temple courtyard. Slowly the procession winds around this platform, three times in counterclockwise direction, for the way of death is opposite the way of life.[5] At last the carriers place the box of bones on the pyre, while the priests relinquish the sacred cord. All guests, in approximate order of their eminence, file past the pyre, make final obeisance, and contribute to the pyre the incense sticks and faggots provided by the host. As each guest descends from the platform, a kinsman hands him a token of gratitude for his work: a handkerchief, a bouquet of flowers, sometimes a book.

All the guests have gathered in a great circle about the pyre, and the moment to light the fire has come. First some honored guest adds a final increment of merit by giving away another robe to each of the priests in the name of the deceased. Then as the flames rise, the undertaker breaks a coconut and pours its milk over the skull. Soon he is dousing the faggots with water to make the fire burn more slowly. Suddenly a hiss followed by an explosion indicates that a fireworks display has begun; thunderous rockets tell the heavens that a soul has departed from the earth. At this time many guests take leave, though the host may have arranged for another evening of feasting and dramatics to please those who wish to remain. A few may still be present on the following morning when the undertaker, accompanied by a near kinsman and a priest, returns to the cold ashes of the pyre. After a blessing by the priest, the undertaker fashions two manikins, one said to represent the former person, the other the future body to enhance rebirth. The kinsman then takes a bone home to keep in an urn, while the undertaker disposes of the remainder.

...sts circumambulate decorated pyres at a cremation rite
...to by Lauriston Sharp

What transformations have been effected? A merit-filled soul has been dispatched from the earth, thereby relieving the people of the dangers of a roaming spirit. It has begun a course of travels that will end, if all goes properly, with rebirth into one of the households of its kinsmen. Thus the cycle of life has been continued. As for the survivors, they have been reminded of the impermanence of life and the importance of merit. Through their stores of merit they have survived the dangers of this period, and they need not yet experience the agony of their own deaths. The host, seeing the great crowds that answered his summons, counts his blessings, and people praise him as a generous host, a rich man, a potential leader.

In the sense that a festivity requires the labor of many to effect a transformation in life, the period since World War II clearly has been a festivity in Bang Chan. The once isolated rustic community has been transformed into something of a suburb. It is still too soon to say whether the ritual actions are producing a transition, as from youth to adulthood, or a transfiguration, as from life to death. Another few years will show the outcome more clearly, yet even now we can observe most of the preparations, the welcoming of many guests, some of the rites, and a few of the transformations.

The Preparation

Even before the cessation of hostilities in 1945 there began a contest for control of the state. In four years two kings, eight prime ministers, two regents, and a variety of constitutions sought to stabilize the nation (Thompson 1948:188). Parliaments debated, but the struggle took place in administrative offices, with money and civil or military positions as the counters (Wilson 1959:55-58). What could not be resolved in cabinet meetings was often settled by tanks in the streets. The economy of the nation, however, snapped back on its pivot with remarkable speed, despite the diplomats and politicians (Paauw 1963:72). Each year the fields were planted. Early in 1946 a crop of unknown size was ready as usual. Rivers and canals floated what could not be hauled over the crippled railroads. Smugglers passed it to the hungry world beyond the Thai frontiers at extortionate prices until legal channels of export were cleared in 1947 (LS 6/6/49; Ingram 1955:87-88). Before tin, teak, and rubber could move again, padi was earning the pounds and dollars necessary to restore imports.

Bang Chan emerged from the war years tattered but not badly battered. Most of the urban refugees returned quickly to the city to begin anew after clearing away the debris of bombs and neglect. Most of the soldiers were discharged in time to help with the harvest. A man complained, "Those animals [the Japanese soldiers] came and ate up all the food" (LS 6/8/49), but the real trouble for the farmers was not food but goods to buy with their money. During that first postwar year the price for padi rose to about 300 baht per kwian, comparing well with the 60 to 80 received during the war. So farmers had money, but clothing, tools, kerosene, and matches were hard to find at any price. Black-market prices for shoddy loincloths left little cash for other necessities. So in 1946 it was not difficult for the district officer to find workers for the road from Laksī to Minburī, the road the Japanese had begun but never finished. A Bang Chan resident recalled: "Every house was asked for one man to help mound up the road. When it was finished, we went to Don Myang to build the airfield. This was during the time we were free from fieldwork. On the road we got ten baht per day and at the airfield fifteen to twenty baht. We slept at the former Japanese camp, but I was not happy because we had to cook our own food. No woman could go along with us" (JRH 10/29/53).

They were not long dependent on wages, for the following year padi prices climbed in the legal market to 770 baht per kwian and then to 1,100 (LS 2/1/49; Janlekha 1957:72; LMH 8/17/57). Within a few years many had become wealthy by local standards. Farmers of the 1950s were receiving ten to eighteen times the price that the prewar rice crops had bought.

Gradually consumer goods began to seep into the markets, and people bought what they could afford:

A little after eight P.M. my wife's brother-in-law dropped by asking me to take some rice to my mother-in-law, who had to feed the workers at harvest. I noticed that he had kitchen utensils in his boat. It seems that these days there are always a lot of kitchen utensils in the farmers' sampans. This is because they have forgone these necessary purchases and the price of padi in relation to the price of goods is quite reasonable. [KY 12/16/48].

Three men went to see a herd of buffalo near Bangkok: "They came back with empty hands since the beasts were too expensive, and most of them were females, thin and old. The price of one big buffalo was between twelve hundred and fourteen hundred baht" (SM 2/16/49). So for the first few years after the war, Bang Chan was still doing without many things, but by 1949 most people were happily buying clothes, rebuilding their houses with new nails and new lumber, replacing thatch with roofs of galvanized iron, and refurbishing the houses of the guardian spirits (LS 10/18/48).

Not everybody was prosperous, as the government was well aware. From the district office came directives for headmen to relay to their hamlets: "The government will arrange to help poor farmers by providing buffalo"; "The government advises householders to grow ground nuts after harvest"; "The District will run a morning market at Minburi and will welcome all villagers who come to sell or buy" (SM 1/12/49). We know of no Bang Chan farmers who received help from the government, nor any who grew ground nuts. The market in Minburī, however, revived. Government was also care-fully stimulating production and held land taxes, despite inflation, at the absurdly low level of 0.30 baht per rai. Not until 1952 were taxes aligned with land values rather than with land use.[6] Then farmers owning land along the road suddenly found themselves paying as much as 25 baht per rai in taxes for land assessed at 10,000 baht per rai. For the most part Bang Chan land was valued at 800 to 1,000 baht per rai, with tax set between 2 and 2.50 baht per rai (LS 9/19/52; 2/12/53; CIW 7/14/54). Landlords, of course, quickly raised their rents by about one-third (Janlekha 1957:62).

Like taxpayers and renters everywhere, villagers in Bang Chan grumbled about new expenses, but they grumbled more because the government did nothing to improve the canals. In the dry season one could neither cross Bang Chan canal by boat nor wade through the sticky mud. District officers were well aware of the needs but lacked funds to act. Finally in 1948 a wealthy farmer organized the people and advanced the money for the digging of a portion of Kred canal, an example of local initiative that was not matched elsewhere in Bang Chan, despite identical needs. Not until 1953, when an energetic new district officer appeared in Minburī with foreign aid funds, could anyone organize the workers again. Only then was Bang Chan canal freed of silt so that boats could move along it during the dry season.

One day in late 1948 the orderly succession of classes at the government school was interrupted by a squall of wind that threat-ened to tear apart the flimsy structure of the fourteen-year-old building, which then had to be abandoned. Months before the formal condemnation by the district authorities (SM 3/25/49), the head priest had already invited the teachers to hold their classes in one of the pavilions of the temple, and soon he assembled a special committee at the temple to address the need for a new school. No one knew how much the new building would cost, where it should be located, or who would pay for it. One teacher hoped that 40,000 baht and donated labor would suffice for the community's share (LS 12/28/48). The District Educational Office estimated a total cost of 86,000 baht when it sent an urgent petition to the ministry (KY 2/2/49). All knew before this petition was ever sent that a favorable reply, not to mention action, might require years, because the ministry's limited funds were needed by many communities. So the teachers set out during the harvest at year's end to solicit donations for the school in padi or cash; by March 1949 they deposited 4,442 baht in a savings bank, where it would draw 7 percent interest (KY 3/4/49).

Local initiative was moving, and was ready for the next disaster. In January 1949 Bang Chan was threatened by attack from spirits of persons who died violently (phī tāj hōng) (SM 1/13/49). A woman died during the night in childbirth. Her body was quickly bound, a coffin prepared, and a boat readied to take the corpse to the temple as soon as the dawn appeared. Her husband, mother, and brother waited tensely in the darkness. As light came, they carried the coffin through a hole in the wall to the boat, then made a gate of mōk branches to prevent the spirit from returning to the house. Branches of the mōk tree lay on the coffin to keep the malignant spirit inside while the family hurried to the temple. Once the coffin was safely there, the boatman sprinkled holy water over his boat to drive away the spirits. A brief blessing was said over the coffin by seven priests before the undertaker removed the body. On the cover of the coffin he deftly cut the child from the womb, and reported that it had two upper teeth. Clearly a spirit of a giant had entered the woman and killed her. The body of the woman was cremated at once and the child's corpse was quickly buried just behind the temple while the spectators steadied themselves with rice liquor (LS 1/12/49). Speedy action had averted disaster.

More remote but also disturbing to the community were the political events in Bangkok, where a king died and prime ministers succeeded each other by force. Since the 1932 revolution, elections had taken place irregularly. Few paid much attention. The monarchy had never sought the advice of its farmer subjects, and after sixteen years of democracy farmers were still not ready to try to tell their superiors what to do. During the election of December 1948, 5 percent of Bang Chan voted (KY 12/4/48). In June of the following year only 17 out of 100 to 150 eligible voters appeared at the polls (LS 6/7/49). Yet at the new store near the temple many farmers listened to the radio, and many of them spoke their opinions.

During the attempted coup in late February 1949 these same men clearly sensed that something was amiss at the pivot of the nation, and they correctly surmised who was behind the trouble. It was discussed in many parts of the village: "In the evening Nāj Mai came to my house and ate a meal with my family. He told me that in Bangkok another coup had taken place, and many people were arrested. This time the scheme was so terrible that the insurgents planned to kill all the ministers. The government knew about this plot and tried to avoid shooting" (KY 2/26/49).

Clearly Bang Chan stood by the side of a virtuous government that sought to avoid murder. A few days later, after the insurgents had presumably been suppressed, the radio reported an "ambush" of a police car carrying political prisoners from Bangkok to Bāng Khen prison in the general direction of Bang Chan; the four prisoners, all prominent people, were killed. The geographical proximity of Bāng Khen, where the incident had occurred, lent immediacy to the topic for many days of discussion. None was deceived by the "ambush." However, order and thus the existing government should be maintained. One coffee drinker said, "I believe the police have done a stabbing-in-the-back kind of business, but from now on there will be no enemy of democracy, and the police will not have to worry about an uprising"; a headman declared, "If it is really police policy to kill accused people, the Department of Police will be criticized. But I think it served these people right because they cheated the country in many ways" (SM 3/8/49).

The very government they espoused had bloody hands from actions that were hard to justify. The group at the store grew so uneasy that two men set off for Bangkok to determine what really had happened. On their return they were able to give circumstantial reports of what had taken place (LS 3/2–6/49), and they vehemently berated both sides and all politicians generally, "those cursed animals, fighting like dogs over a bone under the feet of His Majesty" (SM 3/3/49). The government, too, remained uneasy, ordering all in the region of the capital to be on the alert for insurgents. Accordingly two Bang Chan headmen received orders from the district office to guard the newly built highway bridge that crossed Bang Chan canal. Days before these measures had been taken, ready wits at the store had reduced local tension with satire, saying that the officials' new way of ensuring that police would kill a prisoner was to order: "Transfer that man to Bāng Khen prison" (LS 3/8/49). So Bang Chan turned away with a shrug, but there remained a sense of malaise and a deep concern for the young king.

Living is painful, but less painful if there can be festivities. A

certain Nāj Hem had fared well since the war, so that he could afford
to make merit. He often headed a temple committee; indeed, he was
a grandnephew of Uncle Sin, who had founded the temple and for
whose kindred it was thus of special interest (LMH 9/22/53; 8/7/57).
So it was a gala occasion when the community dedicated the new
congregating hall he had built, complete with golden naga tails at the
roof peak. By this means his wealth grew still more, and his influence
too, so that it was he that was able to have Kred canal dug clear of
mud.

In the same season others also held festivities. They included a
certain elderly man who was said to have served years in prison for
robbery (SM 1/24/49). On his release he had sought the quiet life of a
priest. But when word got about that he was able to make people
invulnerable with tattooing and with the words he could speak into
an amulet, many young men came to him on the festive day he made
obeisance to his teacher (SM 3/2/49). Since the crop had been good,
eleven headmen of Bang Chan and its neighboring hamlets resolved
to pay thanks to Mother Thōranī, goddess of the earth (SM 2/4/49).
Never before had such a great festival been arranged at the temple for
this goddess. The headmen invited from Bangkok a man of clear
voice to recite Pali verses. People from more than eleven hamlets
assembled to hear him sing:

Hail, Mother Thōranī, mother of the earth, of rice, of vegetables, of trees,
and of all the growing plants on the surface of the earth. I beseech you to
enter our presence. May you be kind enough to reside with us at this sacred
gathering.
     Mother, forgive us for having cut you with our sharp sickles, for having
carried you home without special care, for having threshed you without
mercy and taken you to our storage bins and granaries. Do not be frightened
and run away. Come back to live with us. [SM 2/4/49]

That evening a theatrical troupe played for all who came.

The Welcoming

So great was the transforming festival that the guests began to
arrive in Bang Chan before preparations were complete. The canal
still lay clogged with silt. Before the road had been surfaced, the
Bangkok–Minburī buses began lurching and plunging along its
course, except when the rains reduced it to an impassable slough.
When it was dry, farmers were again on their way to Pratū Nām

market for new treasure: flashlights, tins of milk, aspirin. Others with more to spend carried home radios, pressure lamps, and sewing machines (LS 5/17/49; SM 2/20/49). Like the head imam at the surao, some were buying the latest portable gasoline engines at 4,500 baht. In 1948 Bang Chan had only five (Sharp et al. 1953:128), but by 1955 the number had increased to seventy (Goldsen and Ralis, 1957:43). These portable gasoline engines not only could flood a seedbed and drain a fish pond within a few hours but, unlike a windmill, worked when the air was still. In 1953 a Bang Chan man rigged a long shaft with a propeller at the end and set the engine in his sampan. It took him to the temple in less than half the ordinary time. By 1960 the canals were roaring with outboard motors that were a little more convenient than the farm engines (LS 3/27/60).

Bang Chan was developing its own market, too. In 1948, besides peddlers and itinerant traders, there were only two stores. One on Kred canal sold only liquor and coffee and was open only when the landless proprietor was not hiring out to help in the fields (SM 1/18/49). At the temple was Yom's store, where people listened to a radio and discussed the news. The proprietor, once a soldier, had married a Bang Chan girl and moved to work on his wife's seven rai of riceland. This patch he finally decided to rent out in order to devote himself to the store. He too provided his clientele with coffee and liquor. The store stayed open every evening until he, his wife, or his son lowered the heavy galvanized iron shutter. He also sold incense sticks, candles, paper flowers, and ceremonial cotton cord to the merit makers at the temple, and candy, pencils, and notebooks to the children at the nearby school. A kerosene tin held fuel for lamps and an old one cut down held lime to go with betel. His location presumed traffic along the canals, but gradually the highway gained importance, particularly where the bus stopped. About 1952 two stores arose on the road; they began by selling most of the same wares that Yom offered, but gradually increased their stocks with soft drinks, ice with a spoonful of pink syrup, a few vegetables from the Minburī market, cakes, eggs, tins of milk, and fish. By 1953, Janlekha reports (1957:44), there was a total of nine stores in Bang Chan, including the two on the road. By 1963 the highway market had grown to eight stores.

People began worrying less about having enough to eat than about having enough money to spend. Fish, caught for home consumption

The genial proprietor of a store on the highway, formerly a farmer
Photo by Ewing Krainin

since the days when Bang Chan gave up market fishing for farming,
were again being dried and sold, usually by women (SM 2/23/49).
During the early 1950s many housewives were gathering their extra
eggs, lotus seeds, and vegetables and setting off for the early-morning market in Bangkok. They seemed not to be burdened by these
tasks. One woman turned over her farm to her son in order to ply the
canals (SM 2/23/49). In 1953 households were spending between

0.19 and 1.00 baht cash per person per day for food (Hauck et al. 1958:62-64).

New operations and occupations were also coming. The owner of a portable farm engine could rent it for flooding or draining at 40 to 70 baht per day, when a man with just his own hands earned a mere 10 to 20 baht (SM 2/24/48). For a time pressure lamps could be rented from a local farmer for 20 to 30 baht, if one were needed for night fishing or to illuminate the stage for a theatrical performance. A few people earned back the cost of their sewing machines many times over by opening tailor shops (SM 2/20/49). Some found new ways to make an honest baht: "Chit brought the old prewar engine from Jāj's house, where the wedding had been. He calculated the cost of spare parts to be used in reconditioning it. The owner asked two thousand baht. Chit says he will offer fifteen hundred. The postwar engines are of poor quality, and Chit will make money reselling this old one" (SM 3/23/49).

By 1953, when the highway had received its final coat of gravel and asphalt, half a dozen men were engaged to maintain it. Three men set up barbershops near the new highway bridge to earn extra money, and in time they had so many customers that they worked on the land only during the period of heaviest demand. New specialties like the mushroom operations also began: "My husband and I started a part-time occupation, selling clothes and mushrooms. Then we bought with the money we earned straw and spores. We didn't have to borrow money. The expansion came from our earnings. We have low costs and high profit. Last year we netted four thousand baht" (JRH 1/21/54). Some, like this woman, made money until over-production drove down the price; then they sought out new ventures, such as poultry and eggs. By the 1960s water taxis had become a flourishing business (LS 3/27/60). These prosperous years helped the village's single home industry to survive, as the proprietor explained:

Before the war I could not pay the cost of rent and so gave up farming. I sold my buffalo and farm equipment to invest in a store. Then I noticed that farmers have a hard time taking padi to be milled during the dry season. They could use a mill at home. There was a great demand for these mills, which cost five or six thang of padi apiece. But making the mills was hard work. My wife and son had trouble because they could not work hard like this. After the war we changed to making pans, baskets, sieves, and hats. During the rice season I worked as laborer on the farms to earn extra money. Four years ago [1950] I started making mango pickers [*takra*]. I make on the average about three hundred and fifty baht per month with four people working. During the past two years I no longer hire out to work in the fields. A man in Bangkok has a store and will take all I make because the quality is good. [LMH 3/1/54]

Most enterprises required little capital, yet getting started was not easy. The entrepreneurs raised their own funds, like the woman who began trading fruits and vegetables with six hundred baht (Janlekha 1957:45). The would-be barber who needed 1,500 baht to open a shop in Minburi gave up when he could find no source of funds (LS 6/6/49). Minburi mill owners and gold merchants willingly offered money to farmers at 2 to 5 percent per month, but few were trapped into this kind of arrangement (Janlekha 1957:158-161). A woman who needed about 700 baht to repair her house after a windstorm said, "I have to buy new supports and thatch in Minburi. There I must pay cash. Relatives do not help in this. I must borrow money at interest. I'll go to the Chinese lenders at Lōlae for five hundred baht. They charge eight to ten baht per month for one hundred baht. Inside the village here it costs less but it is hard to get. Local people like to lend money outside so that they can charge higher interest rates" (JRH 11/25/53). If one had a rich kinsman, he was lucky.

Once one was started, there were tricks to learn. Even a trader of many seasons made mistakes: "This year we bought thirty-three lots of thatch to resell. We buy most lots at Paknām for eighty to one hundred baht and resell them here at one hundred and forty baht. We stupidly bought the last lots locally at one hundred and thirty baht. Now we have to sell them at local prices and can't make a profit. That's a good joke on us" (LS 1/27/49).

A greater difficulty, however, lay in getting cash for sales and not extending credit too liberally. Most traders spent half their working hours collecting the money for last week's or even last month's purchases: "Later she also dealt in pork, and her daily outlay rose to 220 baht. Out of this, she received 150 baht cash and gave 150 baht credit. To date her credit accounts total 750 baht. Yesterday she was able to collect 150 baht cash and six thang of padi (worth 54 baht) from her debtors" (Janlekha 1957:45). Many went broke after trying vainly to collect their debts, but even when they were successful the hazards had not ended. A former boat vendor complained: "We used our income for making loans rather than reinvesting in the business.

These people say they will give interest, but actually they don't. It's hard to get the money back. If my husband followed my advice, he'd be rich, but he is kindhearted. If anyone asks for money, he helps them" (JRH 1/21/54). Many were uncertain whether they were running a tightfisted commercial venture that loaned its money at interest or whether they were the generous patrons of impecunious kinsmen.

Besides traders and peddlers there were new farmers in Bang Chan. Occasionally, as in former times, they came from nearer the capital to settle, but of the 48 new households that appeared between 1949 and 1953, "18 came from bordering villages and 9 from distant villages in all directions" (Janlekha 1957:34). The rest sprang from within Bang Chan itself. During this same period 38 households disappeared or moved away, leaving a net gain of 10.[7] These immigrants were not the familiar purchasers of cheap land but renters with much of their own equipment, though too poor to buy their fields. Their reasons for moving in were so varied that each had his own tale. One recalled: "I first rented ten to seventeen rai and gave eight thang of padi as rent. The landlord made me pay in advance. Last year I owed him twenty baht, even though I had paid the rent already. So he denied me the chance to rent again" (JRH 10/1/53).

Most newcomers came to Bang Chan because they had distant kinsmen there who might rent them land; most had moved no great distance from their former fields. Laborers also moved in, settling sometimes with a farm operator who needed a hired man; sometimes, with no specific job in mind, they settled where they could build a hut. Four years later, in 1957, the number of new households was 23, while 24 had disappeared from the census rolls. Though population had increased, the migration rate decreased somewhat.[8]

For the average man, the time to buy land had passed. Values rose from 300 baht per rai in 1948 to more than 1,000 in the middle 1950s for ordinary land; along the highway a rai was said to be worth 12,000 (Janlekha 1957:69). Holdings were diminished from our estimated average of 50 rai in 1910 to a median of 20.9 and an average of 30 in the 1950s (ibid.:60). Bang Chan also knew that further subdivision of the land by inheritance was an evil, though leaving equal portions of land to one's children was the preferred practice. A man with six children and 50 rai of land declared, "It's hard to find land to buy now. If you divide land among children, first you decide which is the best worker and the most deserving. If there is only a little land, the best one gets it. If there is a lot, each can get some" (JRH 10/28/53). This man had made up his mind not to divide his land.

Janlekha (1957:52) showed that the acreage planted to rice had decreased in the five years from 1948 to 1953 by nearly 350 rai, or by more than 10 percent. How much of this land was lost to padi by new housing, new fish ponds, or other uses he did not discuss. Rice growers, however, sustain the amount of land under cultivation as much as possible. The acreage planted by a household depended on the supply of labor. Most could not afford to hire help but used their children when they were judged competent to work in the fields. Thus a man with his wife worked only the ten rai he owned while the children were small. When four had grown, the father rented an additional fifty rai in scattered holdings. As the children left home, he rented less. This method of renting a few rai whenever workers were available appears to have utilized well the small landholdings at a time when land was in demand.

Among the transient newcomers of 1948 came the Cornell University group led by Sharp, with Kamol Janlekha and later Singto Metah accompanying him. They stated that they wished to study the life of farmers. Though the headmen who met them did not immediately understand what there was to study, they found no special need to seek further explanations. So they acquiesced with warm smiles. They later discovered that it was no trouble to talk about their parents and grandparents or, in this time of money consciousness, to recall the returns from last year's crop. During an early visit the newcomers brought a generator and a Thai-dubbed American movie about Tarzan to a festival fair at the temple, which happily attracted an unusually large crowd (KY 11/20/48). In the same month, when buffalo began to sicken and die, they brought a veterinarian from the Department of Animal Health and Husbandry in Bangkok to inoculate the local animals (LS 11/23–25/48). Sharp's position as a benevolent patron of Bang Chan became assured, his standing reinforced when high officials from Bangkok, diplomats, and scholars came to visit Bang Chan. Not many years later a headman of Bang Chan told the tale: "Dr. Sharp has helped the Thai people. He asked many officials and royal princes to have a meeting at the temple about the price of rice. Before the meeting the price was very low, but since then it has increased. If we have to get anything from the district office, it takes us two weeks, but Dr. Sharp does it at once. During an epidemic affecting the buffalo, someone told Dr. Sharp, and he sent the veterinarian from Bangkok right away" (JRH 9/24/53). Such facts and legends made the community receptive to physicians from the Ministry of Public Health, whom Sharp invited to examine the health of schoolchildren and study their diet. So the welcome remained warm throughout the decade of the 1950s as the Cornell group, enlarged to twelve, came and went to study nutrition, health, and agriculture as well as the social scene.

With the Cornell group came an assortment of new ideas, many of them perhaps already in the air. The members of the group considered themselves primarily investigators, though they were not averse to an effort at social change, if it were wanted locally and carried out with an experimental interest (see, e.g., Hanks et al. 1955). Their presence gently stirred the atmosphere. What these educated Thai and foreigners had selected to study, and what they said or implied about their findings, often conveyed an idea more adroitly than a lecture could have done. Some reaction was bound to occur when Hazel Hauck (1959: 30) asked whether parents gave their infants boiled water, rainwater, or canal water. Many Bang Chan hosts learned to offer foreign guests an explanation along with a glass of water: it was rainwater. When asked what local people did for sickness, Bang Chan had no perplexities in deducing the confidence of their visitor in "modern" medicine. So Goldsen and Ralis (1957:8) subsequently discovered that 64 percent of the respondents to a questionnaire said they had visited one or more hospitals and 37 percent had undergone treatment. Thus ideas were crystallized, if not introduced, about insecticides, fertilizers, immunization against disease, the reading of books, and many other topics. Something even set a teacher dreaming about a public library, though the dream was never fully realized (KY 10/20/48; 12/2/48).

Awareness of a broader world has a still less clear source. Farmers at this time traveled to and from not only Bangkok but many other parts of Thailand (KY 12/3/49; 10/31/54). A few veterans of the 1941 Indochina war spoke of Laos or Cambodia, and one or two told about Korea (AE 3/8/53). The newspaper to which the schoolteachers subscribed, the radio, movies, and conversations at the store over imported coffee and tea all contributed the names of foreign countries, the friends and enemies of Thailand, and some characteristics of the life led in these strange lands. A sporting event in the United States drew Bang Chan's rapt attention:

At last the day came of the much-talked-of fight for the world bantamweight crown, between Robert Cohen and Chamroen. Bang Chan was enthusiastic, and everyone wanted Chamroen to win. People gathered to listen near every house that had a radio. Some were full to overflowing. While the fight was on, I thought every heart was beating as it never had beaten while listening to Bangkok news. At last came the verdict. . . . It was natural to hear some unrefined mouths speaking words unwholesome for cultured ears. [KY 9/19/54]

If an ordinary person could thus move to America, if one could come in touch with him while he was away, it was becoming easier to think of a single world rather than a vague assemblage of countries, some inhabited by giants and demons, which could be reached only by magic spell or bodily transformation. Some exchanged letters with members of the Cornell group who were away in America. The people of Bang Chan were beginning to see their place in a continuity of lands where the same sun and similar human beings were making their daily rounds in slightly different settings. One evening a glimpse of this thought came while the members of a household were talking with two members of the Cornell group. They asked how one reached America and heard that there were three ways to go: to the west, to the east, and down through the earth. Some were mystified, until the eldest man of the household explained. He took an orange to illustrate the position of America on the sphere and then, using his pressure lamp as the sun, showed the rotation of the world making day and night, eventually ending with the earth's rotation about the sun in true Copernican fashion (JRH 10/23/53).

To be sure, the location of other places in the world was vague. Only a few of the fourth-graders in school knew they would have to walk west or northwest to reach Burma (LMH 5/8/53). Bang Chan had no maps of Asia, but despite the uncertain location of world events during the early 1950s, many people were following the Korean war and listening to the demise of France as a Southeast Asian power. Their sympathies were clearly against the North Koreans and the French, though they did not warm to the South Koreans or their old rivals the Vietnamese, either. Burma, much less in the news, still aroused unpleasant memories of the fall of

Bang Chan, 1953, looking south from 2,500 feet. The temple compound is in the lower center, with Sāēn Sāēb canal leading off to the southwest toward Bangkok. Photo by U.S. Air Attaché.

Ayutthayā in 1767. The recent Japanese occupation, on the other hand, left only slight feelings of pleasure or displeasure. All were glad the Japanese had gone home but a few recalled with delight their first movies, known as "Japanese shadow plays" (*nang nippun*) (LS 1/27/49). America was the land of great "progress" (*khwāmcharoen*) which was helping the Thai people. They knew little about aid from the U.S. government in planes, ships, highways, and rural development programs, with which few came in touch. But the Cornell group maintained a benevolent image of America through contributions of money to help rebuild the school, a new water tank, and a cremation platform.

Devotion to the country they had. In almost every house portraits of the king and queen hung on the wall. A very few were fortunate enough to have a third picture hanging a little lower, which showed a member of the household receiving a token from His or Her Majesty. On every school day blue-uniformed children stood at attention, saluting while the flag was raised. Almost the first sentence of the primary teacher announced: "We are Thai people. We live in Thailand." Among the important attributes of the Thai self-portrait was respect for the Lord Buddha; thereby one became a being more sociable, more cooperative, and less ready to use arms than people of other countries and religions. The other aspect of the self-portrait appeared less often: once a minstrel from Nakāun Nāyok appeared at the temple in Bang Chan (LS 3/3/49), singing the glories of the martial life and of the current prime minister, Field Marshal Pibul Songkrām, who was strong enough to redress the insults of the French who spitefully seized Thai lands. Moslems were Thai Islam and of Thai nationality too, but a little more quarrelsome, a bit less ready than Buddhists to avoid killing animals and people. The Chinese, however, though Buddhists, were not Thai. Despite the adverse propaganda of the government, Bang Chan did not change its receptive attitude toward Chinese rice millers, their agents, and the numerous peddlers. All were grateful to them for having advanced money on crops, given hospitality to visitors, and even written prescriptions for ailing mothers (LS 11/22/48). Bang Chan knew from the radio about the success of the Communist revolution in China and about a horde of people who might invade Thailand (LS 10/7/52). Still Communists were of no particular nationality and came from no single place. That Communists were a threat to the life

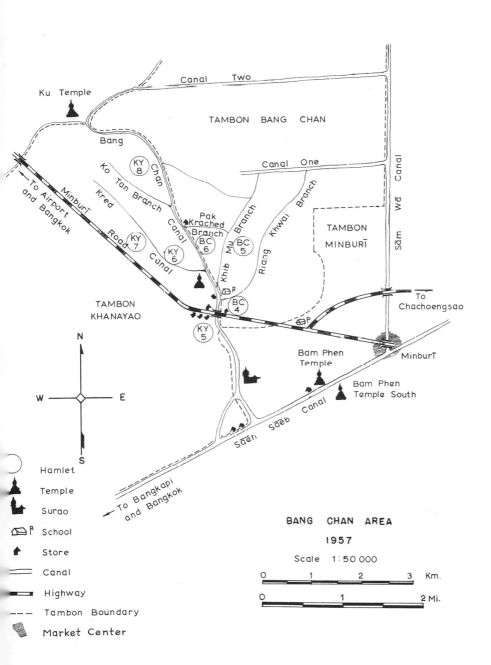

Ku Temple

Canal   Two

TAMBON   BANG   CHAN

Bang

Canal   One

KY 8

Ko Tan Branch

Kred

Bang Chan

Minburī

To Airport and Bangkok

Road   Canal

Pak Krached Branch

Khib Mu Branch

Riang Khwai Branch

Sām Wā Canal

TAMBON MINBURĪ

KY 7

KY 6

BC 6

BC 5

To Chachoengsao

TAMBON KHANAYAO

BC 4

KY 5

Minburī

N

W   E

S

Bam Phen Temple

Bam Phen Temple South

Sāen Sāeb Canal

To Bangkapi and Bangkok

○ Hamlet

Temple

Surao

School

Store

Canal

Highway

Tambon Boundary

Market Center

BANG   CHAN   AREA

1957

Scale   1:50 000

0   1   2   3   Km.

0   1   2 Mi.

of Thailand was clear even to children of the fourth grade, but who they were remained uncertain. A farmer's wife, when asked to identify an amorphous picture in a projective test, declared, "This person has much power. [*What is he doing?*] He is trying to protect the country. He does not care for the enemy. [*What is he doing now?*] He has confidence. Now he is not doing anything, only waiting. [*Who is he?*] He is Hanuman" (Hanks 1957). The monkey god of the Rāmakian was quietly waiting somewhere above Thailand for the appearance of any enemy, and this woman felt assured of her protector's valor and competence.

The Rites

Actions to achieve a given social end may be both sacred and profane, both esoteric and commonplace, both symbolic and technological. Padi growing requires a plowed field but also a prayer addressed to Mother Thōranī, goddess of the earth. The construction of a house requires a special verbal formula to ensure the stability of the posts as well as deep holes in the ground. When an undertaker cremates a corpse he must break a coconut and douse the skull before setting fire to the pyre. We may readily judge what actions are "essential" and what are "dispensable," yet in all cultures a whole gamut of actions is necessary to realize an objective properly. Since each new objective demands a social transformation, we may speak of the actions that effect these transformations as rites.

Agricultural Rites

When the Thai government sought to introduce to the farmers more productive rice varieties and the use of fertilizers and insecticides, it adopted the rites of the agricultural extension services in America. U.S. foreign aid funds, beginning in 1950, had brought together Thai and American agricultural experts, who began, among other programs, the testing of new rice varieties in the varying soils of Thailand (Love, 1954; Min. Ag. 1957:357-366). Elsewhere they had set up American test-demonstration plots in fields rented from farmers. There they grew local varieties of rice alongside new ones, calling attention to the work with large signs. Whether or not the laborers in these plots offered prayers to Mother Thōranī, they did spread fertilizer.

The Cornell group persuaded the researchers at the Agricultural

University to establish test-demonstration plots in Bang Chan. At a meeting at the temple called by the head priest, some dozen farmers chose two persons to rent out land for the tests (LMH 5/22/53). The chosen two were deemed rich enough to be able to make the temporary sacrifice of land. So in a few weeks laborers from the Agricultural University prepared the seedbeds, planted local and new varieties of padi side by side, and set the big green signs in place.

A member of the Cornell group supervised the test plots and gathered information concerning community interest. In certain respects he found the results disappointing. A dozen people dropped by to see one of the plots during its first month; six appeared at the other (JK 6/22/53; 7/18/53), but as soon as the growing season began in earnest, no one came who had not been hired to do the work. Some unknown visitor broke down the signs (JK 9/9/53). Then yields of the new varieties after harvest proved little or no better than local ones, except for one new variety of early rice.

Despite failure of the foreign rite to introduce new varieties, its transforming powers had been released and were taking effect. A young farm renter with growing children had been affected: "People who say education is not important for farming must have old-fashioned ideas. Now education is to help the people, who have increased in numbers while the land remains constant. . . . In the future every person will be a more skillful worker. . . . Ten years from now people will have to farm more seriously, perhaps like an American" (LMH 1/24/54).

One of the landowners where the test had taken place declared, "I am always looking for new varieties of rice that will increase the yield, but what interests me most is the method of cultivation used here. I want to know the best spacing between rows in transplanting. I am also interested in the fertilizer you use, because I never tried any of the chemical ones, only a little dung on the seedbed" (JK 7/13/53). Others were also talking about ways to increase the yield. An old man asked how to use fertilizers while another tried out insecticide on a pest that attacked his seedlings (JK 6/22/53; 8/13/53). A third considered an entirely new crop that might be raised after the rice harvest (JK 7/1/53). A fourth, letting his imagination roam, spoke of a machine to transplant rice (JK 6/17/53). When Goldsen and Ralis (1957:43) inquired about the best way to increase yields, only 5 percent mentioned seed variety while nearly 20 percent mentioned fertilizer and nearly 50 percent mentioned irrigation. During our visit to Bang Chan in 1964 chemical fertilizer was used in the fields as well as in the seedbed. The yield reported by one man had reached 50 thang per rai, nearly double the 28.3 thang per rai reported for 1948-1953 (Janlekha 1957:52).

Rites of Regulation

In 1953 the lumber from the abandoned school building was sold for 2,600 baht (KJ 10/27/53). With the addition of this sum the funds for the proposed new school reached approximately 11,000 baht, as compared with the initial 4,442 baht of 1949. The temple committee dealing with the school had grown uneasy about leaving the money in a bank under the name of a single person, as the bank regulations required. If the signator should die, they knew no way to recover the funds; so they closed the account. Dividing the sum among several committee members, who loaned it out judiciously, they soon doubled the total (LMH 11/24/53). Sharp's return in 1952 with an expanded Cornell group stimulated the temple committee into new activity. The district educational officer approved the building of the new school in five stages, utilizing first the local funds (LS 2/25/53). The temple committee seized the initiative, approved plans for a five-room school, selected a site in the crowded temple compound, bought concrete posts for the foundations, and laboriously installed them. The teachers renewed their efforts to collect funds locally, capitalizing on the evidence of progress to reassure critics who whispered that the money had been lost by mismanagement.

The foundation posts were but partly installed when a director general from the Ministry of Education appeared on the scene. By chance only, he had met a member of the Cornell group, who told about the unfinished school. The presence of foreign researchers in Bang Chan piqued his national pride and helped form his resolution to visit Bang Chan. On his arrival farmers proudly showed him the foundation for the new school. Later he met with the temple committee and asked simply how many children were to be accommodated in the five rooms. A headman told him that the school had 500 children. Suddenly aware of the crowded rooms, another man added that all do not attend school at the same time. The embarrassed teachers, trying to divert attention from absences, declared that the size of the new school was limited by the funds available. Not until the director general had finished the meal laid out for him in the temple pavilion did he reply: The school already begun was totally inadequate; it needed no fewer than ten rooms. It should be located on a larger piece of land (LMH 11/23/53). The only bright note he left with Bang Chan was a promise to help.

Local efforts had gone for nothing. The temple committee and the teachers shrank before the prospect of having to match funds for a school that would cost probably three times as much as anyone could dream of collecting locally. Dispirited people gathered with no zest for the undertaking. Teachers were nonetheless duty-bound to set out in their boats and seek contributions. One man told of a visit: "The teachers came and asked for three thang of padi, but I gave them only three liters, because I do not have enough. Anyway I think the school is going to be too big. Bang Chan cannot build like that when we cannot even raise enough money to build a little school" (LMH 2/2/54).

The official gaze had already focused on Bang Chan; it was too late to back out. The provincial governor appeared to select a site and arrange a road from the highway to the new school (LMH 12/23/53). Though two headmen said at the meeting that the road would spoil the flow of water to the adjoining rice fields, an education official overruled this objection. More official visits finally made clear that the cost of the school would reach more than 200,000 baht. Instead of matching funds, however, Bang Chan was to mound the earth for the road and building at something less than the prevailing wage and from its own resources provide some portion of the furnishings (LMH 1/24/54). While the task remained the same, local responsibility had been reduced to a size commensurate with its capabilities. People turned to worrying less about the ability of the community to contribute than about the capacity of government to provide the necessary money in the face of Communist advances in Laos, which might require sudden transfer of funds to defense (LMH 12/23/54). All felt better when the actual work began, and local entrepreneurs could contract for various parts of the job. In 1955 the flag was finally raised on the new flagpole; a representative from the Ministry of Education pulled aside the lilac veil and revealed the school's name in gilded letters. The name was familiar; it was the official name of Kamnan Phlym: Aphiban, the protector. After all, the school occupied land generously made available for a modest price by the former kamnan's favorite daughter, and this daughter's son-in-law had been appointed head teacher.

As they paddled their sampans toward the temple or toward the highway, farmers were pleased to see the long wooden building, its roof tiles glistening in the sun. There was the loving mother's gift, from Thailand herself. Knowing her love, the inhabitants of Bang Chan would dutifully obey. Once there had been talk of "self-help" while officials calculated the tasks that the farmers should be allowed to undertake. Self-help did not mean, as it turned out, that they should seize the initiative, for they had been shown the awkwardness of their efforts. Instead, it meant that they should strive hard to improve themselves. When in 1957 the director general of the Ministry of Education visited the school, he was disturbed to find that few pupils could recite their lessons smoothly and that there was no demonstration of calisthenics (LMH 7/9/57). The teachers needed to work harder, he concluded, and should attend in-service training classes. Then they would be helping themselves and their pupils, as well as aiding the progress of the country.

Rites of Civility

A Bang Chan teacher prophesied as he spoke of education in the locality, "These families will have *new culture*. Then their children will go to school at least six years. They will speak a better language; their clothes will be better" (LMH 8/10/53). He expressed somewhat more sanguinely the judgment of many outsiders that farmers were crude people with a vulgar language and slovenly clothes. Visitors from the city were offended by the rustic boorishness they found in the village. One from Bangkok apologized to a member of the Cornell group for the uncouth scene: "Thailand is different; it just got civilization from foreign countries. In the village there are only four grades, and the children are taught but soon forget. They are stupid and cannot read" (JRH 3/21/54). The village (*bān*) had always been midway between the city (*nakhāun*) and the wild forests (*pa*) of the periphery, but it should move nearer the center now in this modern era. So civilized people from the cities urged progress: to brush teeth, to make and use toilets, to wear tidy clothing of Western style, to furnish houses with chairs and tables, to speak with refined words, to be literate, to greet one's superiors respectfully. . . .

Schoolgirls of Bang Chan
Photo by Ewing Krainin

The "new culture" emanated from Bangkok. Though Bang Chan people had visited the city for at least a century, fleeting trips to the market had not sufficed to acquaint the farmers with the new culture, even if it had always existed. Through the decades the capital had remained the nearest heaven, the City of Heavenly Spirits, where people did not work in the burning sun in order to eat. There theaters presented performances in all seasons and people ate all day long. With the building of the road Bang Chan moved an hour from this source of radiance, now no longer just a warm beckoning reflection in the sky. The direct rays both attracted and repelled. They illuminated a gentler life but also its contrasts with country rudeness. They warmed with visions of gayer living while they burned with more contemptuous judgments.

After World War II visitors from the country began to linger in the capital a little longer, instead of returning quickly to the padi fields. Acquaintance was renewed with all but forgotten aunts, uncles, and cousins still living in Sāmsen and Khlāung Tej. A sixteen-year-old great-grandson of a former Laotian prisoner of war told of his holiday visit: "I went once this year with friends to Bangkok to visit my mother's younger brother, who works in the finance section of the Railway Department. I saw a movie, the zoo, and the Royal Cremation Grounds" (LMH 6/15/53). Only 20 percent of the household heads of Bang Chan had not visited Bangkok during the year 1955; 35 percent said they had lived in Bangkok for longer or shorter periods, usually as soldiers or policemen but also as laborers and schoolchildren (Goldsen and Ralis 1957:58). Among the new emigrants were young people who simply wished to earn money for a few weeks in the city:

Sometimes there is work in the country; sometimes I have to go to Bangkok to find it. In the country I dig earth for gardens or fish ponds. In Bangkok I take jobs as carpenter or laborer who mixes cement. I earn twenty baht per day working from eight in the morning to five in the afternoon. I have only my food and bus fare as expenses and live with a younger brother of my father in Bāng Krabȳ. I got the job through an old man who is a neighbor there and works for the company. [LMH 12/6/53]

This visitor remained unscathed by the "new culture," but not some of his neighbors, who determined to avoid becoming farmers by seeking out urban occupations. The youngest widow of Kamnan Phlym, living in Bang Chan with her third husband, worked fifteen rai of rented padi land and earned extra money as a peddler of garden produce. Her children, three of them begotten by the kamnan, had left their mother's house, except for one unmarried girl. She told about them:

I have no land to give my children; so I must give them knowledge. I gave them a choice of ways to earn a living. I said, "You can work on a farm or study." But I didn't force them to do either. The oldest became a teacher in the elementary school. The second son tried farming for a year but found it hard work. He changed and went to vocational school. Now he is a soldier in the Air Force. My two daughters are the only ones that helped me. The eldest is married to a farmer, but her sister married a man in the Air Force. The fifth, a son, is working for a foreign firm at the airport. The sixth was adopted, and she is living with me. She is not yet married. The youngest boy is studying in the middle school at Minburi. [LMII 9/29/53]

So these sons and stepsons of the former kamnan were finding their way toward the new culture outside Bang Chan. One of the former kamnan's grandsons told of his achievements and intentions:

I studied in Minburi as far as the sixth grade [*matthayom hok*]. Now I am at technical school in Bangkok studying construction and design of buildings. My father was in this work and liked it. During holidays from school I worked with him planning and constructing five buildings. How far I can go with my studies depends on the money. If there is enough, I'll finish. Then I shall enter government service or join a private company. I'm interested in art, too. Sometimes I paint and draw pictures. I'd like to study fine arts too. [LMH 6/6/53]

Nor was it only the descendants of the kamnan who were being transformed by the rites of civility. In 1955, 28 percent of the household heads reported one or more members living in Bangkok. Most of them had left between the ages of fifteen and twenty-five. From the highway bridge across Bang Chan canal to the most stagnant backwaters, people told of sons and daughters who had studied beyond the four primary grades (see Appendixes A and B). In 1954 only one of five children in the fourth grade at local elementary schools (aged eleven to fourteen) was dreaming of a future in farming (see Appendix C). They wished instead to become soldiers, doctors, teachers.

The Transformations

Bang Chan was perhaps being changed before the rites began. Who is to say whether rite or transformation comes first? The very agent that leads to the performance of a rite may be the one that transforms, rather than the rite; the rite then may stand as a symptom rather than as an agent. So let us say that the agricultural rites were taking place and the rice farmers were becoming technologically more efficient. As rites of regulation were being performed, Bang Chan's initiative in communal affairs was yielding to the passivity of dutiful subjects. So too provincial rusticity was being converted into urban civility during the rites of civility.

In effect the rites were pulling Bang Chan apart. The once intimate neighborhood contained only remnants of the former families. Cousins who had winnowed the new harvest through the night together had now moved away. One sold his land to an investor from the city, and the new tenant was a stranger. Sons and daughters were seeking new lands or new occupations. More farmers were hiring needed workers because it was hard to criticize the work of a neighbor (LMH 2/8/54). Cooperative exchanges of labor existed in only three localities of Bang Chan in 1953, and at least one of these had to supplement the exchange with hired help (Janlekha 1957:111–114). An old lady compared the present with the past:

Bang Chan canal once had few people and few houses. Now there are more of both. The families are larger. More children are born. In my household there were only two. My eldest daughter now has twelve and my youngest ten. The more people, the greater the expenses [kin māg, chai māg]. Life looks like a tree. First it is small, and then the branches grow. Gambling disappeared two years ago. People in the same hamlet used to hear about a game of cards and gather together. Now the money is all gone. There are more poor people. Formerly people without land used to earn one to one and a half baht per day and have some left over. Today the poor earn ten baht per day and have none left over. [JRH 12/3/53]

Another old resident enlarged certain aspects of this picture:

We used to exchange food, coconuts, and borrow money. There was more borrowing in general. We had big gardens and raised all our food. Nothing at all was bought. There was extra food because people were fewer. If someone wanted to borrow money, it was there. Today people charge interest, unless they are dealing with brothers and sisters of the same parents. Now people are poorer, for no one can buy anything for five baht. We used to lend dishes to feed the priests, but now we are afraid they will be broken. Formerly all had money left in the house, but now farming is not enough to support life. [JRH 12/12/53]

While households might not have grown much in size, all agreed that neighbors were meeting each other on fewer occasions and the individual households were struggling to stay afloat financially.

Money rather than food and shelter was becoming the primary concern. Janlekha (1957:170–177), figuring family labor as an expense, found an excess of costs over income and an insufficient supply of credit. Households could no longer look to their neighbors for cash and so had to seek it where they could. The soft drinks, store clothes, home furnishings, and pressure lamps were setting up a more expensive respectability. "Some people do not pay money for food but pick or get it from the canals and gardens. This family cannot live like that because we come from rich houses and cannot live on poor food" (JRH 1/24/54).

Along with the respectability went undeniably greater costs of producing a kwian of padi. Where a plow and buffalo once sufficed, the efficient farmer needed at least engines to pump water, insecticides to kill the worms, and chemical fertilizer. Yet through the 1950s the price of padi remained fairly stable between 800 and 1,000 baht per kwian. Some farmers perceived their dilemma:

My thirty-eight rai of land is enough for my small family. I have three daughters. One of them is married and lives here with her husband. I should have fifty rai for a family of five or six. Most people rent, but if they are not careful, they cannot earn a living. Each household ought to have extra work such as a little business. The return from a farm is not enough. The return from a farm that is owned is about twice as much as from a rented farm. About 40 percent of the crop goes for rent. Farmers are stupid people; if they earned enough, they would not want to work on farms. [LMH 2/23/54]

So tenants were the first to feel the squeeze, but next were the holders of small tracts who lacked the manpower to rent additional lands. Some, however, were able to increase their production to fifty thang per rai (LMH 1964), almost double Janlekha's (1957:52) average for 1948–1953.

As rice producers were moving farther apart, a greater diversity of occupations was also dividing people. Even between 1948 and 1953 Janlekha (1957:45) found the number of persons working outside of agriculture increasing from 10 to 14 percent. Goldsen and Ralis (1957:41) reported only 9 percent in nonfarm occupations for 1955 but drew from a larger population. Diversification increased as the 1950s wore on, as mild inflation drove more people into cash-producing ventures. Local egg producers became more specialized and no longer carried their wares to market on the early-morning bus; middlemen came to gather the eggs from the houses along the canal banks, while instructing in the latest practices of husbandry and selling chicken medicine as well as chicken feed (LMH 7/9/57). Seven young men became water-taxi drivers who waited with their outboard motorboats for passengers at the highway (LS 4/3/60). In the 1960s a granddaughter of Kamnan Phlym established a small rice mill powered by a diesel engine (LMH 1963).

So the good life lay elsewhere than on the farm that had once assured stability with its bulging rice bins. It was no longer the dispossessed and hungry that turned to manufacture, trade, or services, but the rich and able. Bang Chan was changing from gaining nourishment to gaining a profit, from accumulating implements to accumulating goods, from sustaining life to sustaining income, from a way of living to earning a living.

While work bees were disappearing, camaraderie was mounting in new places: the mushroom raisers shared information on the latest techniques, shared spores, and took turns making trips to the market (JRH 1/21/54). The laborers on the highway gathered at the stores to drink and play chess before going home (LMH 11/30/53). Habitués dropped in at their favorite spot to pass the time with a cup of coffee or a bottle of Pepsi-Cola. Along the canals familiar people became "kinsmen": "Chau sold me that buffalo on credit. He trusts me, and he is rather rich, since he owns some land. My father and Chau's father were close friends. So I respect his father and call him 'father.' Chau helps with farming" (JRH 10/1/53).

In one of the groups that still exchanged labor, people sought far for trustworthy persons to help:

We respect Chan; so we call him *nā* [mother's younger brother]. My husband worked with him for many years, but he is only an older friend. Sawing lives in Lam Pak Krached and is a son of my mother's younger sister. Every year we go to help him, and if he cannot come to us, he sends a man. Prasoed is a younger cousin but not a close one. Rāg and Jū are friends. Chyn is a *nā*. We like Prasoed best because he helps most often, and we respect his father. Chyn comes often to chat when we are lonely at night. [JRH 9/11/53]

In these ways some sought to compensate for the demise of the old neighborhood.[9]

The behavior of the young did not add to neighborhood cohesion. They wandered farther afield, to the consternation of their parents. When they earned money along the way, few turned it over to their parents as the older generation had done (JRH 12/12/53). Not infrequently they married across religious lines, to the distress of parents. An old Moslem woman recollected:

A Thai [Buddhist] boy eloped with a Moslem girl. Her parents made her come back, but she ran away again with the boy. He is living in Minburī now and works on the road. The girl's brother works on the road too, but he was not angry. He ought to be angry, but he wasn't. The girl was called home a second time, and now she visits her "husband" when she is in Minburī. There were fewer elopements between Thai and Moslem in the old days. Now boys and girls know how to wander around [paj thiaw]. They take the bus. [JRH 12/12/53]

Some Buddhists and Moslems could not reconcile themselves to these matches, refusing to accept payments of forgiveness. So some households, too, split apart.

The cohesion furnished by the temple was also being strained. Work sessions at the temple during the dry season fell off, as the head priest observed: "It was easier in the old days to get help. Formerly the temple committee got the materials for making repairs. They could get labor and hold it for a month with ease. Today it is hard to ask people to come for a single day. Formerly they came and worked hard, but now if you ask them to work harder, they complain" (LMH 8/3/57). Where former generations had given their labor to the temple, people of the 1950s were making merit with currency. So the more intimate connections between temple and community were lapsing. Fewer people were sending their sons to be temple boys, and the new ones came from households that found it difficult to feed or discipline them (JRH 3/23/54). The age for young men to be ordained seemed to be advancing, though pious elders stoutly denied that the number of priests being ordained had ever varied (see Appendix D).

These were, nevertheless, no sorry times for the temple. Nāj Hem had erected the new congregating hall and furnished it with a canopied preaching chair. A new priest's house was built with money left by old Sud. These new features were more lavish than the memorial pagodas, the old houses torn down and rebuilt for priests' dormitories, and the small shelters on the canal banks that the earlier generation had erected. Wealthier people were making more impressive donations. Yet the new bell tower erected on general subscription within the Bang Chan community remained incomplete for want of funds. Since the war's end the annual gift of priests' new robes (Thāud Kathin) had been made by outsiders, almost without exception (LS 10/25/48; JRH 11/4/53). When the dormitories for the

priests burned down, the head priest looked to government departments and wealthy merit makers to finance the reconstruction (LMH
8/3-4/57). The temple was busy as ever with festivals, but they were
given mainly by a few wealthy families, supported by outside funds.
The head priest, long eager to rebuild the sanctuary (bōt), was
unable to accumulate enough local funds even to finance repairs (LS.
4/2/60).

The community lacked leadership, though not for want of eager
and ambitious persons. A headman who was married to a granddaughter of Kamnan Phlym sought to become kamnan himself. No
doubt the former kamnan's image guided him, for both bought and
sold land for profit; both sought to marry many wives; both expected
to leave their residences to their grandchildren as a group (JRH
12/1/53). The usual route was blocked by lack of vacancy in his
tambon. So he joined with a group of petitioners to revise the
administrative boundaries of the tambon and form a new tambon
affiliated with the Minburī district (SM 2/24/49). The plan made
administrative sense by coalescing Bang Chan into a single entity
under the nearest district center. The headmen of hamlets in the
Bāngkapi district were happy not to have to travel so far for the
monthly meetings at the district office. Evidently the first petition
stalled along the way, for in 1953 the headman was still seeking the
support of the Cornell group as well as that of visiting civil officers
(JRH 12/17/53). He distinguished himself by his industriousness in
building a road from the highway to the new Bang Chan school, thus
gaining the ear of the provincial governor, who was well disposed to
the plan. On the eve of its realization, the governor was transferred
to a new position (CIW 7/16/54). Though the headman sought to
interest the governor's successor, the plan had lost headway, and the
reorganization never occurred.

In the interest of local initiative the district offices, beginning in
the early 1950s, set aside a portion of the land tax from each tambon
for local development (CIW 7/5/54, 7/14/54). The various headmen
gathered together with the kamnan and a representative of the
district to determine how the funds were to be spent. Through five
years in the Minburī district the committee deepened the canals; in
Bāngkapi the results did not directly impinge on Bang Chan. Even if
local headmen influenced the decisions on these projects, the work of
the committee was constantly hampered by the small sums at its
disposal. Here was no avenue for an energetic leader.

The head teacher of the new school also made a bid for local leadership in 1960 as he sought the help of parents to erect a sheltered dining area as an addition to the new school. Though he succeeded in his objective, the expenditures for the project never amounted to more than 5,000 baht (LS 3/29/60). His aims never matched in scope the schemes of the head priest or the headman. No one had sufficient resources to summon the strength of his fellow villagers for an enduring project. The differences in wealth between the would-be leaders and their fellow residents were not large enough to ensure certain command. They properly sought to align themselves with powerful persons outside Bang Chan, but the centers of influence in the towering hierarchy were difficult to reach.

The ambitious ones were feeling their way as best they could. Some sought to marry the daughter of an orchard owner, for orchard owners stood a rung above rice farmers in the hierarchy (SM 4/1/49). A few sent their children to become teachers, for a person with steady monthly pay moved more freely than a farmer: "My son who teaches in the Minburī school was ordained a few weeks ago. His oldest sister is also a teacher. She put in two thousand baht for the ordination; he put in two thousand of his own. Friends gave two hundred baht each; his father gave four hundred, and I gave one thousand. The total cost came to at least eight thousand baht for a one-day ceremony" (JRII 7/30/53). So a few thousand baht could be mustered, yet these people too stood but a few rungs above the farmers.

A far better connection was to a certain father's younger sister: "My husband often visits his aunt who lives in Bangkok. Her husband is a police major. My husband works her lands here in Bang Chan. He manages the land and pays her rent only if the crop is good. She also lends him money without interest when he needs it" (JRH 11/21/53). The country nephew freely came and went from his aunt's well-appointed urban residence, where any kinsman could find food and shelter. Bang Chan was one of the stable pillars that supported that residence with rents, labor, and padi. The aunt's seventy rai of padi land provided work for four households, and when an old man died, the Bangkok aunt and her husband underwrote the major costs of his cremation in Bang Chan. This household offered its clients benefits probably exceeding anything Kamnan Phlym could have offered the preceding generations.

The son of one of the first settlers from Khlaūng Tej formed a

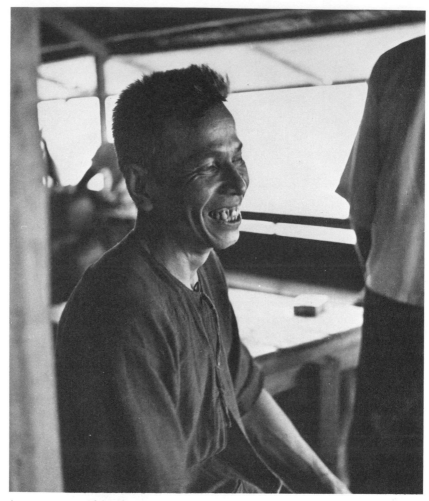

A most respected headman
Photo by Ewing Krainin

comparable center in the city. Known as Khun Lūang, this high-ranking naval officer financed the education of his two country nephews, one of whom became a teacher in a prominent Bangkok school. The other managed Khun Lūang's lands in Bang Chan, which bordered on his own extensive fields. The cremation in Bang Chan of Khun Lūang's brother, the father of these nephews, was long remembered for its magnificence.

If leadership were exerted by any householder in Bang Chan, it came from these and any others with vital working connections to

A headman's wife
Photo by Ewing Krainin

Bangkok. Someone in debt might offer a lien on his land to one of them and receive a loan of money. Through them the temple received substantial support. Familiar with the latest city mode, these people set the style for festivities, and we suspect that their influence raised the wedding ceremony to prominence among the life-cycle rites of Bang Chan, even if many a frugal parent still preferred elopement as less expensive (LMH 8/11/57). Indeed, they may have brought to Bang Chan the urban dictum that a topknot need no longer be worn. Only a few Bang Chan parents continued the practice, especially if a child were sickly (JRH 7/30/53). Yet the urban patron of these scattered groups of households, ordinarily occupied with affairs at the capital, never chose to shape the country community.

Though these were Bang Chan's most brilliant liaisons, there were others. Another naval officer of lower rank had siblings and nephews in Bang Chan but seemed to have little touch with his country kinsmen (LMH 7/14/53). The younger brother of a Bang Chan headman became manager of a Bangkok bronzeware factory that in good times employed a few country folk (Hanks and Phillips 1961). This very headman had a son who, having worked in the uncle's factory, established one of his own in Bangkok and became an employer of his younger siblings. A long-standing connection to the Makasan temple in Bangkok helped ensure a young man's education in the city (LS 10/20/48; JRH 8/14/53). Sāmsen and Khlaūng Tej were still places to spend a sociable afternoon in town. Rather than consolidating life in Bang Chan, these various liaisons pulled the community farther apart.

A few of Bangkok's wealthier circles appeared on the fringes of Bang Chan. Some were speculators seeking to purchase land while prices were still low in comparison with those of Bangkok. A headman spoke about one of them:

Nāj Hau is building the side road in order to increase the value of his land. It will be easy to divide it and sell lots. Government officials will buy the land and build fine houses for foreigners to rent. Originally this man was not rich, but now he is because he was clever. He owns one or two buses on the Minburī line; he first built a factory. He is also building a side road near his property at Kilometer Nine. [LMH 5/4/54]

So these moves from the city increasingly disrupted the rice-growing scene but offered little leadership. Farmers sold their land and used the windfall to change their occupation if they could.

The rites and transformations exacted their toll, as they had always done. Some became floaters without a patron:

When a relative in Bang Chan offered me land to build a house, I moved back here. Then something went wrong between myself and my wife; she left me and married again. Then I went where there was work. Last year I made one thousand baht working here and there for farmers. Just a few weeks ago I moved in next to Nāj In, who is just a friend, but we love each other. He owns three rai of land and is about sixty years old. He gave his farm to his son and daughter and went to live alone. There is nothing between us that can make a fight. He is easy to get along with. [LMH 12/8/53]

People such as this man, petulant and given to drinking, were discarded by patrons during every transformation. Certainly the world of more exacting technology had no permanent place for him. Nor was there place for a young man who served six months in Korea with the Thai army before returning to the padi fields. He had become so insufferably arrogant that even his own siblings avoided him (KJ 11/13/52). Somewhat more complex was the schoolteacher, another son of Kamnan Phlym, who prided himself on his miniature camera and lessons in English. Instead of working faithfully at his job in the school, he began drinking excessively, missed many days of classes, and finally suffered the stern discipline of being transferred to a neighboring school when the new Bang Chan building opened. A year of further discouragement brought about his resignation. He too joined the isolated.

Phillips (1958) illustrated the thirst for a substantial patron in his tale of the elections of 1958. A highly placed official visited the community soliciting votes. On election day 70 percent of the electorate turned out obediently and helped place the official in office. Of course they anticipated his favors in return for their help. Some understood that he would provide funds to rebuild the crumbling sanctuary at the temple. Two boys asked for his recommendation when they applied to enter a vocational school. If he tried to help them, it was not known in Bang Chan, and the sanctuary still crumbled dangerously for ten more years.

The community was again being divided into the haves and have-nots, the floaters and the established ones, the patronized and the patronless, the gentle and the gauche, the convivial and the lonely, the adventurous and the timid, the knowing and the innocent. This had happened before: the Laotian villagers at the Mound of Earthly Splendor drew slaves from their masters and organized them anew. When their village and even the nearby Moslem hamlet at the Governor's Mound dissolved, communities grew elsewhere. The palace workers dispossessed from Khlaung Tej regrouped on Kred canal, while the rise of Kamnan Phlym drew the disaffected from other spots. Each hamlet presented the illusion of stability, though few had fathers who were born in the same hamlet. The majority were always newcomers, and most of them would disappear along with those who had preceded them.

These communities of the central plain still contained no house-holders rooted to the same plot of land for generations like those in Europe. A central Thai, moving slowly but always moving, settled until the food seemed to be running short and then pushed on. Certificates of ownership from the district land office had delayed some of them a little, but they were gathering speed again as urban workers.

The differences between the 1950s and the past lay less in the rate of mobility than in the kinds and amounts of benefits that patrons dispensed. On the Mound of Earthly Splendor the patron attracted and sustained his group of farmers with little more than a buffalo and a plow. Kamnan Phlym had to offer food, shelter, land, and farming equipment to hold his group. The Bangkok patron of the 1950s proffered food, shelter, a job with pay, and a chance to enjoy urban pleasures. Each patron needed somewhat greater resources than his predecessor to manage a more complex organization of clients. A Bang Chan kamnan could deal with persons seeking subsistence but not those who demanded wages. The new urban patron managed clients in various occupations, some the clerks in his government office, some the workers in his factory, some the farmers on the land. His organization might extend over several provinces. Certainly these groups endured longer than the village on the Mound of Earthly Splendor, but it was too soon to know whether these new organizations had the kind of vitality that would survive the life span of their main patron.

It was also too soon to know whether the age was a return of a cycle of greater organization. Most of Bang Chan and considerably more of the surrounding lands once acknowledged Somdet Chao Phrayā Srīsurijawong as patron, that splendid figure who outshone any of Bang Chan's subsequent patrons. Since his day we have seen a cycle of community identity and organization: disintegration of the pioneer settlements after the 1870s followed by a slow rebuilding and consolidation after the 1890s with the separate neighborhoods coalescing during the 1910s and 1920s, when all available land became devoted to rice cultivation. Then followed the austerities of the Depression and World War II and the need to seek more varied sources of income. With radio and new modes of transportation providing improved communications, new forms of liaison between city and county could be explored. Many farm families continued the earlier trend of becoming small but independent business enterprises in a wide variety of economic activities, some of which linked them directly with the capital. At the same time Bangkok people and agencies reached out toward the countryside: villagers felt the impact of rising levels of national economic activity, of tentative political overtures, of a spate of would-be development programs sponsored by the central government abetted and sometimes aided by the technical assistance operations of international agencies and foreign nations. By the late 1950s the golden tail of the naga on the Bang Chan temple roof had become as much a landmark for persons in passage as a bearing for local departures and returns. And in the community this situation permitted a differential acquisition of new values and new status symbols derived from the modern urban environment, and as these urban artifacts, manners, and ideas were acquired by some but not by others, different life styles and an embryonic class stratification began to emerge among the people of Bang Chan.

As city and village networks extended out over wider areas and included a greater range of social levels, Bang Chan's patrons, both internal and external, increased steadily in number and scope if not in splendor, power, or wealth. Salesmen seeking to build a clientele paused briefly at new stores along the highway; the official of the Bangkok electric works came to attend the cremation of his grandmother and engaged himself to sponsor the annual giving of gifts to the monks the next year; a baffled bureaucrat came to improve production of the newly introduced tilapia fish and left again hardly the wiser; patients of the local doctor came each year to work his fields; and the local contractor could give out jobs while building stalls for the Constitution Day Fair in Bangkok's Lumbini Park or while constructing the new Minburī Health Clinic on a profitable government contract. Under these conditions there developed some sense of abandonment by the royal patron, who had once stood above all the minor patrons; or perhaps it was rather a sense of usurpation by the increasingly ubiquitous secular servants of the king. There was certainly a feeling of insecure dependency on a central government that was seen as possibly benevolent and surely pervasive, but quixotic, inefficient or corrupt, and impersonal. For

An annual offering for the temple and its priests
Photo by Lauriston Sharp

the future, a new patron for all of Bang Chan might be emerging.
The royal welfare state seemed the most likely candidate, particularly if it could shed its bureaucratic aloofness and arrogance and
assume an air of greater compassion. But it was difficult for most
Thai officials to view themselves as servants of the people, as the new
Bangkok rhetoric and broadcasts from China said they should be;
unlike the leaders of neighboring nations during and after the war,
they had not had to seek popular support, organize parties, or
prepare masses of people to make decisions and wield new powers.

Again Bang Chan was losing its nebulous identity. Between
households of ambitiously independent farmers with an eye on the
main chance in Bangkok or on possible local commercial or industrial
developments could be found a small neighborhood of equals who

still cooperated in farming rice. And scattered in the smaller houses transient tenants worked scraps and pieces of the formerly broad rice fields. Elsewhere in the central plain, beyond the reaches of Bangkok, there were beginning signs of the transformation to larger rice acreages managed by fewer operators or by absentee owners who hired managers and landless laborers who had not yet fled to urban slums. But in Bang Chan, as an expanding capital city reached the community physically and began to encompass it culturally, more and more people came to rely on the city and to accept its standards as their own or as appropriate for their children. For them the transformation seemed now less concerned with rice than with such urban phenomena as Thailand's first industrial park, planned with workshops and warehouses for the lower reaches of Bang Chan canal with easy access to Saen Saeb canal and realized, not very successfully, in the late 1960s. At the same time many rai of Bang Chan land were being removed from agricultural production at incredibly high prices and some of the windfalls were matched with a government subsidy to raise high above the plain an imposing and resplendent new sanctuary for the temple of Bang Chan in honor of the Lord Buddha and for the merit of the people.[10] As ways of earning a living increased, a way of life was ending, but with some old values retained. The villagers of Bang Chan, whose almost forgotten ancestors had emerged from Bangkok over a century before, would now find themselves again a part of Thailand's capital city, merged once more in their urban source.

CHAPTER 9

Five Perspectives

In this chapter we shall survey our account of Bang Chan from five perspectives. All but one of them grow from familiar ground. The exception is Bang Chan's own view of its past, an ahistorical one. From each of these five perspectives we shall see new shapes and promontories. But first let us spend a moment examining certain differences between Bang Chan's ahistorical perspective and our own. We shall look upon the concept of history as if it were any other cultural feature, be it a joking relative or a trifooted pot, present in one society but absent in another. For our purposes a concept of history is a publicly recognized mode of understanding happenings in the world, by reference to unique events in the past, which are presumed to influence the present. Let us bypass intriguing questions about the ontology of history and examine only this cumbersome definition.

What happens in the world can be understood in many ways, and some of the interpretations that people give are inherited from their cultural tradition. It is perhaps useful to think that the way a people interprets happenings arises from some recurring problem. Over the years these people have defined the problem, and from the definition emerges a solution.

A glance at three Asian civilizations reveals differing problem formulations and solutions, of which one is historical. The Chinese were obsessively concerned with the problem of maintaining social order. In their formulation of the problem they defined or assumed society to be a part of a nature that is orderly. Yet typhoon and drought, war and rebellion occurred. These they considered disturbances of inherent harmony, much as we think of illness: a deviation from the norm. Remedies would return the disharmony to harmony. Chinese history records the varying conditions of nature and society like a doctor's record. Victories against barbarians signified harmony, while comets in the sky indicated disharmony. To the extent that the remedy was effective in restoring order, the disturbing event was nullified and society, again in harmony with nature, continued until the next disturbance. As the disharmony did not necessarily influence subsequent events, there was no history. The record only showed future emperors what to do or not to do when the same sort of disharmony occurred again.[1]

In India a focal problem centered on moral justice. Why were the unworthy so often rewarded while the worthy suffered? Instead of centering the problem in society or nature, Indians focused on the individual. When an individual is presumed to have not just one but many lifetimes, the justice missing in this life may be sought in the sequence of several lifetimes. A transcendental world beyond the perceptible world arose around this concept, and in the unseen boundlessness operated moral law. In such a broad setting history was unnecessary: no happening ever rose to the stature of a unique event; everything repeated itself again and again.

Eastern cities and empires nearer the West were also aware of crime and disorder, yet these phenomena disturbed them less than the changes of human fortune. Why is today's king tomorrow's slave? Instead of relating this question to nature or to a transcending cosmos, the people of the Middle East centered attention on the stability of a social order. Why did some cities and empires endure while others disappeared? Change was assumed, and the problem became how to overcome its inevitability or control its direction. The answer was basically historical. Unique events of the past had brought salvation and others might bring misfortune. Human beings needed to preserve the benign effects of one event and nullify the disastrous effects of others. So each group found its formula in obedience, sacrifice, or perhaps simple faith in some creator or deities who had power to preserve the present bliss, but decreed or permitted disaster when a breach occurred. So Middle Eastern cities rose with hallelujahs and ebbed with lamentations.[2]

History thus offers one of several possible ways to interpret happenings in the world.[3] It emphasizes uniqueness at the expense of uniformity, repetition, or generality. People who use the historical mode of understanding observe not just a rabbit but the first rabbit or the one with the longest ears. The very word "event" implies something unique, and its root, *evenire*, means to come out of.

Immanuel Kant deemed time and space to be categories of perception independent of judgment. We believe it possible to demonstrate briefly that these categories derive from judgments about the continuity and discontinuity of experience. If anything is to be perceived, a change in the perceiver or in the scene is necessary. This change is viewed fundamentally in one of two ways: a change of position or a change of existence. When something moves, the happening is registered as a change of position. When something appears or disappears, the happening is judged to be a change of existence. Though these two manners of perceiving change may oversimplify, agreement about their use is fairly general. When an animal disappears, the hunter assumes it has moved to another spot and seeks to follow its tracks. This is a judgment of change of position, a spatial judgment. A pain disappears, but no one searches for it, since all assume it has ceased to exist; a temporal judgment is required to describe it. Other happenings may be ambiguous. The moon disappears and reappears, we say. Hugo Adolf Bernatzik (1958:127) reports that the Yumbri (Mrabri) of northern Thailand, a remote hunting people, daily regard each sun and moon as unique. A change of intensity may be placed in either the temporal or the spatial class: it is now twilight or it is getting dark. The poet who asked, "Where are the snows of yesteryear?" gained poetic flavor by converting the ordinary judgment of existence into judgment of position. Sometimes we strain to convert a spatial judgment with its implied continuity into discontinuity. Then we emphasize the differences with disjunctives, as *child* and *adult*. When we wish to smooth the discontinuous, in the extremity we may speak of *metamorphosis*.

When happenings are judged as changes of existence, a temporal category is required. The ordering of these judgments may be noted as simply "now" and "not now" (Leach 1961:124-126). From this point the ordering may be elaborated in several directions. A frequent manner of elaboration is the narrative form that introduces a sequence. In turn sequences can be laid end to end to form a chain. The happenings in each sequence may be counted, and by references to other appearances or disappearances, such as day and night, the interval between happenings may be measured. When sequences become linear and related to things that change only in position, one of the conditions of history has been attained. The arrangement must remain linear, however. Bang Chan orders its sequences in a circle, so that the past merges with the future. Then history in our sense cannot exist, for all happenings recur as rhythmic repetitions.

The importance of uniqueness for the concept of history now becomes evident. When people are wont to regard a happening as one of a species, a temporal ordering becomes at best of secondary interest. Then people merely note a recurrence, and for this the spatial category is usually preferred. The comet or rabbit has been away and has returned. For a sequence in time to occur, a people must fasten upon uniqueness. The comet with the long tail or that rabbit with the large ears must be observed sufficiently clearly that it is seen to differ from the comet with a short tail or the rabbit with small ears. Since society and human beings lend themselves better than nature to this treatment, we have a succession of unique kings rather than a recurrence of kings. Nature lends itself to recurrence in space, but history deals with the succession of uniquenesses in time.

We have said that history is a *publicly recognized* mode of understanding happenings; in this regard we have found it necessary to distinguish the manifest prevailing ordering of time in a society from a host of latent ones. Though our culture arranges happenings officially in a linear form, the tendency to circular ordering may be detected in references to the "daily round" and the "cycle of seasons." Bang Chan communicates its time in circular fashion. The temple buildings were erected in the year of the Ox of the twelve-year cycle. A farmer announced that he was born in the year of the Snake. When someone needs to know whether another is his junior or senior and so whether to pay or receive respect, the matter is settled quickly by the cycle of years and the cycle of numbered months. These same farmers, however, reminisce in linear fashion, speaking of "old times" or "twenty-five years ago," though the number only approximates the time span. Some people state their age in years without laboriously adding the cycles of twelve. Thus a latent linear time runs alongside the cyclic, and within their lifetimes people think historically about some things. A chronically sick woman, for instance, traced her illness to an incident in her youth, but she drew upon no "objective" past. The past was personal, of concern only to the individual, like the choice of a particular buffalo for the farm.[4] Without public recognition of a common past and its common influences, history cannot exist.

Most contemporary nations have adopted the concept of history to weld people together in support of the state, but ancient Greece exemplifies a culture that used a concept of history well before our era. Epic poetry celebrated the heroes of a publicly real though vaguely delineated past. Dramatists reminded people of the virtues and errors of this past. History described what existed so that it might not be forgotten. Along frequented routes tombstones proffered piteous words to gain the attention of passers-by. Oblivion was the danger of both individual and state. The present sustained the past with commemorative and reenactment rites; the past in turn lent its strength to the present. Alexander carefully arranged his route so that he might lay wreaths on the graves of Greek and Trojan heroes before setting out to conquer Asia Minor. Augurs, oracles, and soothsayers detected the scent of past events blowing down the winds to crystallize the future.[5]

Through Buddhism some of the same cultural forms came to Bang Chan. The truth that the Buddha taught is still influencing those living two and one-half millennia later. Like Greeks, these farmers commemorate the day of his birth, enlightenment, and death. Certain portions of the ordination rites for a priest reenact the Buddha's departure from princely estate to find the meaning of life. The doctrine of karma, that one reaps the product of one's own past conduct, employs the working concept of history. Yet these clearly historic trappings never produced a concept of history in this scene. We have already encountered one explanation: the past is individual and personal; it has no public significance. Besides, the doctrine was more like a private panacea than a manifesto transforming future generations. Whether a man should avail himself of its powers rested not on a community or kinsmanly obligation but upon the individual. As far as history is concerned, the early Buddhist councils looked back to the original sayings of the Buddha to clarify the doctrine rather than to survey the development of the movement. If a history of Buddhism were written before the nineteenth century by a member of the monastic order, he must have been a Middle Eastern convert.

Of the five perspectives chosen for our examination of a century or more in Bang Chan, only one meets in part our definition of a concept of history. This one deals with Bang Chan's heroes. The remaining perspectives frame our data, almost as if history had never existed.

From a Teak House

We were fortunate during the course of our interviews in Bang Chan to meet a certain Nāj Sin, who bore the same name as the temple founder. He was one of those local philosophers who enjoyed pondering subjects that his neighbors tended to pass over. An afternoon's talk with him always took some unexpected turn. Conversations with the research group seemed to hone his already sharpened curiosity. So when we came to inquire about the past, Nāj Sin set off to make his own investigation. He visited six elders of the community and wrote a brief history. We give the major share of it:

The development of the irrigation equipment during the past fifty years began by using buckets and human energy. The water shovel [chāng lāng] came after this and then the splash wheel [chak]. These two devices still require human energy. When windmills were invented, human energy was less used. Nowadays the windmills are used everywhere, but farmers prefer engines if they have enough money to buy them.

In ancient times people dug a pond with their hands. If the soil were hard, they soaked it with water until it became soft. The first tool was a wooden shovel [phlua]. Then came an iron shovel which was sharp at the forked end and called hāng jiaw. After this another kind of iron shovel was made called phlua sāmred. This is used in the present time.

To separate straw from the padi they formerly used a wooden shovel to toss the grain, also a tray [kradong]. Then the lighter chaff is blown out [by the wind]. Now they send their padi to the mills.

The way they grew rice [formerly] was very primitive. They had no buffaloes and no tools such as sickles and windmills. They used a mattock [chāub] to loosen the soil. They used a stick to make holes, in which they put five or six grains of rice; then they covered them with soil. They did this in the sixth month until their rice fields were fully sown. When it rained the rice sprouted. During this time they had to kill weeds very often until the sprouts grew into clumps which the weeds could not overcome. Sometimes they used seedlings instead of rice grain in this method. If they had buffaloes they plowed their dry land and sowed seeds and waited for rain. When it rained, rice and weeds both grew. So farmers had to kill weeds nearly every day. They said they could hardly remove all the weeds. The pest in those days was weaverbirds [nok krachab], which they had to drive away in the morning and in the evening or sometimes all day long if the sun did not shine bright. They used a pellet [lūk jōn] made of clay held in a string by a leaf of grass [*āu*]. They threw the pellets at the birds when they flew down to the rice plants. The birds came in big flocks; they ate the rice flower and left the husk still on the plant.

The broadcasting method of cultivation [*nā wān*] yielded less than the primitive digging-stick method [*nā dam*] for equal amounts of land. But they could grow more rice by broadcasting in more land in an equal time. So in ancient times they grew two or three rai for a small family and no more than ten rai for a big family. But when they had buffalo and changed to broadcasting, they could cultivate one hundred rai or more depending on the size of the family and the number of buffalo.

The tools for harvesting rice were developed too, from picking by hand to use of the finger knife [*kae*]. Then came sickles [*khiaw*], when they grew more rice.

Yield per rai was not less than forty thangs because the land was rich, for it was just cleared.

They did not need to buy food except salt. They bought cloth because they did not weave their own cloth. But in more ancient times people wove their own cloth. They could make only one to one and a half meters a day. The cloth was very durable. They had no sewing machines.

Women wore a cloth that covered the breast only [*iam*]. It did not cover the back. Then came a piece of rectangular cloth which covered the upper part of the body too [*tabengmān*]. After that they used a camisole [*sabājchiang*]. They wore the dhoti [*chōngkraben*] instead of skirts. Women stayed at home, weaving, mending clothes, cooking, and looking after children. Men went fishing, hunting, and collecting firewood, and sold things.

There were no matches. To make fire they used two pieces of wood rubbed together. They had no lamps. To start a fire they lit a clump of straw called *kob* and let it keep burning. After that, they used stone and steel struck together. They used the lint of a palm tree [*tao rāng*] for tinder. Then matches appeared. They knew kerosene and used it wisely for lamps. But during World War II they had no kerosene, no matches (or they were very expensive), so that they turned back to the ancient methods again. They said the war changed people into primitive men again. They had to use coconut oil, fish oil, and pig fat in place of kerosene. They used a little bowl containing the oil and a knot of thread for a lamp.

In the rainy season they worked in the rice fields. In the dry season they went fishing and sold or hired out to someone as labor. In hiring they received pay of fifty stang [0.50 baht] a day, but they were rarely hired.

Here is a remarkably historical-sounding statement for a man said to lack a sense of history. The events are arranged in a rough temporal sequence going back fifty years or more. In most cases the changes mentioned effect a saving of human energy or some other advantage. The old is associated with the primitive, the new with the advanced. The use of the word "development" [*khwām charōen*] implies a flow, and the term has often been translated as "progress." Certainly the traces of many a nineteenth-century European historian appear again and again. The subject matter is largely confined to technology rather than social institutions, but we may say that Nāj Sin simply chose to observe changing technology on this occasion.

A second look at the document reveals a few peculiarities in the phrasing of "development." Our conception of progress notes the discovery of the gasoline engine, rather than the popular use of it. Whether or not we could afford to buy a gasoline engine for our irrigation has nothing to do with progress in our sense, for it moves along independently of the individual. A similar qualification is to be seen where the change from digging-stick cultivation to broadcasting occurred, "when they had buffalo." During World War II there were matches, if people could afford to buy them. A further qualification of development is noticed along with the observation that people grew rice on 100 rai of land if they had manpower enough.

Once when we were talking about digging-stick cultivation of rice with a farmer, he offered to introduce a neighbor who was still using this method; we had assumed the technique had disappeared decades earlier. An old woman who lived alone was growing rice in that manner. A second glance at Bang Chan revealed that many other "ancient" techniques were still being used. The broadcast method of cultivation still occurs, particularly where the floodwater is deep; some people have no buffaloes. Women wear old-fashioned clothes as well as the more modern ones. The treadmill and windmill exist alongside the gasoline engine.

Instead of giving a history, Nāj Sin revealed part of Bang Chan's scale for judging social advancement. The "primitive ancients" were living alongside the "progressive moderns" and differed from them because they used windmills instead of gasoline engines, harvested by hand instead of with a sickle or finger knife, wore old-fashioned rather than tailored clothing, cultivated their fields with digging sticks or by broadcasting rather than by transplanting. Instead of a "development" of Bang Chan as a whole in our sense, we find changes occurring in the lives of individuals in accordance with economic circumstances, and often in an additive rather than substitutive manner from the community's point of view.

Rather than "progress," Nāj Sin described the ebb and flow of prosperity. Individuals within a household shared common memories of their good years and the hard ones of World War II. Rather than an objective time in the past, here was a compounding of memories of many common events. Instead of history, here were reminiscences of people ordinarily alone with their reveries. Memory of something common might draw these people together as if they dreamed the same dream.

Let us fashion a kind of Buddhist history. Prosperity was due to merit gained in past lives. The meritorious could buy land and gasoline engines, and live in teak houses. The advance of Bang Chan required gains in the merit of most inhabitants. Could Nāj Sin observe the sweep of time, he too would have seen progress for all in merit.

Since the day that the first fisherman stepped from his boat in Bang Chan, the total merit of the area increased. Living conditions became more favorable, mosquitoes fewer, consumer goods more available. As an old man noticed, "people in the past were not so clever as they are now" (LMH 5/23/53). A more meritful being was appearing on the scene. Bang Chan people took individual pride in their improved standard of living, even if Bangkok visitors spoke of the community's rustic backwardness from their more advantaged positions.

If we look from Bang Chan to the neighboring communities and beyond, we find that there too the standard of living has risen over the decades. Today this portion of the countryside compares not unfavorably with many of the simpler sections of Bangkok. Bang Chan is not quite a suburb, but every day the city extends its area. Like many a rural community lying nearer the grand palace, Bang Chan will become a part of the city. The grandchildren and great-grandchildren of the first settlers are returning to the city their forebears had to leave.

This gradient of living standard shows that those souls reborn nearer Bangkok have greater merit than those who live farther away. Over the decades the total merit of all the people has been increasing. To find a place of merit equal to that of Bang Chan a century ago, one would have to go far toward the forested hills near Cambodia. Those many souls who suffered for their previous sins by clearing the wilderness are being reborn to greater ease. Another existence, and those with sins like those of the fisherman brothers may be redeemed, and they will again be living in the city from which their sins too once drove them. Yet when they have again reached the city, no one can say whether their merit will continue to increase. Perhaps they will be reborn to even greater ease, but sins may drive them again from the city or even within the city to equal misery.

The Birth and Labors of a Hero

Clio, muse of history, gave fame to her favorites. In the earlier Greek tradition, at least, history rekindled the deeds of heroes and paid them fresh tribute. Their deeds reverberated down the years, bringing blessings to the new generations. There were also the deeds of such villains as Atreus, whose crimes worked evil for his successors. When the bards no longer sang their epic verse, the exploits of heroes and the accursed were reenacted upon the stage.

Though current fashion in history and anthropology makes little use of heroes, the theme still crops up in disguise. The agents of change have shrunk often to misshapen dwarfs, for behind impersonal innovations, some say, lurk the dissident, indifferent, disaffected, and resentful (Barnett 1953:378-410). Others would shrink the stature of these agents even more, finding a store of wrath and anxiety accumulated over generations that conditions social change (Hagen 1962:217-236). Psychologists are more inclined to let a hero live in natural but not colossal proportions while they search for the mainsprings of Lincolns and Jeffersons. Meanwhile students of culture and personality seek to explain the coming into being of average citizens without regard for either heroes or villains.

Bang Chan's most clear-cut hero was Kamnan Phlym. He built the first teak house, imported the first gasoline engine, and staged the most elaborate festivities yet seen in those parts. Let us assume in Hellenic manner that Phlym was the agent responsible for these and other changes. What molded his heroic proportions?

Brushing past many an entangling qualification, let us pick up a theme and follow its development. Thai hunters, farmers, and kings consider themselves born autonomous creatures. Unlike the Burmans, who battle against obstruction to achieve autonomy (Pye 1962:144-157), the Thai hold that each person comes into life a complete and independent soul. The will is fully developed, though a child's faculties remain feeble for many years. The human problem is not to achieve independence but to build a bridge between monad-like beings. Alone, life is impossible; true existence occurs in society.[6] The lonely soul (*winjān* or *khwan*) is pictured waiting in a tree outside a household to be born. The child that dies may be a soul that came to the wrong family. Mothers are kind persons who out of pity offer opportunities for souls to be born (J. R. Hanks 1963).

Childhood, as we have already observed, offers a constancy of parental attention to very few. Children circulate to grandparents, aunts, and uncles, forming attachments that are apt to be broken. Few human contacts are dependable. Children of the poor are farmed out early to households where they must work hard just to remain sheltered. While sons of the wealthy enjoy more prolonged succor, all boys know that eventually they must make their own way. Curiously, the Thai word *pliaw* means both mature and abandoned; when compounded with the word for heart (*pliaw chaj*) it means lonely (McFarland 1944:534).

Ambivalence toward others builds up quickly. Phillips (1965:329-353) found few instances of empathy in his sentence-completion tests. Another person is a constant potential threat. Rebuffs are always possible. A pleasant exterior offers the safest defense. Hostility may never be expressed, for anger exposes sensitivity to further shafts. One must learn to live with his failures, and one is helped to accept them by knowing their source in the sins of a previous existence.

The lonely young man nevertheless needs human contact, despite wounds of past rebuffs. Some are anxious and strive the harder to gain acceptance. A young man who moved from his parental household to live with his wife's parents told of his experience:

I had to look out for many things. I had to be out of bed ready to work before the others. If I got up late, it would be shameful for my wife's parents. When I was hungry, I could not do as in my own parents' house [simply ask for food]. I was afraid of imposing on the people in this house. I had to be the first to work. No one forced me, but I felt forced in order that everyone would love me and no one would hate me. [LMH 12/6/53]

Some cannot overcome their fears and remain timid dependents throughout their lives. Others, however, learn that anger may send the sensitive ones scurrying. A woman told of her father:

One reason for not living too near a neighbor was that father wanted to be independent. He could not cooperate easily with the neighbors. One day he even quarreled with my mother and tried to beat her. There was no reason for the quarrel, but he was drunk. Mother ran away to the neighbors, and father could not do anything about it. Then seeing himself frustrated, he returned to the house and burned it down and the crop too. Then mother escaped by boat with us children to Bangkok. Father sold the remaining buffalo and a boat and followed mother, wanting to kill her. We hid in Bangkok. Father could not find us, and about two years later he died. [LMH 9/29/53]

Not all of these people are equally prone to violence; indeed, a little less aggressiveness might have gained this bold man some of the socializing respect that Chyn the martinet enjoyed. He stood much nearer than Chyn to the Thai hero, who enjoys a happy balance between anxiety and anger. Such a hero cultivates indifference to acceptance and rebuff. Within himself he overcomes his gnawing loneliness and fear of abandonment. He acts without the usual restraints and with assurance of his own power. Such a person may well epitomize the ideal of Buddhist learning.

Like every Thai hero, Phlym passed the tests that came his way. In the temple as a priest he overcame some of his fears of abandonment and discovered strength within himself. When he moved to live with the parents of his wife, he worked through his fears of rebuff toward approbation and respect. With his bride he learned to manage household resources so as to be always able to reciprocate a neighbor's help abundantly. Then when he returned to care for his aging father, his talents at management could be put to work on his father's more ample resources. His enterprises flourished. In the contest for supremacy in his hamlet, Phlym's benefits and ability to command others outshone his older brothers'. He won the office of kamnan and with it the commune (tambon) while his brothers moved off, leaving him supreme. His guardian spirits showered further benefits on him, and he returned their favors in lavish ceremonies. He erected the first teak house; probably his gasoline engine, radio, and written will were the first ever in Bang Chan. His hand brought these technological improvements and symbols of prosperity; others imitated his example.

In this same sense we may sing the praises of other local heroes and quasi-heroes. Though we know him little, the unnamed prisoner of war who in the 1830s or 1840s gained the favors of the prime minister and led the Moslems into the Bang Chan wilderness was certainly of heroic stature. More familiar was Uncle Sin, who overcame his loneliness and fears of rebuff before reaching Bang Chan. Through kindly charm and pity he gained the respect of others. Thereby his trade and wealth grew so that he could found the temple in Bang Chan. Chyn, the martinet, had certain heroic proportions. His eye pierced the external politeness of other people and saw their timidity. Perhaps after many brawls his hostility became blended with pity. Certainly his tests were no less numerous than the labors of Hercules, and never was Hercules required to employ quarreling workers to complete his tasks.

We may find many lesser heroes. Lī, the freed slave, brought the first buffalo and plow to his village on the Mound of Earthly Splendor. Three grandnephews of Uncle Sin hitched a windmill to one of the irrigating pumps popularized by the government during the late 1930s (KJ 3/12/49). A certain dispossessed farmer made and sold rice mills for home use during World War II. Later, when people again began taking their padi to the mill for grinding, he changed to making implements for picking mangoes. This was the first "factory" in Bang Chan. A prominent farmer who gave up agriculture even before World War II and became a builder heralded the era of nonfarm occupations. A few years later a woman with little land started a briefly profitable rush to produce mushrooms for the Bangkok market (JRH 1/21/54). Minor innovations took place in many households, just as Barnett avers (1953:17-18). A housewife improvised a binding to hold together a cracked pot. A husband neatly fashioned devices to mend broken harnesses, so that buffalo might not be delayed in their plowing. His neighbor bought a farm cheap because the former owner could not grow a good crop on the soil; the new owner invented ways of making the heavy soil produce more abundantly (JRH 7/23/53).

There were villains, too. The priest who stole money from the temple left the community (LMH 2/16/54). The farm renter who could not get along with his wife and children lived alone (LMH 12/8/53). A certain Phun made his livelihood by robbing distant communities and lived in Bang Chan until he was killed (KJ 2/26/49; LMH 7/7/53). Wian was shamed by his wife, who accused him of stealing her property and spending it on a secret mistress; he killed himself (LMH 8/30/53). A lonely Singto kept live snakes, experimented with opium, and sold charms (LS 1/12/49, 6/7/49). Group living was a rescindable privilege. Those who, despite a broad range of permissible conduct, could not hold up their ends in community arrangements were isolated or exiled. Their traces quickly vanished.

The bubbling spontaneity of life goes on, meeting the new and making the old do. Some of the new lasts but a season and is forgotten, like the footbridge built across the canal so that priests from the temple on their morning rounds might visit the builder's household more easily. It disappeared the following year and was not rebuilt. A shelter emerges in the padi field at planting time, and tomorrow it disappears. So perhaps most changes in Bang Chan appear and disappear without notice. Even the simplest change requires some fashioning of materials and their adaptation to the particular scene.

Other things last a little longer, perhaps because they are associated with a particular person. Chyn the martinet's gang of protectors grew under his care and lasted until his death. Even the household compound that Phlym built dissolved after he died and could not continue without him. In this community we can hardly look for permanence as the criterion for the hero's work.

We are dealing with individually introduced changes that appear to fall into one of the following classes: (1) fads and amusements—gambling games, coffee drinking, the drape of the scarf; (2) symbols of prestige—the radio, the wrist watch, the teak house; (3) instruments—irrigating pumps, bridges—and even occupations—farmer, fisherman, market producer. These classes appear to form the most malleable and least enduring parts of the social scene. The fads and games continue as long as they amuse or until some more entertaining pastimes replace them. The symbols of prestige change along the lines suggested by Rowe's phrasing of Tarde's law of imitation, a movement downward of the new along lines of declining prestige (1962:75–80). The technological changes involve mainly economic activities. The familiar psychological laws of learning—reward and punishment—dictate these changes. Of course, each category, like a color of the spectrum, shades fuzzily into the next. A new shoulder scarf worn by a young woman may add prestige as well as amusement, and some symbols of prestige may help produce a better crop.

So the heroes and quasi-heroes of Bang Chan may be gamblers or dandies, rich men or government officials, mechanics or organizers.

They are welcomed or neglected but rarely opposed. Since Bang Chan looks to the present, they and their contributions are soon forgotten.

Force and Process

As long ago as the first Babylonian empire, some genius linked the happenings of history to disinterested, inanimate forces in nature. Today the astrological influences of Mars, Venus, Saturn, and the other planets have been largely replaced by a medley of social forces. Our abundant vocabulary proffers terms that, multiplied by modifying adjectives, become political powers, social tensions, economic pressures, psychological resistances, and so on and on. Though they lack the specificity of the older concepts, they too are viewed as causing sequences of happenings. When these new types of forces are detached from the sequences that they produce, we speak of "processes"—"political," say, or "inflationary." Even when we omit the word "process" and speak baldly of "modernization" or "Westernization," we anticipate finding a sequence of regularities brought about by certain forces as yet undefined.

Let us then view our material ahistorically, as specified or unspecified forces producing regularities. We shall speak of three: population pressure, commercialization, and urbanization. While in Bang Chan these forces interact, we may also consider them independent of each other. Population pressures may alone have led to migrations in unurbanized Polynesia. Similarly many a tropical agriculturalist far from cities and people participates in the present market economy. Furthermore, such cities as Sumer and even Bangkok have grown in open country without benefit of commercialization and little beset with population pressure.

Population Pressure

Bang Chan is located today in one of the most densely populated regions of Thailand, with more than 300 persons to the square mile (2.6 square kilometers). In the 1850s the density was less than one person per square mile. What effects may be attributed to this mounting density?

Until the 1920s farmers had much unused land. The ordinary fifty-rai holding was only partly tilled; the remainder was rented or left for buffalo pasture. After the inflated prices of World War I, farmers extended their areas of cultivation and frequently worked their entire holdings. At this point population density in Bang Chan declined briefly, but it increased again, mainly through natural reproduction, during the next two decades. Migration seems to have been small and any population movement during this period was outwards, into the more peripheral parts of the central plains. During World War II the population swelled with refugees from Bangkok, but most of them returned to the city after the end of hostilities. In the late 1940s, despite more intensive cultivation and utilization of labor, population density was just beginning to be a problem. Bang Chan began to export people as well as padi to Bangkok.

Population pressure during the late 1940s and 1950s was not sufficient to prevent a person from finding land to rent. Each farmer worked land up to the limit of his labor force. A parent of husky children, ordinarily a man with more labor than land to work, rented from another who could not work all he owned. It might be necessary to travel in order to tend scattered holdings, but some land was still available.

As land became more difficult to locate, kinsmen could no longer count on living next to each other. Neighborhoods became mixed with nonkinsmen, and labor exchanges involved increasing numbers of friends. The former hamlet or neighborhood cluster of siblings and their children became the exception. Kinship designations continued to be used when intimacy reached a sufficient level, and it would appear that the available kinsmen were more warmly greeted than formerly. The endearing term for the young siblings of the mother (nā) was sometimes used in reference to the father's younger siblings (JRH 9/11/53, 11/26/53). Once all children of a parent's older siblings were deferentially called elder sibling (phī), while the children of younger siblings of a parent were known as younger sibling (naūng). Without the presence of these elders to form the needed reference, cousins frequently came to address each other in reference only to themselves, like siblings under a parent's roof (Warin Wonghanchao, personal communication). So cousins became elder or younger siblings depending solely on their age in relation to the speaker; deference to the household of an absent uncle bowed before readier convenience.

Commercialization

The hamlet at Kred canal was made up of rice growers who in the 1900s sold only a small portion of their harvest, in part because the harvests were never very large. Besides, selling even a small share made them uneasy, as Rama IV had felt uneasy when, fifty years earlier, Bowring urged him to export padi. There might not be enough to last until the next harvest. Often mice or floods left scant supplies for a toiling household, and housewives nervously set out in their boats to earn inedible money for a living.

The commercial growing of rice reached Bang Chan in the wake of World War I, with its high prices for agricultural produce. Suddenly the returns from the sale of padi lifted many toward the style of living of Kamnan Phlym. They had only to work a little harder and harvest a larger crop from their land. Then all drank deep from the pool of market produce and services—not only new food, tools, clothing, and storage cabinets, but buffalo, houses, and boats. They became rather independent of their hamlet neighbors, for they had changed from subsistence farmers to entrepreneurs. As some householders hired hands to plant and harvest, labor exchanges languished. Work festivities gave way to merit making and elaborate life-cycle celebrations paid for in cash. Parents took care to arrange a daughter's marriage with a young man of good standing rather than let her elope with the hired man.

At the beginning of the 1930s, as world rice prices slipped and fell, the giddy moments of prosperity vanished. Labor exchanges were revived, since few could afford a hired man. Life-cycle celebrations declined as proud demonstrations of affluence. Humbled people shared again with their neighbors and reciprocated services. Yet something had changed, for none could quite return to the folkish past. People still thirsted for market produce, even as home manufacture was revived. They no longer shared money with neighbors but carefully loaned it interest-free to trusted kinsmen, to non-kinsmen only if fully secured and enriched with interest. They strove to recapture their former prosperity with more efficient cultivation of more marketable padi. Few succeeded until World War II had run its course. Then unbelievable prices for padi confirmed the way of commercialization with fresh flows of status-giving consumer goods. People lit their houses at night with pressure lamps, drank American soft drinks, and bought edibles in the food market.

Women traders overcame their dependence on baskets of real food; money too could satisfy hunger.

Urbanization

Besides a return of high prices and increased market purchasing, the war brought a highway to Bang Chan. For years the capital had stood at a half day or more by boat along Saēn Saēb canal. Suddenly buses moving along the highway brought city streets within an hour's travel. Bang Chan moved cityward; whereas in 1948 many had never visited the capital, by 1955 four-fifths of all household heads had visited Bangkok once or more during the past twelve months (Goldsen and Ralis 1957:59). Some women made trips two or three times a week with market produce to sell. Bangkok also visited Bang Chan, though less frequently. Children of farmers returned from city jobs to help parents during periods of heavy work. Friends of young men in military service accompanied Bang Chan sons on home leave. Sāmsen and Khlāūng Tej kinsmen came more frequently to ordinations and cremations of greater elaborateness. Government services became more available, and high officials as well as foreigners visited to satisfy their curiosity about the community that foreign ethnologists were studying. Clerks came for religious holiday outings, jobbers to sell goods, and sometimes speculators to buy farmland.

A former generation had moved eastward to find farmland, but youths of the 1950s with half a degree of self-confidence moved into the city to find "easier" work. If they had enough education, they took salaried positions, but most farmers' sons and daughters knew only unskilled work. Some returned after a time and became farmers again; some never returned (Goldsen and Ralis 1957:60). In Bang Chan a variety of new full- and part-time occupations appeared. A small number of residents (12 percent) were engaged in trade and service occupations in a community where a few years before all were farmers. The number was mounting as stores, barbershops, restaurants, and even a small mill sprang up along the highway. The habits of farmers were changing. While women sold produce in the Bangkok markets, husbands during the dry season earned extra money as laborers.

Intercourse with the city made Bang Chan more self-aware. Farmers saw themselves as "ducks" who waded in the water, while citified "chickens" kept their feet dry (KJ 4/7/49; Sharp 1950). The more self-conscious bought new tailored clothing, shoes, pens, and watches. They began to regard education more as a means of personal advancement than as moral training. Some of their children were sent to Bangkok schools and some of their sicknesses were treated with Western-style medicine in Bangkok hospitals. They built hygienic privies, listened to radios, read magazines, and pinned on their walls cut-out pictures of state officials and beauty contest winners. Many became curious about foreign countries; a few spoke of wars, communism, and problems of the world rice market. Bang Chan has not just returned to a heightened period of prosperity with more feverish marketing and ostentatious life-cycle celebrations. More important, Bang Chan was metamorphosing from a farming community to a suburb (Sharp 1950).[7]

What of other forces? There were many, but the foregoing were the chief ones. The direct tidal forces of the West never surged long in Bang Chan. Until the arrival of the anthropologists, the West had always reached Bang Chan indirectly. The freeing of the slaves, the new economy of goods instead of workers, the remodeling of government, all had affected Bang Chan, but only via the central government or commercial circles.

The indirect effects of the West first appeared when Laotian prisoners of war established themselves in Bang Chan. Slavery had become abhorrent not just in the West but in the ruling circles of Thailand. Later, government reorganized itself into a central bureaucracy with salaried officials who held territorially limited authority. In keeping with this trend, individuals came to own precisely described areas of land. Between 1900 and 1920 irrigation and education also reached Bang Chan. Then came programs of agricultural improvement, canal maintenance, road building, public health, and information, as the Thai government grew attentive to new definitions of welfare.

The West sent steam rice mills and steam launches, later trucks and buses to move more things and people more easily. Bang Chan also brought the West into the home as people returned with shoes, alarm clocks, flashlights, and bicycles. The declining rice prices of the 1930s only whetted appetites for this new merchandise. Not only did the world become more accessible; it became better known through magazines, movies, and the radio.

Direct contact with the West came late and briefly when the Cornell anthropologists arrived. To these rice farmers, Westerners had been something like those grotesque statues of Europeans with stovepipe hats and beakish noses that guard the portals of some royal temples. Sharp, with the assistance of Janlekha and Metah, established Westerners as friendly persons able to influence levels in the government hierarchy inaccessible to villagers. The seven foreigners who followed showed their interest in rice production, education, household management, nutrition, and health. They talked of America, assisted with the sick, spoke about democracy, and brought other foreigners to visit.

They reinforced, perhaps obliquely, the pressures of urbanization. City people said country people were ignorant; Westerners said nothing about ignorance but plugged for better schools. City people said country people were dirty; Westerners merely advocated use of the Western-style medicines available in Bangkok hospitals. City people said country people were lazy; Westerners kept Bang Chan talking day and night to answer their questions. Urbanization by anthropologists merely lacked acid.

The relation of Westernization to the processes we have been discussing in this scene are clear only in the case of commercialization. Though population increases have been attributed to Western influence, particularly in the colonized portions of Southeast Asia, the application of this thesis to Thailand before 1960 is difficult. Population growth in the Bangkok area was continuous through the nineteenth century, long before the introduction of modern medicine or the opening of trade relations. Food resources sufficed in most years and agriculture easily expanded with the population. At best it could be argued that Western influences helped preserve the political order in the valleys of central Thailand. Wars between neighboring states ceased and so did the removal of people; population could continue its silent growth. As for urbanization, the building of palace, temple, and fortress has long occurred in this region; Westernization mainly added impetus.

An Organism Grows

The organic perspective on society has intrigued observers for centuries. Ancient India considered society to be the organic combination of the four castes, with the Brahmins as the sacred head, the Kshatriya as the arms, and so on. In the *Republic* Plato spoke of the state as if it were an individual, so that we may infer this penchant among some Greeks. The organic perspective continued with Hobbes, Hegel, and Engels. Today those of us who speak of *development*, *adaptation*, *fluorescence*, or even *decay* perpetuate, perhaps deliberately, this image.[8]

The standard criterion of living matter is its potential for adaptive response, and it appears that groupings of certain species, as well as individual organisms, can meet this standard. Under attack by antibiotics, bacterial colonies on a watch glass erect common defenses. Ants and wasps, too, meet threats, by organizing themselves into custodians of the queen with her eggs, while others become counterattacking warriors. Similarly some primate bands designate certain members to harass the intruder while the remainder retreat to safety. Human societies, of course, meet threats of crisis in even more varied ways: the disciplined Zulu regiment, the Inca warning system of fire relays, the Maginot Line.

Let us use this organic metaphor as we view some of the changes undergone by Thai society from about 1850 to the present day.[9] During much of the last century Thailand's societal organism resembled a sea anemone. The capital was its central neural ganglion, which communicated intermittently with its many provincial members. By and large, each of these members sustained itself and responded more or less independently of the central ganglion. Attack upon a segment of a member released immediate local reflexive defenses, and if the attack proved formidable, messages to the provincial nucleus aroused the entire member to the emergency within a short time. If this response were inadequate, messages to the central ganglion activated the total societal organism. Though attacks might lacerate a member badly, the organism as a whole survived, and eventually the crippled member regained its former vitality.

This neuromuscular system of the whole was sustained by a massive but certainly inefficient nutritive system. Structurally each provincial member consisted of varying numbers of clustered substructures made up of household cells that formed the predominant tissue of the entire organism. These household cells were of a nonspecialized type that might function as contractile muscular tissue in emergency but ordinarily nourished the organism. They occurred typically in clusters in direct contact with the environment, converting the products of soil and water into nutrients. Most household cells sustained themselves, yet they did pass a small portion of their produce to neighboring cells in the cluster by osmotic transfer. Another small portion also went by special channel to the substructure center and thence to the nucleus of the provincial member. Each member then passed some of the stored nutrients to the central capital nucleus of the organism. Thus many hundreds of household cells were necessary to support the limited neuromuscular system. Generally, household cells sustained themselves and received nutrients from the nucleus of the provincial member only in case of crop failure or attack. An equilibrium existed, however, for the neuromuscular influences maintained a kind of order within the member that permitted the household clusters to produce nutrients.

Of course, societies as organisms have characteristics that are unmatched in the biological world or at least matched only to a limited degree. Grafting, a delicate operation among higher animals, takes place readily among societal organisms. Thus the sultanate of Trenganu was severed from Thailand in the 1830s and joined to the British overseas protectorate that became the Malay States, subsequently Malaysia. The relative ease of separation from one societal organism and incorporation in another constitutes a special property. Another special property is the ability of the parts to move and reorganize themselves within an organism. During the 1780s in Thailand, Rama I moved thousands of household cells to provide nourishment for his newly organized capital at Bangkok. These clusters functioned as well around the central ganglion at the capital as they formerly had in the provincial member. A third special property is sensitivity to symbolic as well as physical-chemical stimulation. A proclamation from the capital nucleus can activate the entire organism as readily as hunger or thirst. A fourth property is the ability of these organisms to reproduce themselves by cell division and reclustering rather than by sexual procreation. Thus here is a special class sharing certain properties with protozoans and coelenterates, namely, a fluidity of structure, mobility of parts, and manner of reproducing; yet, unlike them, societal organisms are responsive to symbolic stimulation. Furthermore, they can alter their internal structures in a manner quite impossible among creatures limited to ordinary biological processes. Reorganizations that require thousands of years to accomplish through organic evolution can occur within a few decades among societal organisms. Let us examine some of these changes.

In the mid-nineteenth century the provincial members, as we have seen, consisted of relatively compact groupings around the central nucleus or one of the substructures. The small bulk and slow flow of nutrients between cells made this arrangement effective in sustaining the organism. Then suddenly in the 1870s, as if a sustaining membrane had broken, household cells began to diffuse from the large clusters around the central nucleus and form many new clusters at increasing distances from the center. The once compact organism became extended and diffuse. This change began at the capital but over the succeeding decades spread to the other members. While the immediate stimulus for this change was the symbolic edict ending slavery, nutritive imbalances appear also to have weakened the metabolic equilibrium within the member.

In isolation these clusters could not sustain themselves and so had to exchange a portion of the nutrients they produced. Under this stimulation mobile market cells grew up in many areas, and with them circulatory systems moving nutrients from center to household clusters and back. Though long present, particularly in the capital ganglion, these mobile centers of exchange gradually became fixed at the nuclear centers of the members as well as at the capital. Structurally these markets and the associated organs for the manufacture of nutrients consisted of migrant cells from China. Without these structures the diffused household cells could not have survived.

Subsequently the small ganglion at the capital began to grow to encephalon size, gradually extending a neural network to control the muscular system of the outlying members. Then the total organism responded more quickly and with more coordination. As this control increased, the circulatory system expanded, converting paths into roads and rivulets into canals; later came the railroads. The port of Bangkok, long a minor orifice for ingesting and disgorging nutrients from abroad, began in the 1880s to handle increased volumes. The flow of these products to and from relatively remote centers along the circulatory channels raised the nutritive level of the entire organism. By 1920 specialized organs for processing raw materials into nutrients were already contributing further vitalizing ingredients: the rice mills, the electric works, the tin mines, the cement plant, and innumerable households manufacturing special articles. The stimuli for these changes appear to be enzymes from Europe which affected the neuromuscular system.

Our observations of Bang Chan allow some view of the concomitant microphysiological changes that occurred over the same period. There is a general rule that migrating cells move from points of low nutritional level to points of higher nutritional level. Access to nutrients, however, can occur freely only when a cell affixes itself to the soil as a single cell. Otherwise it must become integrated into a cell cluster before it can gain access. Thus, ordinarily, migrating cells move from one point of access to another point of access in a cluster with a higher nutritional level. When the first household cell moved to Bang Chan from the capital ganglion, a region of high nutritional level, it must have lacked a point of access in a cluster. With the arrival of additional cells in Bang Chan, a cluster was formed, and the nutritional level increased through osmotic exchange within the cluster. As its size continued to increase, its nutritional level also increased, thereby attracting more cells.

Specialization and differentiation took place along with integration. The first household cells not only produced rice but fished and manufactured household implements. For the market they supplied fish, rice becoming acceptable in exchange only at a later date. After 1917 a sudden change took place. Fishing and manufacture all but ceased and rice became the chief product for exchange. Before this date household cells consumed about four-fifths of the rice produced, using one-fifth for exchange. After this date a cell consumed one-fifth and exchanged four-fifths of the rice produced. This change became possible by an increase in the amount of land cultivated, from ten to about fifty rai per household. Almost simultaneously there arose in the Bang Chan region new specialized organs for the transportation, processing, exchange, and manufacture of nutrients. Thus these cells became integrated into the nutritive system as a whole. As we have seen, a cell's nutritional level varies with the vitality of the nutritive system as a whole. The dysfunctions of the 1930s resulted in severe deficiencies for the household clusters of Bang Chan. Those that survived tended to compensate by producing more rice and a random variety of other nutrients. Conversely during the period of restored vitality of the 1950s the cells also increased production of rice and a somewhat less random supply of other nutrients.

Neuromuscular changes also took place in Bang Chan. In the 1890s a temple cell appeared and helped draw together the separate cell clusters into a more coordinate unit. Shortly thereafter a single household cell became transformed into an effector responsive to neural messages from the capital ganglion. Household cells further increased and coalesced under this influence. By the 1930s a school cell began secreting enzymes that, like those of the temple, promoted the coalescing of household clusters and also increased sensitivity to symbolic stimulation. Subsequently certain household cells became specialized into the neuromuscular type associated with education, no longer sustaining themselves from the soil. Other functions of the neuromuscular system (police, public health, agriculture) affected Bang Chan but made no structural changes within it.

So Bang Chan grew as a part of a societal organism, in particular under the influence of the capital ganglion. Without this center Bang Chan would never have developed. A differentiation and special-ization of its tissues took place as it became integrated into the systems of a more coordinated societal organism.[10]

Kaleidoscopic Transformation

History is the influence of unique events on subsequent events. Ayutthayā, once fallen, precipitated the founding of the capital at Thonburī. Such events are unpredictable, each one leaving a wake that contributes in turn to a new and equally unpredictable event. No one could foretell whether Ayutthayā would rise again from its smoking ruins, or whether a new capital would rise somewhere else, or whether no capital would rise at all. The connections between events can be traced only in retrospect. Projection of a sequence into the future is the work of theologians, not historians.

This view of history can be traced at least to the three fates, whose unseen hands guided events in the Hellenic world. During the subsequent centuries, when all in the West assumed the presence of an omnipotent God in control of human affairs, the view continued amid prayers and protests. Even in our present era of reassuring predictability, who can tell which of the scientific laws will apply or what seeming trifle may divert the lawful outcome of a familiar sequence? So we still bid historians make the connections between events into plausible tales.

Like Adam and Eve driven from Eden, the first household that moved to Bang Chan looked back at what it had left. A foreigner who passed along Sāen Sāeb canal described the route these people had taken:

This canal is 55 miles long and connects the city of Bangkok with the Bang Pa Kong River and is made through a flat alluvial country devoted entirely to the culture of rice. The natives, like the rest of the Siamese, appear to be a branch of the Malay family. The floors of their bamboo-thatched houses are raised some four feet from the ground; their clothing is simply a cloth around the waist; and, whatever they may be engaged in, one hand is generally actively employed warring against the swarms of mosquitoes [King 1860:177–178]

This traveler did not pause to learn that he was passing the huts of prisoners of war, vagabonds, ruffians, and the frightened dispossessed. Here was the dump for the City of the Heavenly Spirits. Clusters of households banded to survive the alternating floods and droughts. At night the occupants lay exhausted from their labors and in the morning they awoke still exhausted from their battles with the insects. Between the neighboring clusters indifference reigned except toward theft and insult. So was released the stealthy venom that left corpses with broken skulls to be claimed by some passing kinsman.

As more people moved in, temples began to spring up here and there across the plain like stars in the evening sky. In 1892 a temple roof glistened above the tall grasses of Bang Chan. People in quest of merit gathered with their offerings to listen to sermons. Hamlets of farmers arose, and their work songs sounded down the waterways. Stony faces of fishermen began to soften as two boats approached; they paused alongside for a joke. When the rivulets were dried by the hot-season sun, fishermen joined farmers to make rice liquor over the fire and gamble goodheartedly until the cooling evening descended. Both fishermen and farmers sent their boys to serve the priest at the temple and their grown sons to learn the doctrine.

One day notice came for one of the fishermen to appear at the nearest government office; he returned a few hours later as kamnan, chief of the area. He then took the responsibility of showing newcomers where to find vacant land, helping stake out their borders, and settling their disputes. In turn people paid him their land tax, from which he extracted his fee. Soon the canal between his house and the temple was filled with the boats of those who wished his protection. His household grew with wives and children. His orchard yielded abundant fruit at the hands of his servants. Baskets of grain came to his storehouse from the toil of his tenants. When the crops were in, musicians gathered in the courtyard of his house to begin the songs for the jeweled dancers. Across the fields trooped householders bearing trays of food for the kamnan; they would savor for a moment something of the courtly life. Farmers and fishermen rejoiced in their protector.

The scratching of signatures in a railway car not far from the reeking trenches in France in 1918 transformed the scene again. The seas were safe for commerce and hungry people awaited the grain ships. In Thailand there sprang up along the canals teak houses of an elegance that matched the kamnan's. Within them householders turned to admire their newly purchased chiffoniers and then their own smiling images in the mirrors. Everyone would be as rich as the kamnan, or nearly so. They too could hire broad-cheeked boys from the northeast to till their fields. Priests might chant blessings in their houses and be feasted from their kitchens. They too could stage a cremation ceremony with a gilded bier and send off rockets to announce the arrival of a prominent soul at the gates of heaven. Money solved many problems.

When it vanished in the 1930s, money left problems, too. Of course, money could still be found if one mortgaged the land, the house, the plow, or the buffalo. When worse came to worst, hands were blistered in the digging of a fish pond. Those who salvaged plow and buffalo set off in search of fields to rent. Those with their houses and some land felt the security of a little more merit. But none had the merit to achieve their dreams of fun and ease. All had to learn to deny themselves, to work harder, longer, and more wearyingly. Neighbors still met at times of transplanting and harvest, though none wished to sing the old songs. All felt shy wearing faded loincloths to the temple. Indeed, a few months after the next war began, they were happy to have a single tattered rag in the house for the man who went hawking eggs. As strong young men patrolled the railway bridges, the aged struggled in the heat to till the fields. Padi piled up in the godowns at the port until it became bait for incendiary bombs. Even city people sought refuge out in the padi fields.

The Japanese army left a strange memento: an undulating dyke grew eastward across the fields, deepening the water here and there but leaving other stretches high and dry. It passed within a few hundred yards of Bang Chan's temple. When the soldiers departed, the dyke lay neglected. Farmers turned to readying the padi for another hungry world; workmen hastily patched homes, railways, and docks. Once the more pressing work was done, people turned to grading the dyke into a road, and by 1952 green buses were rolling over its tarred surface.

An urban tide lapped against the house posts, bringing on the flood: retail stores, cafés, sewing machines. Housewives waited at the bus stop in the morning to take lotus buds to market. Young men and women joined them to seek jobs in the glistening city. Old women struggled with baskets of rice for their city-dwelling children. The return bus let out soldiers on leave from the regiment, housewives with betel and lime for sale to their neighbors, and bewildered youths happy to return to the quiet countryside. Along the same road came government officials to inspect the crops or the newly built school. Trucks with movie projectors and screens drew up to show the causes of malaria and the fortunes of a Memphis gangster. A buffalo was accidentally killed by a truck, which limped back toward the city with broken headlights and dripping radiator. Farmers along the road were suddenly rich if they sold their land to storekeepers or Bangkok speculators.

Some incident or cataclysm will change the scene again. It may be a passing peddler, a war, or another sweep of the market. But perhaps none of these or all of them will have the same effect when the parts are ready to shift. Then the flick of a cat's tail in a passing sampan could send the parts tumbling.

Retrospect

Now what is to be done with this basket of odd-shaped bundles, each neatly labeled a history of Bang Chan? Following the tradition of science, we should resolve the many to one, for no scientist leaves his laboratory without reducing his data to simpler terms. Yet we propose to do without this customary finale on several grounds.

We cannot reject one or the other view on grounds of error, since we are dealing with cosmic views. They are systems for making order in the world that a people knows. Each adopts a few basic metaphors to make its world understandable, meaningful for living, or at least sufferable, and somewhat manipulable. The systems are more or less self-contained, each specifying what is real, what is fiction, what is nonexistent, and offering in its own terms proofs for each category. In this sense they are, like languages, complete at any moment but extendable. As no linguist or cosmopolite criticizes a foreign language for using the "wrong" word or for its strange idiom, so we may not claim on the basis of a single system that another is in error. We can prefer one system with its metaphors to another because of its capacity to express our problem, its poetic flavor, its consistency, its apparent completeness, and so on. Like Kluckhohn and Strodtbeck (1961:1-48), one can gather schemes for comparing two or more, and eventually some may grow skillful in translating from one system to another. Yet we cannot eliminate another on the grounds that, according to our system, it contains an error; there are only differences.

Elimination must take place on other grounds. If a world view and its metaphor fail to cover the problem of interest to us, it may be rejected. With respect to coverage, three of our views seem incomplete. History, considered to be the resultant of individual human action, clearly fails to consider the social base of human action that lies for the most part outside of human awareness. Though the metaphors of force and organism deal with these very backgrounds of human action, they bypass the individual actor. Most systems are extendable to cover new problems, but tasks this formidable lie beyond our present scope. Certainly the Buddhist view of a morally determined world encompasses the whole, yet having turned the job over to a learned Buddhist, we still face the problem of translating his results into our naturalistic world. The view of haphazard stages avoids this problem but lacks clarity and precision for those who would analyze a continuous set of processes. So none of the proffered metaphors suffices for the task. To construct a new view embodying the subject in its entirety is a job in itself.

We also refuse to reduce our hypotheses on special clinical grounds. Certainly had someone brought in a totally new creature from outer space, we should probably be able to ask it more questions about its structure and functions than could be answered. This raw slice of history is not so baffling as a space creature, yet even this relatively simple subject exceeds the conceptual tools of any one system. To describe in this eclectic manner is systematically disconcerting but certainly more useful for finding out about the specimen.

Finally, we would let the multiplicity stand on humanistic grounds. If knowing Bang Chan enriches the soul, this enrichment probably comes not from the fascination with any particular actor, the beauty of the scene, or the impressiveness of the end product. Rather we might feel some awe at the complexity of this microcosm. To describe it with a single metaphor suggests simplicity; to use only two or three implies the completeness of our knowledge; but five views offer the possibility of a dozen or a myriad more before we reach an understanding.

Schooling of Bang Chan population by age and sex, 1953

Age group	No schooling or unknown		Temple school		Government primary school (grade reached)								Middle school		Total any school		% any school	
					1		2		3		4							
	M	F	M	F	M	F	M	F	M	F	M	F	M	F	M	F	M	F
5–9	68	68			27	34	4	3			1				32	37	32	35
10–14	33	23			10	11	14	16	22	19	38	31	1	3	85	80	72	77
15–19	13	15	2		1	4	4	4	13	14	43	57	7	3	70	82	84	85
20–24	14	12			2		6	4	17	11	52	43	1	2	78	60	85	83
25–29	7	26			2		2	3	12	11	32	32	5	2	53	48	88	65
30–34	10	36	12				5	6	4	2	13	7	2		36	15	78	29
35–39	19	39	13	1		1	2		1	1	1	1	1		18	4	49	9
40–44	31	45	7						1		2		1		11		26	
45–49	27	34	15	1									1		16	1	37	3
50–54	27	26	6	1				1	1		1				8	2	23	7
55–59	23	29	3										1		4		15	
60–64	17	24	10												10		37	
65–69	14	11	1												1		7	
70–74	8	6	1												1		11	
75–79	6	7																
80–84	2	5																
All ages	319	406	70	3	42	50	37	37	71	58	183	171	20	10	423	329	57	45

Bang Chan school enrollment, fourth-grade enrollment, number graduating from fourth grade, and number entering middle school, 1937–1960

Year	Total enrollment	4th-grade enrollment	4th-grade graduates	Entering middle school
1937		12	12	
1938	195	8	8	1
1939	189	22	22	3
1940	202	19	18	1
1941	217	15	15	
1942	203	24	20	
1943	233	17	15	
1944	225	28	25	
1945	227	18	13	
1946	235	25	24	2
1947	244	15	12	1
1948	259	18	10	1
1949	249	21	15	1
1950	240	21	14	1
1951	241	31	12	1
1952	254	46	28	8
1953	229	54	27	4
1954	202	45	33	11
1955	189	32	31	9
1956	210	20	20	8
1957	242	32	31	9
1958	251	26	26	12
1959	262	45	45	13
1960	288	35	35	14

Responses of 363 fourth-grade rural and urban schoolchildren aged 11–14 in 1954 to question: "When you are 25 years old, what kind of work would you like to be doing?"

| Desired occupation | Sex | Students in rural schools | | | | Students in urban schools | | Students in all schools | |
		Bang Chan	Bang Chan Islam	Bang Khuad	Min-buri	Public	Private	No.	% of sex
Farmer	M	3			10		2	15	9
	F	4		12	5	4		25	13
Merchant	M	1					2	3	2
	F				3		3	6	3
Policeman	M			5	12	2	4	23	13
	F	1						1	
Soldier	M	3	6	2	24	23	24	82	47
	F	4	2	1			2	9	5
Civil official	M	3	1		3		3	10	6
	F	1	2			1	9	13	7
Laborer	M	1						1	
	F	1						1	
Teacher	M			1	2		1	4	2
	F				11	13	20	44	23
Physician	M	8		3	5		16	32	19
	F			1	3	2	6	12	6
Nurse	M				2			2	
	F	9	5	9	30	11	6	70	37
Actor	M					1		1	
	F			1	7		1	9	5
All occupations	M	19	7	11	58	26	52	173	98
	F	20	9	24	59	31	47	190	99

Religious affiliation and experience of Bang Chan males, by age group, 1949

Age group	Total males	Moslem males		Buddhist males		Buddhist priests[a]	
		No.	%	No.	%	No.	%[b]
0–4	78	3	4	75	96		
5–9	108	8	7	100	93		
10–14	98	3	3	95	97		
15–19	109	7	6	102	94	10	10[c]
20–24	93	9	10	84	90	39	46
25–29	58	5	9	53	91	37	70
30–34	52	6	12	46	88	32	70
35–39	45	4	9	41	91	27	66
40–44	47	3	6	44	94	35	79
45–49	44	1	2	43	98	35	81
50–54	28	3	11	25	89	21	84
55–59	23	3	13	20	87	14	70
60–64	22	3	14	19	86	13	68
65–69	14			14	100	10	71
70–74	8	2	25	6	75	5	83
75–79	2			2	100	2	100
80–84	3			3	100	3	100
All ages	832	60	7	772	93	283	
Age 20 and above				400		273	68

[a]Have been or are ordained priests in Bang Chan or elsewhere.
[b]Of Buddhist male age group.
[c]Became priests between 1949 and 1953, by which time the number of Buddhist males aged 15–19 had been reduced to 92.

Price range of padi, land, and land rent in Bang Chan, 1880–1953 (in baht)[a]

Period beginning	Rice (per kwian)[b]	Land (per rai)[c]	Rent (per rai)[c]
1880	12.50 (1)		
1890		1 (1)	0.50–2 (3)
1900		4–8 (3)	1–3 (2)
1910	20–160 (7)	16–40 (3)	3–4 (2)
1920	60–200 (3)	300–500 (2)	
1930	25–40 (5)	60–250 (2)	0.30 (1)
1940	40–300 (5)	210–300[d]	1–50 (2)
1948–1953	650–1,100[d]	1,500–12,000[d]	40–90[d]

Unless otherwise indicated, figures have been culled from the field notes of JRH, KJ, LMH, and LS. Prices and dates are approximate. Figures in parentheses represent the number of times a price has been mentioned and assigned to the given period in field notes.

[a]1 baht – U.S. $0.05 in 1953.

[b]1 kwian = 2,000 liters or 1,000 kilograms.

[c]1 rai = 0.40 acres or 1,600 square meters.

[d]Figures from Janlekha (1957:62–63, 70), who notes that for the most recent period the highest prices for land were for plots along the Minburi road to be used for residential or other than agricultural purposes.

Glossary

ā	อา	Younger sibling of father
amnād	อำนาจ	Power, influence
amphōē	อำเภอ	Political subdivision, district, made up of tambon
bāht	บาท	Basic Thai currency unit, same as tical; about U.S. $0.05 during 1950s
baj jiabjam	ใบเหยียบย่ำ	Preemption certificate for land
Bān Dāūn Sī Phūm	บ้านดอนศรีภูมิ	Village of the Mound of Earthly Splendor
Bān Lāb Siri Khun	บ้านลาภศิริขุน	Village Receiving Splendid Bounty; a hamlet of Laotian war prisoners
Bāng Chan	บางชัน	Name of the community studied
Bāng Khuad	บางขวด	Name of a community
Bāng Sȳ	บางซื้อ	Name of a community
bāw	บ่าว	Slave, servant
bon	บน	To address a spirit or guardian
Borisad Khud Khlāūng lae Khū Nā Sajām	บริษัทขุดคลองและ คูนาสยาม	Siam Canal and Irrigation Company
bōt	โบสถ์	The sanctuary building in a Buddhist temple compound
bun	บุญ	Merit of the Buddhist variety
Chāēm	แฉ่ม	Name of a man, first settler in Bang Chan
chāj (phī chāj)	ฉาย (พี่ฉาย)	Man, male (elder brother)
chak	จักร	A splash wheel for irrigating a field
chāng wāng	จางวาง	Royal deputy
changwat	จังหวัด	Political subdivision, province, made up of amphōē
chao myang	เจ้าเมือง	Local lord of a town or region

Chao Phāū Sāēn Sāēb	เจ้าพ่อแล่นแล่บ	A spirit guardian of Sāēn Sāēb canal
Chao Phrayā Srīsuriya-wong (also Somdet Chao Phrayā)	เจ้าพระยาศรีสุริยวงค์ (สมเด็จเจ้าพระยา)	Prime minister under Rama IV, regent under Rama V, Chuang Bunnag
chao thī	เจ้าที่	Lord of the place, an earth spirit
chāūb	จอบ	Mattock
chāūng lāūng	ฮ่องลอง	A water shovel for irrigation
chēdī	เจดีย์	A stupa, a memorial
chētaphūd	เจตภูต	Ghost, life, soul
chōēj	เลย	Calm, cool
dāūk bia	ดอกเบี้ย	Interest on money; "cowrie blossom"
dek wat	เด็กวัด	Temple boy
dip	ดิบ	Raw, immature
hua mū	หัวหมู	Pig's head
imām	อิหม่าม	Moslem religious leader
īpōē	ฮีเปอ	A magical device confirming power
jā	ย่า	Father's mother and her sisters
jāj	ยาย	Mother's mother and her sisters
jām	ยาม	A system of medical diagnosis involving hours of the day and days of the week of a patient's visit to a physician
jāū	ยอ	A fishing device
jū faj	อยู่ไฟ	The fire rest for postparturient women
kab khāw	กับข้าว	The curry or flavoring added to rice for eating
kabīkabāūng	กะบี่กะบอง	A sword dance
kam	กรรม	Karma
kamathān	กรรมฐาน	To concentrate mentally
kamnan	กำนัน	Chief of a tambon or commune, elected by other phū jaj bān

kamsith	กรรมสิทธิ์	Ownership
kapī	กะปิ	Shrimp paste
"khao duen" [khaw dyan]	เข้าเดือน	Translation uncertain; possibly to enter the month (of corvée service)
khāthā	คาถา	A verbal formula with magical efficacy
khāū raeng	ขอแรง	Summon strength
khāūb khun māk	ขอบคุณมาก	Thank you very much
khāw	ข้าว	Rice
khāw mao	ข้าวเม่า	Green rice, roasted
khiaw	เคียว	A sickle
khlāēw khlād	แคล้วคลาด	Amulet with power to divert an enemy's blow
khlāūng	คลอง	Canal
Khōk Chuan	โคกจวน	Governor's Mound, a place name
khrāūb khrua	ครอบครัว	Family or household
khun phra	คุณพระ	A magical device giving power in combat
khun thāūng	ขุนทอง	Rich man; "Mr. Gold"
Khwāēng Amphōē Khlāūng Sām Wā	แขวงอำเภอ คลองสามวา	Name of former district prior to organization of Minburī District
khwan	ขวัญ	Soul, one of several
kōēj (nāūng kōēj)	เขย (น้องเขย)	Male in-law (younger brother-in-law)
kog	ก๊ก	Neighborhood, group
kot	กฎ	Law
krēng chai	เกรงใจ	Imposition; to fear, respect
Krom Dāūkmaiphlōēng	กรมดอกไม้เพลิง	Department of Fireworks
Krom Khlāūng	กรมคลอง	Department of Waterways
Krom Mahād Thai	กรมมหาดไทย	Department of the Interior
Krom Māū	กรมหมอ	Department of Medicine

Krom Nā	กรมนา	Department of Lands
Krom Sinlapākāūn	กรมศิลปากร	Department of Fine Arts
Krungthēp Mahānakhāūn	กรุงเทพมหานคร	Formal name of Bangkok
kwian	เกวียน	A measure of padi, a cartful, standardized as 2,000 liters
lān	หลาน	Child of a sibling; grandchild
lao	เหล้า	Alcoholic liquor
Lāūj Krathong	ลอยกระทง	A November festival
leg laj	เหล็กไหล	Magical device to prevent being cut
lūk krāūk	ลูกกรอก	A device to help win in gambling
lung	ลุง	Older brother of parent
Māē Pōsob	แม่โพสพ	Rice Mother, spirit of the rice
Māē Sī	แม่ศรี	Mother Splendor, a spirit
Māē Thōranī	แม่ธรณี	Spirit of the Earth
makanājok	มรรคนายก	A layman in charge of maintenance of a temple and certain ceremonial offices
māū	หมอ	Curer schooled in traditional Thai medicine
Mēkalā	เมยลา	Spirit of the Water
mūbān	หมู่บ้าน	A hamlet; smallest political subdivision
myang	เมือง	Town, country, region, place
nā	น้า	Younger sibling of mother
na chang ngang	นะจังงัง	An amulet compelling fright in an enemy
nāj amphōē	นายอำเภอ	District officer, appointed by Minister of the Interior
naj nām mī plā, naj nā mī khāw	ในน้ำมีปลา ในนามีข้าว	In the water, fish; in the fields, rice
naklēng	นักเลง	A rogue; a rough, sporty fellow

naklēng tō	นักเลงโต	A martinet; a leader who maintains order by his strength and threats of violence
nāmchan	น้ำจัณฑ์	An elegant royal term for liquor
nāūng	น้อง	Younger siblings, children of parents' younger siblings
nēn	เณร	A novice in a Buddhist temple
nitsaj	นิสัย	Habit, psychological propensity
pā	ป้า	Older sister of parents
paj thiaw	ไปเที่ยว	Wander, look around, go sightseeing
palad amphōē	ปลัดอำเภอ	Assistant district officer
parāūt	ปรอท	A magical device to prevent being cut
phak bung	ผักบุ้ง	A common water vine (Ipomoea aquatica); the leaves are a popular vegetable food
phak phuak	พรรคพวก	The indefinite group of kinsmen
phākhāwmā	ผ้าขาวม้า	Loincloth
Phansā	พรรษา	Buddhist "Lenten" season
phathammarong	พะทำมะรง	Jailer
phī	พี่	Elder siblings, children of parents' elder siblings
phī	ผี	A ghost, a spirit
phī pūjātājāj	ผีปู่ย่าตายาย	Ancestral spirits
phī yngāng	ผีอึ่งอาง	A spirit invited to possess a person
phra	พระ	A Buddhist priest or monk
Phra Phūm	พระภูมิ	Earth guardian; occupant of spirit house
phra thudong	พระธุดงค์	A wandering priest
Phraborom Wongsānuwong	พระบรมวงศานุวงศ์	Royal relatives; Supreme Council
Phrachao Phāēndin	พระเจ้าแผ่นดิน	Title of the king; Lord of All the Earth

phrāhuad	พร้าหวด	Sword
phraj luang	ไพร่หลวง	Commoners
phraj som	ไพร่สม	Perpetual bondsmen
phū jaj bān	ผู้ใหญ่บ้าน	Hamlet headman, elected by other members of his mūbān
phū wā rātchakān myang	ผู้ว่าราชการเมือง	Former title of provincial governor
Pī Mamia	ปีมะเมีย	Year of the Horse in cycle of twelve years
plā chāun	ปลาช่อน	A kind of fish
plā salid	ปลาสลิด	A kind of fish
pliaw (pliaw chaj)	เปลี่ยว (เปลี่ยวใจ)	Abandoned
pō	โป	A gambling game
pratū nām	ประตูน้ำ	Water gate or lock
prȳ	ปรือ	A coarse grass used for making mats, walls and roofs
pū	ปู	Father's father and his male siblings
rai	ไร่	A measurement of area; 1 rai = 0.4 acres or 1,600 square meters
ramwong	รำวง	A circle dance, now modernized
ratabān	รัฐบาล	The national government
rātchakān	ราชการ	Affairs of the king
riak khwan khāw	เรียกขวัญข้าว	A ceremony performed at harvest, calling the soul of the rice
sakdi	ศักดิ	Power, authority
sakdinā	ศักดินา	A former measure of honorific grade
sālā	ศาลา	A pavilion
salyng	สลึง	Unit of currency: one-fourth of a baht
sampan	สำปั้น	A type of small boat

sāo (nāūng sāo)	ลาว (น้องลาว)	Woman, female (younger sister)
saphaj (phī saphaj)	ละใภ้ (พี่ละใภ้)	Female in-law (elder sister-in-law)
sīsa	ศีรษะ	Head
sī sak mongkhon	ศรีศักดิ์มงคล	An elegant expression to address a spirit in offering a pig's head
sitthi	สิทธิ	Accomplishment, success
Somdet Chao Phrayā Srīsurijawong	สมเด็จเจ้าพระยา ศรีสุริยวงศ์	Prime minister under Rama IV, regent under Rama V, Chuang Bunnag
Somdet Krom Phrayā Damrong Rāchānuphāb	สมเด็จกรมพระยา ดำรงราชานุภาพ	Prince Damrong, a younger brother of Rama V
Songkrān	สงกรานต์	New Year
sug	ลูก	Cooked, mature
sum	ลุ่ม	A fish trap
surao	สุเหร่า	School and place of worship for Moslems
tā	ตา	Mother's father and his male siblings
tambon	ตำบล	Political subdivision, a commune, made up of several mūbān
tamlyng	ตำลึง	A discarded unit of currency; 1 tamlyng is 4 baht
thang	ถัง	A measure of padi, a bucketful, standardized as 20 liters
tham khwan nāg	ทำขวัญนาค	A portion of the ordination ceremony for a priest
tham mȳ, kin mȳ	ทำมือกินมือ	To live from hand to mouth
thāt luang	ทาสหลวง	Royal Slave
Thāūd Kathin	ทอดกฐิน	A Buddhist annual ceremony in which robes are presented to priests
Thēp	เทพ	A man's name
thid	ทิด	Form of address for lay men who have been Buddhist priests

thuad (jāj thuad)	ทวด (ยายทวด)	Great-grandparents, mother's mother's mother
thurian	ทุเรียน	Durian, a popular kind of fruit
tog raeng, chaj raeng	ตกแรง, ขอแรง	Offer strength, use strength
Tō	โต	A man's name
trā chāūng	ตราจอง	Certificate of possession of land
tua	ถั่ว	A gambling game
Uparād	อุปราช	Second King
waj khrū	ไหว้ครู	A ceremonial paying of respect to one's teacher
Wan Kon	วันโกน	Day prior to Wan Phra
Wan Phra	วันพระ	Weekly holy day, "priest day"
Wang Nā	วังหน้า	Second King
wat	วัด	Buddhist temple or monastery
Wat Rādsadthātham	วัดราษฎร์ศรัทธาธรรม	The name given Bang Chan temple by Rama V
wihān	วิหาร	The reliquary of a Buddhist temple compound
winjān	วิญญาณ	Soul, one of several
Wisākhabūchā	วิสาขบูชา	The day of the Buddha's birth, enlightenment and death

Notes

Chapter 2: *The Dispensable Ones*

1. We reckon the rough air distance from Paknām to Pitsanulok and from the Korat escarpment to the beginning of the western hills on a line running east and west through Ayutthayā.

2. The Māē Nām Chao Phrayā is referred to in the *Phongsāwadān* simply as the Māē Nām (see Thiphakarawong 1934b:70).

3. We have not yet found a description of the flora and fauna of the central plains prior to cultivation. The technical description of the area as "jungle" interspersed with savannah, especially to the south, corresponds with the accounts of old informants, who speak also of tiger, deer, and small herds of elephants roaming the plains (LS 10/22/48). The savannah-like flora, annual inundation, and sedimentary clay soil make these plains similar to the "veal" described by Jean Delvert (1961:127–131) for Cambodia to the east. We have been able to identify from field notes the following flora in early Bang Chan: *Imperata cylindrica (ja kha), Cyperus sp. (prȳ), Bambusa sp. (phai), Arunda donax (mai āū), Ipomoea aquatica (phak bung).* Some present flora are listed in Sharp et al. (1953:App. G). Wilhelm Credner (1935:119) describes what may be comparable vegetation in the Māē Khong region and includes *Thyrsostachys siamensis (mai ruak), Ocytenanthera sp. (mai pak), Homonoiariparis (takrai nam), Eugenia ripiscola (wā nām), Bambusa arundinacea (mai pai).*

4. The most common among these burrowing fish are the *Ophiocephalus sp. (plā chāun).* Janlekha (1957:App. E) lists thirty-one species of fish found in Bang Chan today, but we do not know which were there earlier.

5. Field notes refer to *Arca granos (hāūj khareng)* (McFarland 1944:928) and *Trichopodus pectalis (plā salid)* (ibid.:828).

6. Khā is a generic Thai and Lao term for tribal people rather than for a specific tribe. An informant at Bang Chan reported that the people living at Khōk Khā, tambon Bang Chan, amphōē Minburī, were formerly animists (LMH 9/18/57). Bastian (1867:100) reports Khā in or near Bangkok who called themselves Khāmu. These would presumably have been a Khmer (Cambodian) group using a name similar to that used by Khmu in Nan Province and Laos today, or they could have been Khmu proper moved south after some campaign toward Laos.

7. The population of Thailand in 1850 ranged between 5 and 6 million people and of Bangkok between 300,000 and 500,000 (Ingram 1955:7; Skinner 1957:81). Even if three-quarters of the Thai population lived along the banks of the Māē Nām, Māē Klāung, and Māē Bāng Pa Khong rivers, one might expect many miles of uninhabited shoreline.

8. Our Thai documentary sources, Thiphakarawong's *Chronicle of the Third Reign* (1934b, 1937) and a description of various works constructed under Rama III by an author unknown to us (Thailand, Royal Academy 1957), agree that the digging of Khlāūng Sāēn Sāēb began, or rather that royal orders for the digging were given, on the fourth day of the waxing moon of the second month of the year of the Cock, B.E. (Buddhist Era) 2380, and of the Sakrād cycle, 1199. There is agreement, then, that the order was given on 30 December 1837.

But there is some question as to when the canal was completed. An edition of Thiphakarawong's *Chronicle* published in 1937 gives the date of completion as "year of the Rat, second of the decade, 1202 of the Sakrād," or 1840/41. But in another edition of the same work published in 1934, the date is given as "year of the Rat, second of the decade, 1212 of the Sakrād." The 1212 is clearly a misprint for 1202; the year 1212 (B.E. 2393 or A.D. 1850/51) was a year of the Dog, whereas years of the Rat were 1202 (B.E. 2383 or A.D. 1840/41) and 1214 (B.E. 2395 or A.D. 1852/53).

In the volume detailing the various constructions of Rama III (Thailand, Royal Academy 1957:69) it is stated that the canal to Bāng Khanak, begun "toward the end of B.E. 2380, year of the Cock" (late 1837 or early 1838, as we have seen), was finished in "B.E. 2381, year of the Rat." But B.E. 2381 (A.D. 1838/39) was a year of the dog; the nearest year of the Rat was B.E. 2383 or 1840/41. Further, it is difficult to imagine how a canal the size and length of Khlāūng Sāēn Sāēb could have been dug in a year or a little more. We thus accept the year of the Rat in our second source, but reject the B.E. 2381 as an error for B.E. 2383 or 1840/41.

But one may ask how an operation of the magnitude of the construction of the thirty-four-mile-long Sāēn Sāēb canal could have been completed even within three years. The local context of the times suggests that the job had to be done in a hurry. Construction was begun just at a time when the tangled affairs of Thailand and Cambodia were building up to their final crisis before French intervention. Rama III had ordered Chao Phrayā Bōdin to fortify Battambang and then praised him for his speed in completing the task in a single year. Then Phrayā Srīphiphat Rā-tanarātchakosa (That Bunnag, brother of Chao Phrayā Phraklāng, Dit Bunnag, who was busy with rebellion in Malaya) received his orders to begin digging Sāēn Sāēb canal in early 1838. In that same summer Phrayā Rātchasuphawadi fortified Siemreap, finishing within nine months in early 1839. Clearly, speed was the order of the day. Early in the year in which the strategic canal was finished, Bōdin was sent back into Cambodia with an armed force, and later that year full Thai mobiliza-tion was ordered. The canal running eastward would have been conceived as an important logistic aid to both military and construction operations on the far frontiers of Cambodia. Prince Bōdin, the Thai military leader in the east, would often have come this way before his death in April 1849. A century later, at Lōlae on the banks of Khlāūng Sāēn Sāēb, the chief (kamnan) of Kannā Jāo commune informed us that the canal "was dug by Chao Phrayā Bōdin" (LS 12/31/48).

Establishing the date 1840/41 for the completion of Sāēn Sāēb canal, rather than a date a twelve-year cycle later, is of relevance not only to the mighty affairs of state of the Thai and Khmer or the humble early history of Bang Chan, but also to the development of the modern rice export trade of Siam. It is safe to assume that the canal was originally planned primarily for military purposes, as we have noted, and its potential role in helping develop the lands between the Chao Phrayā and Bāng Pa Khong rivers was at first perhaps hardly appreciated. Yet this area rapidly became a major Thai rice basket, and still is, contributing heavily to the outstanding position achieved by Thailand as an exporter of quantities of high-grade rice (Silcock 1970). It has been too easily assumed that this process, one of "reproductive development" in which essentially unchanging technologies are simply expanded in quantity, did not begin until the middle 1850s under Rama IV, abetted by his land policies, the Bowring Treaty, ocean steamers, and the Suez Canal. Our reconstruction suggests the process started eastward of Bangkok some fifteen years earlier. It involved the old Southeast Asian state pattern of settling captured, often alien populations on strategic empty lands. In this case, a major facility was provided, the new canal that gave easy access to the Bangkok market and helped to make the capital the primate city of the realm.

Perhaps another important factor in the early agricultural development of this eastern subdivision of the central plains was the Chinese population, which helped link rice farmers and fisher folk to Bangkok and eventually to the world market. Some five thousand Chinese workers were hired by royal authority to help dig Saen Saeb canal (Thiphakarawong 1934b:179; Min. Ag. 1956:133). Some who had not fallen by the wayside would have seen the canal's busyness during its first years and would have established themselves along its banks as entrepreneurs and brokers between their own city business kin and the new Malay, Lao, and Thai settlers in the countryside, thus contributing eventually to the commercialization of rice growing in the area.

Somewhere in our field notes we have information on the quantity of central plains muck that can be dug by a worker in a day. This figure might enable us to work out some estimate of the amount of time it would have taken five thousand Chinese to excavate Saen Saeb canal. We have not embarked on this endeavor because we do not know that the canal work force was limited to the Chinese. We note that Rama III's decree made Phraya Sriphiphat Ratanaratchakosa, who had quasi-ministerial status, director of the canal project. As such, and if he were under pressure to rush the work, as he apparently was, he could have called upon clients of the *phraklang* to serve as workers in addition to the Chinese he had authority to hire. Clients of the Interior Department (Mahad Thai) would presumably have been engaged in military service and thus not available.

9. While prisoner-of-war slaves were owned by and brought to the king as his right, he frequently rewarded his generals by giving them prisoners (Wales 1934:60).

It is our assumption that the area near Bang Chan canal was awarded by Rama III to Chao Phraya Phraklang (Dit Bunnag) rather than to some other of the illustrious Bunnags. Our reason is simply that both he and the land were so closely associated with the Moslem prisoners from the south who would have been acquired during the Third Reign, and mostly before 1840. In the 1840s he would also have been interested in the eastern defenses, the new canal, and the need to settle empty lands in that direction. He died in 1855, during the Fourth Reign, having been inactive for some time.

Another Bunnag, That, brother of Chao Phraya Phraklang, would also have had an interest in land lying along Saen Saeb canal, for as Phraya Sriphiphat Ratanaratchakosa he was in charge of its construction. The Bang Chan site might well have been given to him by Rama III as a reward for his work.

Our Bang Chan informants tend to associate their Governor's Mound (Khok Chuan) with the most famous of the Bunnags, Chuang, who in 1851, on the accession of Rama IV, received the title Chao Phraya Srisurijawong, and who served as prime minister and also, during the early years of the Fifth Reign, as regent. His great power might have been sensed and remembered even by country folk who had little to do with him on his visits to a family residence in Bang Chan. We suspect that in referring to him they may have sometimes meant his father; and this would seem explicit when they speak of "Somdet Chao Phrayā Srīsurijawong the elder" (LMH 8/6/57), for the father was often called the "elder Somdet Chao Phrayā" (*Somdet Chao Phrayā ong yai*). Nevertheless, the land in Bang Chan may have been given to the more recent Bunnag by Rama IV.

10. Aside from the testimony of Thiphakarawong, we base this estimate on: (*a*) our evidence for a tendency to settle the more accessible areas first; thus the Moslem village was settled before Chāēm, Bang Chan's first resident, moved to a more inaccessible spot upstream on Bang Chan canal; (*b*) the local tradition that a man, Lō, had married a woman, Lae, and settled at Lōlae, now at the junction of Sāēn Sāēb and Bang Chan canals, *before* Sāēn Sāēb was completed (LS 12/31/48); they would have formed a local nucleus of settlement; (*c*) genealogical testimony of Nāng Dāēng Tongridtha, said to have been born in Bang Chan in 1867 (JRH 2/18/54; LMH 7/30/57). She was the twelfth of fourteen children, all born in Bang Chan, so that her parents could not have reached Bang Chan later than 1857. Her father's brother (Chāēm's older brother) reached Bang Chan after her father, but this uncle had a child born in Bang Chan in the 1850s, according to our Sangthāūng genealogy. Thus the first settler could not have come later than 1857 and may have come some years before that.

11. There are routes by which one could proceed more directly, but we have not determined just how much of the present canal system was in existence in the 1850s. Padungkrungkasem canal was finished in 1852 and may have connected with the present Bāngkapi canal (Thiphakarawong 1934a:77).

12. It would seem likely that a person seeking a new residence in this area would come during the hot season in order to locate permanent water. Besides, a household should be ready before the rains in June to plant a rice patch and garden.

13. This type of house occurs today as it occurred a century ago (see Pallegoix 1854, 2:208–209).

14. Janlekha (1957:104–120) shows labor distribution for a family of nine on a modern wet rice farm of about twenty acres(forty-nine rai).He ascertained the man-hours devoted to rice cultivation. Four adults of the family studied spent 5,478.5 man-hours over 248 days. This averages 4.5 hours of work per day per person, but workdays are much longer at the beginning and end of the growing season. Work includes plowing and harrowing with buffalo, planting, uprooting, transplanting, and harvesting. Weeding is not a major problem in modern Bang Chan.

15. Hauck et al. (1958:78) found that for the preparation of meals an average 3.5 hours were required for a sample of eleven households. The range was 0.8–4.1 hours. These figures do not include time spent on the tangential tasks of gathering fuel and certain foodstuffs that grow wild. The work is done by one person.

16. As far as possible, we use the categorical terms "grandparents" and "aunts and uncles." Only when the distinction is important according to Thai usage shall we differentiate the grandparents further, as the villagers do. Thus the Thai distinguish between father's father and his male siblings (*pū*), father's mother and her female siblings (*jā*), mother's father and his male siblings (*tā*), and mother's mother and her female siblings (*jāj*). Similarly we shall not follow Thai distinctions within the category "aunts and uncles" unless necessary: mother's or father's older brothers (*lung*), mother's or father's older sisters (*pā*), father's younger siblings (*ā*), and mother's younger siblings (*nā*).

17. We offer the following definition: Inheritance occurs when established procedures exist for a donor to convey property to another person, ordinarily a kinsman, when the donor is dead. Automatic transfer, as under Islamic law, meets this definition. We believe that the customary Thai procedures fail to meet this

definition. Property abandoned for anyone to claim is not conveyed and hence is not an inheritance. A Thai who intends to give an object to another must do so before he dies. Dead men cannot give, and Thai custom seems to provide for no such role as that of executor. The so-called laws of inheritance merely supply rules by which the survivors divide residual property on a share basis. Strangely, the Thai word for inheritance (*maundok* or *māuradok*), translated literally, means the abundance or returns or product of death.

18. The word *phī* refers to siblings elder than oneself and to children of parents' older siblings. The word *naūng* is used for siblings younger than oneself and children of parents' younger siblings. These names have now been extended to refer to an indefinite variety of cousins, according to whether they are one's juniors or seniors. These designations are variously modified by *chāj* and *sāo* to distinguish sex; e.g., phī chāj = elder brother, naūng sāo = younger sister. Prefixed to *saphaj*, they refer to the wife of a younger or elder brother; with *kōēj*, they indicate the husband of a younger or elder sister.

19. The term "nuclear family" generally implies husband, wife, and unmarried children, but in our usage the unit may also comprise the following: widows or widowers and children; man or woman with a second spouse and the children of one or more marriages; a childless couple. The ages of the children and the ages of the parents are not important, though the definition may include a very aged parent being cared for by unmarried adult children. Using this definition for nuclear family, we found, in our 1957 census of hamlet 7 in Kannā Jāo, 22 nuclear families out of 44 households. They include the following composition of nuclear families:

15 households of husband, wife, and children
3 households of husband, second wife, and children of present and/or other
  marriages
2 households of husband and children
2 households of husband and wife

The view that equates "family" with "household" is expressed by Prince Dilock: "Unter Familie versteht man nach siamesischen Begriffen nicht nur die Familienangehörigen als solche, sondern auch die ganze Gesinde einschliesslich Sklaven, Hörige und deren Angehörige" (1908:96). Herbert Phillips reaches somewhat the same conclusion:

> . . . the question of who lives with whom simply is not one of overriding importance; as long as individuals can live together without discord, act in terms of the household's established patterns of superordination and subordination, contribute labor or money to the family larder commensurate with their ages, and not inconvenience each other, they will be welcomed into the household; if unable or unwilling to fulfill such elementary obligations, they may take their leave, even if they are in fact full-fledged members of the nuclear household. [1963:49–50]

20. Janlekha (1957:28) found in 1953 that of the 298 households of Bang Chan, 5 percent consisted of single persons, 60 percent were made up of nuclear families, 8 percent of nuclear families plus at least one parent of the older generation, and 27 percent of nuclear families plus at least one parent of the older generation plus collaterals of any generation plus married children's spouses and children. These last two types we recognize as stem families.

21. See notes 16 and 18. We are indebted to George Murdock (1960:5–7) for pointing to the plethora of kinsmen that these cognatic kinship systems of the Eskimo type may offer a person. Neither Murdock, his contributors, nor Davenport (1959) have dealt with the necessary auxilliary devices for selecting from these

kinsmen the ones to receive special intimacies. For secondary or further removed members of ego's personal or sibling kindred, the central Thai kinship system does not clearly provide well-defined roles, such as the mother's brother in Australia and the Trobriand Islands, or indicate relationships preferred for reinforcement, such as parallel cousin marriage among the Jews of Genesis. Instead, it seems to provide models for intimate relations between any two people. Thus when men of the same age group are intimate, they act like brothers; when men further apart in age are intimate, they act as father and son. We and our wives have acted as "parents" for visiting Thai students, and these students have often responded by signing letters as sons and daughters. Phillips (HPP 7/18/57) quotes a father who told his son as he went to live with a relative: "Now you are your uncle's boy."

22. The various forces, influences, and entities to which Thai refer in connection with life, mind, and spirit are far from systematized. The *winjān* soul is sometimes said to enter a child when it first stirs in the mother's womb, sometimes to enter with the first breath. Villagers in Bang Chan do not readily distinguish it from what Robert Textor (1960:336–341) calls *khwan-soul*, which also enters and may leave a child, causing sickness. There seem to be few references to either of these entities at death, but many to what Textor (1960:312–323) calls "suppressed corpse ghost" and to ghosts, possessed by everyone, called *chētaphūd*. George McFarland (1944:256), however, translates this word as "self; life; soul."

23. Collective terms for persons in the great-grandparental generation occur in the kinship vocabulary. *Thuad* compounded with the grandfather terms indicates parents of paternal grandfather, paternal grandmother, and so on (McFarland 1944:399; Kingshill 1960:235). Sharp also reports collective terms in the great-grandparental generation for all males (*thuad*) and for all females (*chuad*) (LS 12/5/48). In the grandparental generation kinsmen are distinguished by sex and by relationship with ego through either the father or the mother, as indicated in note 16.

24. Sharp et al. (1953:78–79) report for Bang Chan: "Of the 288 households in the community there are twenty-nine which include a son's wife (patrilocal) and twenty which include a daughter's husband (matrilocal)." By 1953 the proportion was about even (Janlekha 1957:38). As we have observed previously, the majority of households contain various additions to the nuclear family.

25. Some hunting spears were still preserved in Bang Chan in 1948, and the pellet bow was used not only to frighten birds from ripening rice but occasionally for hunting (LS 1/28/49). Old Nāj Sud still had a reputation as a hunter, as his father had before him (LS 9/20/48).

26. The record is silent on whether these Moslem slaves had to raise pigs for their lord. Pig culture in Bang Chan hardly survived the Pacific war (Sharp et al. 1953:199; Janlekha 1957:22).

Chapter 3: *Newcomers*

1. A thorough comparison of the differing forms of contractual arrangement would be appropriate at this point; we wish it lay within our capacities. We note only that the European tradition invokes a force superior to the contracting parties to enforce and legitimize agreements: God, power granted by a king, truths held to be self-evident. Thai contracts are made directly with an office or officeholder having well-known and established rights and powers. Questions of legitimacy are simply answered by reference to the existence or absence of an agreement made by an acknowledged office, as if we were dealing with leases or rental agreements held by an established owner. Questions of enforcement do not arise because of the re-

ciprocal form of the agreement: failure on the part of one of the parties automatically terminates the agreement. It then may be renegotiated, as when a landlord whose tenant cannot pay the rent asks, "What rent can you pay?"

Thai law (*kot*) is traditionally not a restraint or a regulation in the sense of a threat of retribution by a superior power in case of breach. A royal decree stated an arrangement of nature and society arising from an office with appropriate powers, and it followed that this was or would soon be a fact. In this sense, like the word of God, the decree was merely descriptive. All other promulgations were contractual offers, such as leases or sales that a citizen might accept or reject to his own satisfaction or regret. In this case law is voluntary, a contract freely entered into. David Wilson (1959:12) quotes a statement of Rama V which reveals these meanings: "There is no law which specifies the royal power in Siam because it is believed to be beyond the law, that there is no rule, thing, or person which can regulate or prevent it. But in truth any act of the king must be appropriate and just. For this reason we have no objection to law." Though clear about the regal decrees, Rama V struggles with the European concept of law. Clearly a king is a being of the world who is constrained to act justly. Law in the Thai sense of contractual agreements entered into voluntarily is nothing to which he objects.

2. A half-dozen types of boats used by the farmers in Bang Chan in the 1940s are described by Sharp et al. (1953:128–129), of which the most commonly used is called sampan. This and two other types are illustrated in the Appendix to Kaufman (1960). To these must now be added the fiberglass boats with outboard motors which since about 1960 have been speeding passengers and goods along the canals of Bang Chan and destroying the quiet that had marked the village waterways since the beginning (LS 4/4/60). Just what types of boats were generally used in the 1850s and 1860s we do not know. We thus employ the word "sampan" to refer to any of the boats rather than to a particular type.

3. The prices of dried fish and plā salid exported from Bangkok are given by Dilock for the decade 1896–1905 (1908: App. to S. 191). The price and quantity vary widely from year to year, suggesting considerable annual variability in the availability of fish, both salt and freshwater varieties. Whether or not the inland price varied equally, we do not know.

Charges for handling fish in the Bangkok markets are now stabilized at rates that villagers feel are reasonable. In the late 1940s owners of private landings in Bangkok charged villagers 7 percent of the price obtained for their fish in exchange for a landing place, coffee to drink, labor for unloading, and a place where purchasing agents could buy from the villager (LS 6/10/49).

4. Loebongse Sarabhaja kindly sought to determine the precise date of the founding of this temple, now known as Bam Phen Temple North (Wat Bam Phen Nya). The precise dates were not given in any source available to him; it was variously considered to have been built as early as 1824 and as late as 1851. If our estimates for the building of Sǣn Sǣb canal are correct, it could not have been built before 1841, the date for the completion of the canal on which it stands. We guess that it was not built before 1860.

5. One reference only to this village in a report by Vichitr Saengmani during 1957 gives the name of the Laotian village as Bān Dāun Sī Phūm, or Village of the Rise of Earthly Splendor. It seems quite likely that this was the actual name used by the inhabitants. Today the few who can remember anything of it refer to it as Mound of Earthly Splendor (Khōk Sī Phūm), giving it a name as a landmark. We believe it consistent with the habit of Laotians to name their villages.

6. Certainly *Bangkok Calendar* (1865:129–132) and other publications, as well as

the American consul, helped keep the capital informed of events in America. Bastian (1867:15) even reports a conversation in an outlying district with a provincial official in 1863 during which the two spoke of world events, among which they mentioned with some distress the American Civil War.

7. Van der Heide (1906) notes the increased value of lands during the nineteenth century, and James Ingram (1955:63) comments:

> The suggestion has been made that the relatively painless elimination of slavery was possible because the wealthy class could, after trade began, receive income from the rent of land, while before trade began land had no value and could earn no contractual rent, and the wealthy class had to receive its income from slave labor. It is certainly true that the price of land increased during the last half of the nineteenth century and the first decades of the twentieth, and that there was an increase in tenancy by contract, but for neither of these facts is there much detailed evidence.

As will be shown in greater detail in Chapter 4, rentals in the city of Bangkok seem to have been common for many years, but rents from rural lands as a source of income were rare because of the availability of uncleared land. The Rangsit project was an exception to the general rule. We suggest that the value of slave labor declined during the nineteenth century as imports increased. The wealthy slaveholders needed cash rather than extensive services. The cost of large retinues of slaves, who were often tax liabilities, became uneconomical in a money economy.

8. As we have observed in Chapter 2, note 18, Thai kinship nomenclature does not distinguish siblings from children of parents' siblings. Children of parents' elder siblings are called "elder sibling," of parents' younger siblings "younger sibling"; age with respect to ego has no bearing. The social scheme implied by this usage appears to limit the effective group of cooperators to siblings with the same parents, i.e., real and half brothers and sisters, when status in the group of siblings is determined by actual age or birth order with respect to ego. When cousins of a remoter degree wish to join a venture, however, the sibling category, particularly that of younger sibling, seems to be exploitable (See Chapter 5 for documentation). Also available are the children of all siblings or cousins of the same generation as ego, who together with ego's children's children are collectively called *lān*. We shall translate this as "nephew" or "niece" in the Thai sense when the connection to ego is chiefly lateral. In un-Thai fashion we shall use the term "grandchild" when the connection to ego is predominantly linear.

9. Of the twenty households said to have once lived in the Village of the Mound of Earthly Splendor we have been able to track down only three from their descendants. Memories of the other households have disappeared. The relationship between these three households cannot demonstrate at this time in Bang Chan's history the kindred nature of a hamlet. This point will become evident as we explore the developments in other hamlets of the area. Here we simply call attention to a tendency for intermarriage within a hamlet, as well as the tendency of kinsmen to settle together.

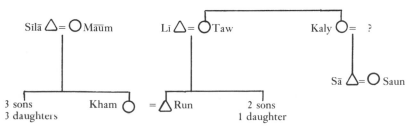

10. The comparatively tight control of behavior found in Moslem communities is described by Thomas Fraser (1960:153–154). In Bang Chan, too, the committee of the surao functions in many ways as a board of elders for all religious and many secular affairs. The imam, having religious charge of 147 households in three tambons, compared his position to that of a district officer, proudly ranking himself above local hamlet headmen or commune chiefs (LS 11/17/48).

This organization is related to the concept of society as part of a superhuman organization in which the leaders enforce the will of Allah. Theravada Buddhism, with its reference to salvation by individual choice, and not in one life only but in many lives through repeated reincarnations, proffers no such tools to any social authority. A subject obeys his king or his lesser patron because of the benefits he derives, and, at least with regard to the patron, he is often free to alter his allegiance (Wales 1934:53; Rabibhadana 1969). To be sure, Thai society is a portion of the cosmic order, but all rules are voluntary, and if a man wishes to risk reincarnation as a woman or a dog in the next existence, individual salvation is merely postponed. The cosmic order is not the enforceable design of affairs as they ought to be but instead a setting for all varieties of creatures with all varieties of impulse, who, through acquiring or losing merit, may now or later move up the scale of progress toward salvation or down away from it, fluctuating as they move from one life to another, or following a more steady course in either direction as they choose to behave consistently through their many lives.

Chapter 4: *Migration*

1. Unfortunately we are unable to reconstruct the picture of land tenure and rentals within the city of Bangkok from studies, if such exist. Our description has been inferred from accounts of foreigners who secured land in the past and from our own experiences with rental arrangements in the present city. Housing seems to have been chronically in short supply, and hence being allowed to live in a given location has long been a privilege, for which one willingly pays a special fee to some agent able to evict one person and admit another.

2. To the statement of Wales we add that of Dilock:

> The smallest landholdings have an area of 3 rai, the largest about 10,000 rai, rarely more. The smallest landholdings of 3–4 rai are not very numerous. They serve mostly for personal use as kitchen gardens for such persons as officials who are prevented by their occupation from busying themselves with cultivation. . . . A [peasant] family uses generally 80–100 rai, sometimes also up to 200 rai, if the land is low and lies on the shore and is favored by annual flooding. In the higher lying neighborhoods, however, where no flooding occurs, or where this stops at the same time as the rain, there are few families that can work more than 30 or 40 rai, at most 60 rai. [1908:72]

In Bang Chan few farmers initially held more than fifty rai. These lands were flooded every year, though before the erection of water gates in 1910 the water was not so deep as it is today. Farmers tell us that few worked more than ten rai of rice because little more than that acreage could be kept free of weeds (LMH 8/4/57). Indeed, until 1890 a plot of five rai or less seems to have been the common area of cultivation in Bang Chan for a single household.

3. When one considers that during all Thai history until very recently all land except that in urban areas had little or no value and that most Thai assumed a casual attitude toward it, it seems anomalous that position in the government hierarchy was measured in terms of land (*sakdinā*). Wales recognizes this anomaly but treats it as a survival of a feudal era (1934:46–50). If we may believe that land was no scarcer

in the past than in the nineteenth century, it seems unreasonable to infer an earlier land-based feudal system. All are clear in affirming that *nā*, though meaning literally an open field, refers in this context to labor force rather than to acreage alone (see, e.g., Pramoj 1955) and thus to a man-land ratio. Why a ranking system uses as its unit a measure of worthless land rather than one for valuable people, until recently always in short supply, is a good topic for further study.

4. George McFarland (1944:16) translates *kamsith* as "a monopoly; a just claim of ownership." We may gain some further sense of its meaning by tracing its roots: *kam* is a word of Sanskrit origin meaning "labor, toil, work, deeds, 'karma' "; *sitthi*, also of Sanskrit origin, means "accomplishment, success, prosperity, affluence, happiness" (McFarland 1944:15,865).

5. We agree with Wales's suggestion (1934:122) that "usufructuary" comes close to the Thai concept of landowner. We would add, however, that the power and the right to control land, in the sense of an exclusive monopoly on its use, is also an element. Perhaps monopoly has further ramifications in the Thai concept of power (*amnād*) and its delegation; the right of others than the king to tax and to fish were delegated monopolies during the reign of Rama IV, with appropriate powers of enforcement also delegated and supported by the king.

6. These phobias seem to gain some of their force from their association with historic moves by which many of these nations were founded. The successful Saxon, Norman, or Ch'in invader feared invasion; the successful unifier of a people under his power feared being conquered by the people themselves, while the declarers of independence declared a moratorium on further such declarations.

7. On the village level this fear of abandonment becomes the fear of loss of household members. Birth rites from contemporary Bang Chan are filled with devices to keep a child home: the blessing enjoins a child "to stay at home like the bottom of the house post"; the umbilical cord is buried under the staircase or a tree so that the part may hold the whole (J. R. Hanks 1963). As a child grows up, parents worry about "roaming" (paj thiaw) and hint of dire consequences. People caution against adopting children lest they leave home. Those whose grown children remain at home are deemed most fortunate. Later, parents worry about whether their children will look after them during their old age. A well-known Thai aphorism runs: "One parent can look after many children, but it takes many children to look after one parent." In the declining years this fear of isolation becomes so great that parents attempt to retain a claim over their children by withholding considerable amounts of property from distribution until after death. An old lady complained about the taxes on her land but said she could not divide up her land among her children because then they would not take care of her (LMH 8/17/57).

8. Hanks (1962) enlarges on a nuclear conception of Thai society in which the majority of clients are ideally attached to patrons high in the hierarchy. These clients change patrons less often than clients attached to patrons lower in the hierarchy. Stability is greatest at the top of the hierarchy and diminishes at lower levels. During periods of disorder and population decline following military defeat, the size and stability of social units decline as clients exercise their right to change patrons more freely.

9. In 1870 the fear of a vanishing population was expressed by the editor of the *Siam Repository*:

> Immigration should be encouraged. The uncultivated wastes of prolific Siam can sustain an immense population. This population can be acquired only by offering inducements to other races to come and make their home in Siam. . . . People will want to come and stay and not as now wish to run

away and escape burdensome taxation and requirements of personal service. There would be no need of groups of officials at all the mountain passes to prevent the escape of Siamese subjects fleeing a country where they can never become independent of greedy masters who are protected by the laws of the country. [*Siam Repository* 1870:351]

Government was again taking no chances that the populace would vanish. Indeed, the encouragement of Chinese immigration and the favorable terms extended to them, far more favorable than the conditions under which the Siamese themselves lived, may have been related to this fear.

10. Einen ausserordentlich grossen, aber nicht günstigen Einfluss auf das ganze Wirtschaftsleben in Siam hat die buddhistische Religion. Die philosophische Lebensbetrachtung dieser Religion hat das Volk gänzlich betäubt. Sie leistet Widerstand gegen jeden Fortschritt und gegen jede Entwickelung [sic] zu höhere Kultur, gegen die Steigerung der Bedürfnisse und der Bedürfnisbefriedigung, gegen jedes Bestreben, durch höhere Bildung, durch energische und intensive Ewerbstätigkeit, durch grössern Arbeitsfleiss sich einem höheren Lebensgenuss, eine bessere Existenz zu verschaffen und Vermögen zu erwerben, gegen jede wirtschaftliche Konkurrenz u.s.w. und hierin liegt auch ein Hauptgrund dass in Siam wie die Volkswirtschaft überhaupt so auch die Landwirtschaft noch nicht auf einer höheren Stufe steht. [Dilock 1908:108]

David Wyatt reminds us that Bowring (who saw much of the prime minister in Bangkok) was the literary executor of Jeremy Bentham, collector of his works, and his biographer.

11. The term *Nāj Kāūng*, though harmless to the eye of a foreigner, acquired an unsavory character. Applied in Bang Chan to the agent who collects rents for a landlord, it came to imply exploitation of tenants. None wished to be addressed as Nāj Kāūng.

12. Ingram (1955:55–56) states: " . . . they [the Thai] have left most other [than agricultural] entrepreneurial functions to foreigners. The cultivation of rice is an ancient and honorable occupation, however, and they seem to have preferred it to all others. . . . The Thai have preferred the communal life of the village, and it is not easy to break the ties of culture and tradition which have induced him to become a rice farmer." We would rephrase Ingram's appeal to tradition as follows: Most Thai consider agricultural work disagreeable and would avoid it if possible. Many, however, commonly grow their own food, much as most American households of the nineteenth century did. Living in a city and working for wages—in other words, living without produce of one's own—seemed excessively hazardous, for most Thai, unlike the Chinese, were unaccustomed to highly developed service occupations. Many urban Thai depended on country cousins to produce their rice and send it to them, rather than buying it through commercial channels. Thus it was not agriculture that Thai preferred but the security of a plot of land in the face of urban uncertainties.

Skinner accounts for the scarcity of ordinary Thai in commercial life by saying that they (a) were held as clients by noblemen and (b) lacked the skills necessary for urban life (1957: 96–97, 103). Certainly some clients were held, for it became necessary in the late 1890s to set terms that ended bondage (Lingat 1931:272). According to Rama IV, others had become so dependent on their patrons that they did not wish to leave (see p. 82). Yet were anyone seriously eager to seek a new job, it was not out of the question to transfer from one patron to another, and freemen, according to our understanding of the patron-client relationship, could be deserted by patrons or could leave a patron. For Thai on the lower ranges of the economic scale, being bound to a patron was not the chief problem; rather, and we agree with Skinner on this point, it was the lack of marketable skills. A skilled person, like the Laotian carpenters, could always make his way in the city (see p. 87).

Thus the majority of migrants into the countryside were clients displaced for one reason or another. Without patrons or other means of making their way in the city, they sought to live as cheaply as possible by growing their own food and marketing enough surplus to buy a few extra things.

This argument, of course, is not relevant to the problem of why Thai on the upper social and economic levels failed to become entrepreneurs, leaving to foreigners, and especially at all levels to the Chinese, the crucial economic operations that would provide so many needed bridges and structural links over which the traffic of all traditional Thai society could move in slow transition toward a modern polity. This problem we have discussed elsewhere (Sharp 1968).

13. Dilock (1908) gives the wages for Chinese workers about the turn of the century as varying between 625 and 937 baht per year. These figures, strikingly high, agree fairly well with those quoted by Skinner (1957:217–218) for the period 1930–1937 for Chinese skilled labor (craftsmen, foremen, office workers), while they are well above the pre-Depression wage of about one baht per day for Chinese unskilled labor. As Ingram (1955:56) states that wages in the city around 1900 were indeed high, conceivably few changes occurred during the intervening thirty years.

14. Further indication of the organizing power of the Chinese is shown by a series of short work stoppages beginning in 1889 and the general strike of 1910 (Skinner 1957: 116–117, 162–163).

15.   In the rear of Wat Leap inside of the city walls is a settlement of Laos. The original settlement was composed of Laos taken by the Siamese at the capture and overthrow of Wiang Chan [Vientiane], one of the eastern Laos provinces, some thirty years ago. Those brought to the capital were nearly all made slaves to the king and put into mechanical departments. A few were blacksmiths, but the greater part became carpenters. A large part of the carpentry work on the palaces and public buildings has been done by the Laos slaves. [*Siam Repository* 1870:335]

16. We consider a corporate society to be one in which all members are organized ultimately under at least one single superordinate institution, such as church or state, which endures longer than any individual's term of office or membership. Traditional Thailand was not so organized. The king's rule was indirect, for people owed allegiance to their patrons, and only those patrons who stood next to the king owed him direct allegiance as vassals. And allegiance, like all traditional Thai relations between patron and client, was a voluntary affair; the volition of vassals at a distance from the capital, the nuclear core of the kingdom, might sometimes waver and require some coercive reaction from the center.

Not until late in the nineteenth century, during the reign of Rama V, were efforts begun to unify all people under a national state ruled directly from the throne. The Conscription Law of 1904 exemplifies one facet of the trend toward a corporate society; then the state undertook to levy troops directly; earlier each of the local rulers had levied troops on demand. Such local, often hereditary chiefs as the *chao myang*, or lords of towns, were incorporated into the national civil service or deprived of the office, which was officially abolished.

The function of the state as well as its organization changed. The state made social life possible by upholding the Buddhist religion (see statement of Rama II, p. 81) as well as by exercising its superior powers (Heine-Geldern 1956). The people contributed to social order by building fortifications against external enemies and temples against internal ones. Kings, so often named Rama after the hero of the Indian epic, symbolized a defense of morality and social order. Not until the middle of the nineteenth century under Rama IV did the state consider that its duties included the nourishment of its people (and itself) through public aid to trade and production. Only under Rama V did this concern extend to education, health, transport, and other social services.

17. Among the various ways of claiming extra land illegally the following are mentioned: (1) clearing into the land of another and claiming the land cleared; (2) using neighboring land for pasturing buffalo; (3) taking land by bribing a local official (VIC 7/18/57).

Chapter 5: *The New Life*

1. We have never heard the claim made by any scholar, yet it is possible that some of the fables, traceable as literary forms to India, may once have had among their purposes instruction in the analysis of events that befell people in everyday life. Through these tales the moral forces in the universe might be more clearly perceived. The *Panchatantra* can be regarded as a lampoon of what may once have been a serious set of tales told by teachers to their pupils. The parables of Christian tradition seem to share the same instructional purpose, even though the moral forces are not the same.

2. In a physical sense the Thai have a history, for there exists a goodly catalog of inscriptions, annals, and chronicles. Such documents were not written, however, to quicken a dead past or to instruct in its lessons. We surmise that these materials sought to glorify Buddhism, certify the pious achievements of a monarch, or record unusual events, such as comets, which portended future events. Camille Notton (1926:ix) suggests that the Northern Annals seek to restore a former paradise. By Thai standards most events recur in dull and obvious rounds that nature has foreordained. People are born, live, and die to be reborn in slightly different circumstances. A few events are exceptional: bounteous years, foreign invasions. Some of them might be anticipated if one could read the signs correctly, but fundamentally they arise as rewards or punishments for past conduct. The events selected by Western historians overlap these exceptional happenings to some extent, but also include many that Thai do not consider unusual: economic and social events, for example. Another criterion of history, the search for naturalistic antecedents of events, did not come to Thailand until late in the nineteenth century; Prince Damrong Rāchanubhāb was the first Thai historian in this sense.

3. Traditional Thai medicine was not a single discipline but a collection of specialties: expelling spirits, setting bones, preparing medicines. Most Bang Chan practitioners of traditional medicine today know half a dozen or more specialties, learned from practitioners who were willing to share their information. One practitioner enumerated his teachers:

> A priest in Bangkok taught me [as a temple boy] to make medicines for children and later how to cure adults. I spent seven years with this priest. Later, when I resigned, I lived in Bang Sȳ and assisted my mother's brother who was a practitioner (*māū*). After retiring from the police, I entered the priesthood and learned from Phra Jim how to make holy water. Later an old man named Nāj Jiam, who lived in Thonburī, asked me to live with him. I

spent fifteen days there and learned to make holy water. Next Phra Phlāj, a priest at Bang Chan who came from Petchaburī Province, also taught about making holy water. His elder brother, Phra Plasai, also taught me how to make holy water and mix medicines. He lived in Kanchanaburī Province but came to Bang Chan from time to time. Phra Tung lived at a Bangkok temple and taught me how to set broken bones. [LMH 6/4/53]

From each teacher he learned unique formulas and subsequently paid annual ritual thanks (waj khrū) to these teachers in order to keep the knowledge fresh. Doubtless Sin had specialties of these kinds; a man who met him from time to time described another one of these specialties: "People came from all over to get Sin to cure them. He was keen in every disease. In the case of cholera he made a spirit house and then a storm would come. If the house collapsed, the patient would recover. If there were no wind, the patient would die" (LMH 2/6/54).

4. In general, Bang Chan people today turn toward religious contemplation and devotion most intensely after retiring from active farmwork. Sixty years, the fifth return of the twelve-year cycle, is a frequent but by no means fixed time for the change. Instead of attending services only on major holidays, these pious elders begin to attend every week on Priest's Day (Wan Phra). In the 1950s a group of ten to fifteen elderly men and women followed the discipline of priests in certain ways by meeting at the temple for a special sermon, and eating no food between noon and the following morning. Such elders commonly are more devoted to the temple than younger people, and are given to contributing a new building or some new adornment as a mode of making merit. Some say very literally that gold given to the temple may be used in the hereafter (LMH 7/30/57).

5. A priest (phra) differs from a novice (nēn) in age at entering the monastic order and in number of ascetic vows taken. Though in northern Thailand most young men who enter orders do so as teen-aged novices and occasionally become priests at twenty-one, most young men in Bang Chan and the central plains enter after twenty to become full priests. Temple boys (dek wat) take no vows but offer to serve a given priest for an unspecified period. Priests and novices are credited with a year of devotion if they live in the temple one "Lenten" season (Phansā) of approximately three months beginning in July.

6. Households settled on the land they worked. Every house required access to water for transportation as well as domestic use. Married children often located their houses on extensions of the mound of the parents; sometimes they built separate but adjacent mounds for their houses. Thus the spaces between the original settlers gradually filled with new houses located on strips running back from the waterfront.

This plan differs from that of the residential hamlet, where houses are clustered together and farmers travel to and from their fields each day. The earlier Laotian and Moslem prisoner-of-war hamlets in Bang Chan were of this latter type, but both hamlets gave way to dispersed living, presumably during the 1880s. We suggest that the change was brought about by the following factors: (1) Canal or river settlements using water transport, as contrasted with land settlements using wells or ponds and trail or road travel, predispose toward dispersed living. (2) When ownership controls access to land, rights can best be protected by settlement on landholdings. Though the clearing of land rather than residence on it was the legal criterion for preemption, often a man could ensure his claim only by living on it. (3) In the absence of slavery and defensive considerations, anyone with the requisite economic means might form a social nucleus.

7. Our informants' poor recall of detail makes it nearly impossible to find agreement on the precise number of households in the hamlet on any particular date.

When lists of informants' near contemporaries were compared, it was found that about 20 percent of the names on each list—usually the names of members of the informant's own kin cluster—appeared on no other list. Agreement on the principal persons of any kinship cluster was much better.

We offer the following diagrams of three of the four kin clusters that settled together. The two Laotian households probably consisted of kinsmen, though we were unable to confirm this assumption.

Unspecified cousins are indicated by broken lines. A household exists when the spouses are named.

1. Khlāūng Tej kin group of Sin (LMH 8/7/57):

2. Khlāūng Tej kin group Sathānsab (LMH 7/25/57; Sathānsab genealogy):

3. Bāngkapi kin group (LMII 8/26/57):

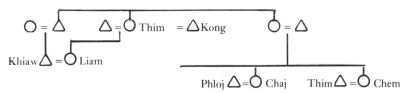

The formation of kin clusters depends on the cooperation of laterally connected kinsmen, usually of the same generation. We may observe that cousins, probably beyond the first degree, may be included. More frequently, however, kin clusters are made up of children of the same parents.

8. We have not attempted to establish the dates of the first trading establishment in the area of Sāēn Sāēb canal. We would expect the first area with shops to have been at or near Bam Phen temple, founded in the 1850s or 1860s. Probably the region's producers of fish and padi had to deal with markets nearer Bangkok until the 1880s. Our earliest reference to shopping in Minburi may be set in the 1890s; the informant, who speaks of her husband's buying and selling in that market, could not

have married much earlier than 1885 (LMH 8/4/57). By 1902/03 the town of Minburī apparently had enough importance as a market center to be chosen as the administrative headquarters of a province (*myang* or, later, *changwat*) of the same name within the Bangkok Circle or Region (Monthon Krungthēp), according to a report by the Education and Religious Director for the region (Thai National Archives, 5 S, 26/12; Phra Thammatrailōkāchān, 31 August 1903). Our earliest reference to stores at Lōlae, the junction of Bang Chan's rivulet with Sāen Sāeb canal, gives an approximate date of 1910, though these commercial establishments, like the settlement itself, may have been in existence much earlier (LS 12/31/48; LMH 3/1/54).

9. The main concern was with the timing of the rain rather than with the total quantity that would fall during any wet season. Some contemporary farmers claimed that the total amount of water made available by the nagas (in this context primitive rainbow serpents in charge of the heavenly water department and able to send rain by spurting water from their mouths) was the same from year to year, but that sometimes the nagas neglected to distribute their rain properly through the growing season. Others pointed out that in certain years only one large naga reigned; as he received all offerings and prayers, he provided a proper return. Only in the years when many small nagas were in charge was there confusion and bad timing (LS 7/2/49).

Present-day rice varieties thrive in the normal rhythm of precipitation in the central plain: heavy rains in June soften the soil; in July and August rainfall is more moderate as the young plants get their start; in September and October come the heaviest daily rainfalls as the rice rapidly shoots upward and reaches full maturity. Variations in this pattern, in floodwaters flowing down from the north, in temperature, in sunlight, and in plant disease and pests create variations from year to year in the crop harvested per unit of land, and these may seem more serious to the rice grower who seeks a maximum surplus to sell for cash than to the subsistence farmer who seeks to produce what he would like to consume, but may have to consume only what he produces. Complete crop failures appear to have been rare; Ministry of Agriculture records show four years of damaging floods and four years of extreme drought since 1831 (Min. Ag. 1950). Anxiety concerning rice may be more closely related to social tensions than to technological disabilities.

10. Alcohol is usually drunk for conviviality, and the later stages of drunkenness result in no more than increased amiability. Two or three cases of habitual drinking could be related to personal distresses. During the 1950s one of the best educated young men of the area took to drink during a period of depression and eventually lost his government job because of irregularity at work. A second man drank excessively when his farm and his domestic life were failing. People also brace themselves for theft or violence by drinking. In explaining why they rated fellow members of the community high or low in general prestige, informants gave avoidance of liquor as a most important attribute of persons judged to have much prestige, while drinking (associated with troublemaking, gambling, and poverty) led to lack of respect and low prestige (Sharp et al. 1953:105–109). Nevertheless, drinking is not considered a totally unsavory habit. According to the Sentence Completion Test data collected by H. P. Phillips, drinking may be regarded negatively, as in the following examples: "*He wanted to be:* a person who did not drink and gamble"; "*He is unattractive:* because he drinks and takes drugs." But the following responses were also given: "*A wonderful thing was:* liquor. When he drank he was intoxicated; it was fun"; "*Most like him because he:* drank whiskey and because he works well" (HPP 1957).

11. The traditional Thai calendar sets a lunar year with extra days added every

four years. Each of the thirteen months was divided into numbered days of the waxing and waning moon. The religious calendar introduced to this system a variable week with Priest's Day (Wan Phra) at the first of each moon and each subsequent quarter. This calendar was used at the Bang Chan temple and the local government school through the 1950s. Years are variously designated: in Bang Chan the building of the sanctuary of the temple was dated according to a system that counted years from the founding of the present Chakkri dynasty of kings, A.D. 1781; the inscription reads: "125 Ratana-kosindi-sok," or "Bangkok Era 125," that is, A.D. 1906. In translating such a date for foreigners, or in naming a year for most events, people of Bang Chan commonly refer to the year in their version of the Chinese twelve-year cycle, such as the "year of the Horse" (1942, 1954, 1966). More recent signs in the temple bear dates in the Buddhist Era, counted from the Lord Buddha's death, which in Thailand is equated with 543 B.C. This system is used by the Thai government, together with the Western solar calendar of twelve months; today all Bangkok and most businesses throughout the country operate on this calendar.

12. Two of the many gambling games were described: (1) *Tua*: A cross is marked on the ground with quadrants numbered 1 to 4. Each of four players chooses a quadrant and bets to win on that quadrant. Bets are equal. A dealer deals an unknown number of counters into four equal piles. The number of counters left over when four or fewer counters remain designates the winner. If one is left over, the first quadrant wins; if two, the second quadrant; and so on. (2) *Pō*: A cross is made on the ground. Each person chooses a quadrant and bets are placed as in tua. A counter covered by a container is shaken over the intersection. The quadrant in which the counter lies when the cover is removed designates the winner. (LMH 12/22/53).

These games seem to have lost favor in recent years, and a game in which playing cards are dealt for high- and low-card winners is now popular. Success in gambling is magically induced by small pieces of wax over which a priest has said the proper words, and by certain unusual objects called *lūk krāuk*:

My father liked gambling. One night a cat bore a kitten but not a normal one; it was small and dead. When this happens, it is a good sign. So father made a little pillow to put the dead cat on and kept it under a glass. I dreamed of the cat, that it came with its neck broken and asked me to set it. The cat said that if I set its neck, it would give me all I wanted. I did not do so, and then I awoke. One day my father took the cat to Bangkok to gamble but did not win. It was because the cat had a broken neck. So the cat at last rotted and no one wanted to keep it, and it was thrown away. [LMH 7/7/57]

13. It was said that on the three days of New Year (the final two days of the waning fourth moon and the first day of the waxing fifth moon of the lunar year) the spirits were permitted to roam about freely. A special cannon was fired in Bangkok to announce the holiday to the spirit world. In the evening in villages throughout the central plains a girl was blindfolded and seated on an inverted rice mortar, while the company sang to invite one of a number of spirits to enter her. Mother Splendor (Mae Si) was the favorite, according to our Bang Chan informants. Textor (1960:368–376) lists five other frequently invited spirits ("windborne monkey ghost, fish ghost, coconut half shell ghost, winnowing basket ghost, creeping snail ghost"), to which we would add two more: one named Phrām Keson, and frog spirit (*phī yngāng*) (JRH 11/25/53).

The following is a translation of the song inviting Mother Splendor:

Mother Splendor, youthful one, people will admire you when you lift up your hands together to show respect for the priest. You have wonderful eyebrows that join together and round-shaped delicate hairs at the nape of your neck. Be praised when covering your breasts with a sheet of cloth. Mother Splendor, heavenly youth, may you be invited to come down. Mother Splendor, the golden rod, may flutes and drums be invited down with you. May the gods of all eight directions be invited, especially the eminent ones. [JRH 11/25/53]

14. By 1910, twenty-odd years after the first settlement, intermarriage had occurred between three of the four clusters of kinsmen. The Khlaūng Tej group, led by Uncle Sin, married only within its own cluster or outside the hamlet. The other group from Khlaūng Tej intermarried with the Laotian descendants and the group from Bāngkapi. We have no explanation for this divergence between the two clusters of kinsmen from Khlaūng Tej. Both were fairly large, in contrast to the one or two remaining households from Bāngkapi and of Laotian descendants. The two Khlaūng Tej groups addressed each other as kinsmen, though neither claimed a traceable relationship to the other. If antagonisms arose, we have not learned of them. (Genealogies of the Sathānsab family show marriages with the Sāsunthra and Phumsab families; marriages among Phumsab, Dithmonkol, and Uamchān are recorded in the Phumsab genealogy [LMH 8/28/57]).

15. The transition from debt slavery had already been made with apparent ease in this locality before 1900. Land had become a substitute for labor as a means of raising extra cash. A man's fields, not his potential as a worker, secured his debts. One informant commented on this transition:

[Then] most people were foolish; now people are cleverer. They did not care about interest when they borrowed money.

When did interest payment start?

Many years ago, about the time of my older brother, about a generation ago [i.e., about 1890]. It began when people started mortgaging land. In the old days when someone owed money and could not pay, he had to work for that man until the next generation or until the creditor was satisfied. . . . My grandfather had slaves when he lived at Khlaūng Tej, but when the household moved here, we had no more of them. If one owed thirty tamlyng (120 baht), the creditor might take all the family to work for him. If he were owed thirty baht, he might take one person. . . . The poor families often did not have enough to eat. They had to add *phak bung* [a vegetable] or sweet potato to extend their rice. They had land originally in certain cases, but it was lost through mortgaging. Poor families might not have any land. [LMH 2/16/54]

Certainly this informant did not mean that interest on debts was unknown before 1890, because debt slaves were responsible for repaying both interest and principal. Rather, he seems to have meant that until this time local land was not mortgaged at interest. Slavery was legal until 1905, and a slave's debts might continue his servitude two or three additional years. We conclude, however, that the mortgaging of land for small sums had already become the poor man's manner of obtaining credit in rural areas like Bang Chan.

A further factor is rural land value in terms of rental income. By the decade of the 1900s we note rentals at three baht per rai for cleared land.

16. The sole account of kinsman killing kinsman runs as follows:

Nāj Jan killed Nāj Phan. They were cousins. Phan's father's older sister was maternal grandmother of Jan. Jan and Phan lived near each other and went around together. On that day they were drunk. Phan talked too much. Phan went home at the request of Jan. Then Phan ate; he had no tobacco and went back to Jan to ask him for some. Jan thought Phan had come to challenge him. Jan took a long sword and stabbed him. At first Phan ran away while Jan chased him. Phan fell, and then Jan killed him. [LMH 7/7/53]

We judge Phan's death to have been a result of misunderstanding; Jan acted in what he thought was self-defense.

In our notes only two other murders occurred. One victim seems to have been killed when he resisted men who were trying to rob him. The second murder took place when five kinsmen conspired to kill a man from another hamlet:

Pun was working as a farmer at Headman Mae's hamlet. He was at the same time a robber and was robbing at Pāknam. He committed adultery with the wife of a headman in another hamlet. The headman did not know what to do. He consulted with his nephew Sawāj [son of older brother]. Sawāj told Pun there would be a feast at his uncle's house and invited him to come. Also invited were his [Sawāj's] mother's younger sister's son, headman's wife's older brother's son, headman's father's younger brother, Sawaj's wife's older brother. All knew of the plan. Pun was dangerous because he carried an old-fashioned pistol with him always and was protected from wounds by amulets. They had a lot to drink, and Pun got very drunk. Sawāj left the house as if he were going to piss. When he came back he had an iron bat and hit Pun over the head with it. Then they removed Pun's amulets and cut the body into pieces, which they buried. [LMH 7/21/53]

Disputes and grievances against kinsmen are frequently settled by suicide or attempted suicide: "Rim had two wives. About nine o'clock at night the second wife and husband slept together. Pum, the first wife, slept nearby. That night Rim heard noises where his first wife was sleeping. He found her trying to commit suicide by tying a blanket around her throat. . . (LMH 6/29/53).

A jealous husband was more successful in his effort to kill himself: "Before Wien died, he asked his wife, 'Do you love me?' Wife: 'Yes, I love you.' But Wien did not believe her. He took a razor and touched it to his neck. Wife cried and prayed to him. She then ran into the field to call her parents, who were working in the field. Suddenly she heard the sound of a gun. . ." (LMH 6/30/53). Here the objective was apparently the indirect revenge of anguish and remorse, through assigning responsibility for one's death to another.

17. The word *naklēng* usually connotes a bandit, hoodlum, or generally bad man given to violent and malevolent action. But the term may also be used for a benevolent deviant given to wild, irresponsible, but essentially harmless behavior, the jovial free spender, gambler, jokester, or even trickster, who nevertheless may be a pillar of the temple, as Chyn eventually was. Thus we prefer the translation "rogue," with its dual connotations, to any other (McFarland 1944:447).

18. Most persons wear a certain number of devices to help them gain supernatural assistance in meeting life's difficulties. Amulets containing written formulae to ward off illness are common. Women often wear amulets to make people kind to them. A person in Chyn's position needed aids to overcome his enemies and protect himself. We do not know Chyn's devices, but the son of another rogue described his father's inventory:

(1) *Mak chang ngang* (compel fright): spells to make the enemy afraid; (2) *khlaēw khlād* (miss): to turn enemy's blow before it strikes (see Textor 1960:57); (3) *ipoē*: a picture of a woman worn together with a female garment soiled by menstrual blood to confirm power (ibid.:104); (4) *leg laj*: to prevent being cut (ibid.:63); (5) *paraūt*: to prevent being cut (ibid.:111); (6) *khun phra*: if a man uses it, he cannot bathe at the same place as a woman; he must bathe

separately. He cannot hang his clothes on the same rack with a woman's. A woman's shirt is an exception. He cannot flirt with the wife of another person. If he wants to sleep with his wife, he must wear new clothes and cannot wear the shirt he uses outdoors. If he does, the power of *khun phra* disappears (ibid.:523). [LMH 11/23/53].

19. A sanctuary is almost indispensable for a temple. There the candidates for priesthood are received into the monastic order; the most precious images, in front of which the important chapter meetings take place, are stored; and the ceremonial robes are received at Thaud Kathin. Ernest Young (1907:284–285) offers the following ceremonial details of the building of a sanctuary:

> Around the 'bote' [sanctuary], the most holy of all the buildings, are placed eight stones, one at each of the eight chief points of the compass. They are called 'bai sema,' and are cut in the shape of the leaf of the *Ficus religiosa* or Bo tree. They mark out the boundaries of the consecrated part of the 'wat' [temple]. They are erected when the temple is first consecrated. Eight round smooth stones are first buried a little way below the ground, together with the relic or image. Holy water is sprinkled over them, and across the boundary thus formed the spirits of evil intent have not the courage to intrude. Small, solid, cubical platforms of brick are built over the stones, and on the platforms are placed the gilded or painted stone representations of the sacred leaf. These again are covered with a canopy of stone cut in a similar shape, and often elaborately carved or inlaid with mosaics.

20. According to Buddhist doctrine, an individual's store of merit from past lives sets the limits attainable in the present life. This doctrine is clearly demonstrated when a person continues to hold the same station throughout life. Similarly, if a person rises from poverty or falls from riches, his store of merit from the past acted to reward or punish him. The case of Chyn, who rose from an initially sinful life to respected prominence, poses a special problem for the moral law (*tham*), since in his case evil deeds appeared to lead to reward.

Without benefit of special counsel on Buddhist doctrine, we suggest two possible ways of reconciling Chyn's rise with the moral law: (1) A store of merit sets limits only for the subsequent existence or existences. Present sin affects only future lifetimes. Thus Chyn rose because of a good store of merit from the past and will be punished for his youthful sins in the future. (2) Though the limits of present attainment are set by the individual's store of merit, the choice of doing good or evil remains ever present. Chyn was bound to rise because of past merit but eventually chose to do good in the course of his rise. He might have robbed other hamlets at the same time that he protected his own hamlet residents and their temple; he might have ruled the hamlet by ruthless terror; but he chose more virtuous means.

21. David Wyatt and Loebongse Sarabhaja have kindly supplied the following information concerning the local government administrative structure: In 1895 the area that now includes Bang Chan was organized as the Area of the District of Sām Wā Canal (Khwaeng Amphoe Khlaung Sām Wā). Its precise boundaries were not specified. Sām Wā canal runs south from the town of Thanyaburi through the area of the Rangsit irrigation project to join Saen Saeb canal at the town of Minburi. The Sām Wā Canal District designation seems to have been replaced by 1902, when Minburi Province (Myang Minburi) appears, and to the north of it Myang Thanyaburi, each containing four districts (amphoe), none of which is named Sām Wā. Minburi retained its provincial (myang, later *changwat*) status until the Depression, 1931, when it was reduced to a district (amphoe).

Our information is confused by an Ecclesiastical Affairs report for 1902/03 which mentions a Bang Chan Canal Temple School (*Rongrian* Wat Khlāūng Bang Chan), not in Myang Minburī but in Myang Thanyaburī, presumably in its southernmost district (Amphōē Lam Lūkkā). Either the report misplaced Bang Chan's new temple school by clerical error or an old border of District Lam Lūkkā (and Thanyaburī Province) extended as far south as the junction of the Krcd and Bang Chan canals. Certainly the location of Bang Chan temple has not changed, nor can we find any other Bang Chan canals or villages in the region. Lam Lūkkā and Thanyaburī are now districts (amphōē) of Pathumthani Province (changwat).

The date of Phlym's appointment as kamnan seems to lie in the decade between 1895 and 1905; we cannot fix it more precisely. No specified number of households is necessary to organize a governmental hamlet (mūbān) or commune (tambon) according to law.

22. In general Moslem and Buddhist households of Bang Chan lived aloofly separate. As the near Moslem households seem to have grown specialty garden crops for the market—lotus, for example—there may have been few common activities to facilitate the exchange of labor and goods. We have but one account of borrowing between the two groups, and in that case it was money that exchanged hands (JRH 12/3/53).

Hostility toward the Moslems always lay close beneath the surface, first on the grounds that Moslem people lived in sin because they slaughtered the beef they ate. Whenever a buffalo disappeared, it was alleged that the Moslems had stolen it and killed it for one of their feasts. Intermarriage seems not to have begun until after 1905, the approximate year when the Moslem community began to grow with returning settlers (LMH 8/8/54). Since either bride or groom had to convert and invariably became alienated from the parental community and was deemed to be living in sin, tension further increased after an interfaith marriage took place.

Both Moslem and Buddhist households were invited to the festivals given by Kamnan Phlym, who even invited a special cook to prepare food for the Moslem guests (LMH 8/6/57). Moslem families seem to have lived quietly under Buddhist officials at this time. In the 1950s two hamlets of mixed faith near Bang Chan experienced no difficulty under Moslem headmen.

23. As has been observed elsewhere (see Hanks and Phillips 1961:654–655), the Thai social system offers moments of both dependence and independence, affiliation and hostility. One can be a loving client or reject clienthood to emphasize the status of independent patron. Of course, all persons are both patrons and clients at the same time. Rejecting clienthood and striking out on one's own are emphasized at marriage. In childhood and old age the client role predominates. Each person or household seeks the setting that best suits his frame of mind.

In the household of Tō we should expect Kham, the eldest, to have acted as patron over his juniors. At marriage each became patron over his own household, yet in matters of common concern Kham probably decided the course of action after varying amounts of consultation. The possibility of conflicting authority was surely present when the younger brother became chief of the entire commune and officially superseded the elder. Kham's departure provided a ready solution for this potential conflict between the rules of kinship and government administration.

We can conceive of circumstances in which a junior sibling might patronize a senior, but in fact we cannot clearly establish the existence of any such cases. A certain Lōng returned penniless to Bang Chan after the failure of his farming operation elsewhere and moved in with a junior sibling (LMH 7/29/54). Aun became a widow with small children too young to work and moved to the vicinity of her more affluent younger sister to work land inherited from their parents (LMH

7/23/57). With independent land the two households could preserve at least the fiction of autonomy and minimize common problems. In the 1940s a widower returned to Bang Chan with a very young daughter and took up residence with his aging mother and younger brother, who was married. The younger brother's wife brought up the child and cooked for the older brother. No effort was made to have separate kitchens. The older brother paid rent to the younger (JRH 7/23/53). The presence of the old mother may have modified the nature of this relationship, and we do not know the precise lines of authority followed by the two brothers. We conclude that whenever possible Thai avoid conflict between authority based on age and authority based on wealth, social position, or office.

24. Our estimate is based on the count of five houses in the immediate neighborhood of Tō's household and ten additional houses in the hamlet (Pheduraj, Maūsuwan, Pūrahong) about the year 1892. By 1910 the neighborhood around Tō's household reached fifteen households (LMH 7/22/57; 7/29/57). The original number of households had tripled. We have no direct knowledge of hamlet size at this time. An informant estimated that two to three hundred buffalo were once kept in a common corral (LMH 7/30/57). Assuming this figure to be excessive and that there may have been as many as one hundred buffalo, we reach an approximate hamlet size of fifty, on the basis of two buffalo for each household. If we assume that not only the neighborhood of Tō's house but that of the entire hamlet tripled, we reach an estimate of forty-five houses. Indeed, this estimate may fall on the low side, if we consider that houses are placed on or near the land one intends to work, and the new lands were peripheral to Tō's neighborhood. Thus the internal growth at the center may scarcely have represented the extent of the changes in the hamlet as a whole.

25. The sum of sixty baht said to have been paid per year does not correspond very closely to the presumptive price fixed by the laws of January 20, 1899, and March 31, 1905, which set the rate of debt amortization by labor at eight baht per month without keep and four baht per month with keep (Duplatre 1933:119–120). If the figure of sixty baht is correct, Phlym was setting more generous terms than the law required.

26. Phlym's occult powers, with emphasis on benevolence, curing disease, reducing friction between people, and love, differed from the magical forces of a rogue. Chyn's powers were aimed mainly at the defeat of an adversary. As many of these powers depend on the strength of words breathed into an object, such powers can be tailored to one's particular needs. Other forms of power depend on spells (verbal formulae, or *khāthā*) that one can cast by uttering the proper words; these, however, are probably less amenable to specific circumstances. Textor (1960:71) deals at length with verbal formulae and shows the forms of objects associated with various occult powers. Differing powers may be breathed into objects of like form, however.

Chapter 6: *Patrons and Their Work*

1. During the 1950s control of the market operations was usually tight but not always. One of Phillips' informants worked with a Bangkok manufacturer of bronze cutlery until he quarreled with the person in charge of retail sales in the market. Then the factory, lacking alternative access to the public, reduced its output and laid off a number of employees (HPP 7/16/57). A Bang Chan woman described how she formed a relationship with a retailer in Bangkok:

> I collect eggs daily and go to the market near the Ministry of Education in Bangkok, where I sell eggs to my aunt, who sells there every day. All this

was arranged at the ordination for Waen's son. I knew this aunt previously but did not know her house. So Nang Sin took me there. My aunt pays me forty-five satangs per egg and sells them at seventy-five satangs. Then I buy betel nut, chilies, and limes to bring back to Bang Chan. I earn five baht profit every day. I go twice a week to Bangkok. [JRH 4/29/54]

As the ordination referred to had taken place only a few days before this statement was made, the informant was describing in part a prospect.

The following account of the marketing of mushrooms makes clear that access to a retailer is not always restricted:

I sell every day; there are about ten purchasers. I know how to speak Chinese and so can get a better price. I walk around and ask who gives the best price. None of them are relatives, just other people. I now know them because I have sold there a long time. I spend only three to seven baht in Bangkok and bring back between sixty-five and eighty-five baht each day. [JRH 1/21/54]

This was a new enterprise in Bang Chan. Had the mushroom production become stable, we should expect the appearance of a middleman who would mediate between producers and retailers. By 1957 mushroom raising disappeared because the price had fallen when many people produced them. A fairly stable egg business had begun. These local egg raisers were served by a man who appeared once or twice a week to buy eggs. He also sold chicken feed and certain poultry medicines as a sideline. Egg producing seems to have become controlled.

2. The Thai kinship system has no equivalent of "grandnephew." The word *lān*, grandchild or nephew/niece, would be used.

3. Buddhists would probably have commented that the store of merit of the two older brothers was less than that of the youngest. The eldest died early, and the second, suffering some misfortunes, could never advance beyond Bang Chan to higher status. Only the youngest achieved high status and lived to old age.

One of the writers discussed this problem with a group of farmers at the temple in Bang Chan:

I raised the question about why should a man who is wicked achieve honors. No one answered then, but S. wondered why a lowly dog like the dog of Rama VI could live in a palace and sit beside a king. Another commented that he thought the dog had a soul of high merit which had sinned once or twice. Another illustrated the law of Karma by describing a farmer who does not look after his fields well and then does not get a good crop; even if he happened to get a good crop, he would be loaded with debts. Conversely the low person who works hard and does good will be reborn to his reward in his next existence. Someone added, a person in high station who has sinned greatly has no real happiness. Real happiness comes from cultivating peace of mind (*ubekkhā*) and avoiding the pleasure-pain of the world. [LMH 3/9/54]

4. Kamut Chandruang (1938) tells of his father, a country boy, who reached Bangkok after a long boat trip and fell asleep at the gate of the temple. There in the early morning he was discovered by a priest, who invited him to remain at the temple. This tale of entry into a temple without introduction sounds to Thai quite miraculous.

5. We believe that students of government under the Thai absolute monarchs have misunderstood a key element in its nature. Accustomed to the European, functional style of government, they have attempted to find a system that carries out the king's will to the ends of the kingdom. All are impressed with the monarch's powers to compel others, yet they are invariably perturbed by the apparent limitations on his effective powers. They seek to explain the discrepancy on the basis of the king's isolation (Horrigan 1959:62) or bureaucratic rigidity (Wilson 1959:6).

The fact that the monarch granted outright monopoly of power to his client princes in the remote dependencies is easily grasped. That the same plan was followed in his inner provinces is not so readily understood. The royal directions to provincial governors (see Wales 1934:125–133) lead easily to the assumption of a bureaucratic organization. The central government administrators placed in each province as judge and overseer further suggest a limitation on any local monopoly of power (ibid.:106).

A variety of testimony, nevertheless, points to a high degree of autonomy in the provinces. Wales (ibid.:105), quoting the Palatinate Law of fifteenth-century Thailand, says, "The various newly subjected regions were governed as independent states but owed allegiance to Ayuthia." When the control of the central government was extended to the provinces during the 1890s and 1900s, the main problem was to curtail the power of the provincial governors (Graham 1913:251–254) or local lords (chao myang) (Keyes 1966). Half a century after Prince Damrong's reforms, provincial authorities are still credited by the people with near absolute powers:

> Public relations and ceremonial functions occupy a considerable percentage of the governor's time. As the chief official of the province, he is expected and requested to serve as president or chairman of a large number of quasi official and informal groups. He is invited to be the chairman of literally every committee formed in the province. [Horrigan 1959:156] Under the general heading of public relations activity can be included the long hours spent by the governor in meetings with individuals and committees who come to see him for every conceivable reason: to complain about district officers; to request funds for village projects; to petition for contributions to repair local wats [temples]; to seek clemency for individuals under arrest, etc. One governor in a busy province estimated that fully one-half of his time is devoted to the kind of ceremonial and public relations activity described here. [Horrigan 1959:158]

In the name of democracy these officials encourage people to help themselves rather than depend on government aid, but the amazed populace cannot explain why a powerful government official asks the people to do a job that he himself can do more easily and effectively.

As in the allocation of property control in nineteenth-century Bangkok and the organization of contemporary markets, in the making of appointments traditional government gave an absolute monopoly of power to its provincial officials. The royal edicts specifying the duties of various appointees fixed conditions of their monopolies but in no way limited their power. An official from the capital may have reported what was going on in the province under his surveillance, but such spying did not limit the sovereignty of the governor as long as he held office. His power could be curtailed only by dismissal or recall. As long as the province was quiet, the royal power did not ordinarily retract its monopoly.

Royal power was no more curtailed in Bangkok than it was in Moscow or Tokyo. The isolation of kings, their dependence on their courtiers, may lead to a Peter the Great as readily as to a ritual emperor and shogun. The curtailment of the royal power in Thailand came from its being given away as a local monopoly.

Further limitations on despotic power in Thailand are worthy of mention. Instead of a territorial state encompassing all persons living inside a fixed boundary, the Thai state was until the twentieth century more like a voluntary association (Sharp 1960). It was held together by the royal patron's skill in retaining his clients and in turn by these clients' ability to retain their clients. All enjoyed in principle the freedom to seek new patrons or to withdraw altogether from the state association if they wished. Land was always available. The present Thai territory contained many small groups of people who lived outside the effective jurisdiction of a national central government. If they caused trouble, they risked enslavement, but otherwise they might live entirely in peace. Generally membership or participation in the state association was considered a privilege of civilized people. Though certain offenses against the state were punished by death, the ordinary social offender was simply ostracized. And loss of territory in war was less distressing than loss of population to people-hungry neighboring states.

Karl Wittfogel's hasty judgment that Thailand is a hydraulic society in external form has some plausibility (1957:32, 425). The country has and had a canal system, monumental public works, a sizable bureaucracy, corvée labor. We believe, however, that in the case of Thailand, Wittfogel has not properly stated the question of freedom versus despotism. Civil liberties need be sought only by residents forced to belong to a territorial state. In the voluntary state association, the ordinary man yielded up individual liberties to his patron but always retained the right to withdraw himself or his services when the despotism became excessive. Of course, the territorial concept of state has now come to Southeast Asia, and we may well expect questions about civil liberties to arise.

6. Nāj Loet Setthabutr (1872–1945), from a family of civil officials, was employed by several foreign firms and founded a boat line and subsequently a bus line in Bangkok. He received the official title of Phrayā Phakdinoraset (Loebongse Sarabhaja, personal communication, 1960).

7. Of twenty-five men born in the early 1890s and living in Bang Chan in 1953, ten said they had attended the temple school there, apparently on or soon after its establishment in 1901. But of the fifteen who said they did not attend any temple school, we do not know how many were in Bang Chan at the turn of the century. Thus we cannot even guess what proportion of all village children attended the new school. Even if our census in 1953 provided more information on individuals, it would show a bias in favor of those who had attended the temple school, since more poor children would have moved away from Bang Chan in the interim than children of wealthier families, who would certainly have provided a disproportionate number of students in spite of the pattern of community support for poverty cases and orphans as temple boys (dek wat).

Reports of the education and religious director for Bangkok provide suggestive data for the Bang Chan region, although we find specific information on the Bang Chan school only in his report for 1902/03. In that report we are told further that 10 of the 32 temples in the adjacent new provinces (myang) of Minburī and Thanyaburī had schools, with 291 pupils attending and some 518 other known boys of school age in these two provinces not attending. Without an accurate census the last figure is doubtless an underestimate, but it suggests that at least two-thirds of the youth of the region were not registered in one or another of the new temple schools. By 1907 the 10 original schools in Minburī and Thanyaburī provinces had dwindled to 6; but again, by 1911 things had improved and local temples, whose numbers had more than doubled in a decade, were operating 56 schools with 1,161 pupils. These students now included a scattering of girls, originally excluded because of the monastic rule forbidding contact with the opposite sex.

In the old official reports and in the recollections of villagers, the new secular schooling in temples initiated by the government cannot always be distinguished from the older traditional form of religious education designed to train boys for their role as priests, with emphasis on the Pali language of the sacred texts. Such training had gone on for generations and continues today (Wyatt 1969). The director's report for 1902/03, which noted how many of 809 school-age boys in Minburī and Thanyaburī provinces were in school, goes on to register some 676 boys as "temple students" (*sitwat*) in all 32 temples of the area. These were presumably older boys who were undergoing the traditional religious training. But five years later, the report for 1907/08 specified that in the 75 temples then found in the two provinces there were 466 temple students (sitwat) and 203 temple students "living at home" (*dekbān*), a total of 669, all of whom were categorized as "studying Thai in temples." It would appear that these are secular temple school students and are to be distinguished from the traditional temple students, who are listed separately, although the absence of some overlap is not absolutely clear (Thai National Archives, 5 S, 26/12, "Reports on Ecclesiastical Affairs in Monthon Krungthēp," Phra Thammatrailōkāchān, R.S. 121, 127, 1902/03, 1908/09). We are indebted to David K. Wyatt for these references.

8. Parents will give up a child not only for their own convenience or to please another person but also to assist the child. A man spoke of his father's departing and leaving him in the care of his aunts when he was still a boy: "My father moved to Bāngplī and bought two hundred seventy rai. It is better land than here and yields between sixty and seventy thang per rai. He moved about eleven years ago. I did not go because of my aunts. I have three aunts. They never married and do not farm. So I have lands here from my aunts" (LMH 5/28/53). This was a very satisfactory placement of the young man, for he would be able to look after and eventually own the lands of his aunts.

Another informant complained that his parents failed to allow him an opportunity: "I believe my parents had a small degree of love for me. Otherwise I might have been a district officer or an official. Once a district officer wanted to adopt me as a son, and when he told my parents about it, they objected. So they made me miss my opportunity" (LMH 3/1/54). Such criticism of parents is most unusual, and parental kindness to a child was certainly emphasized in the sentence-completion items on parents (Phillips 1965:308–312).

9. Under this tax law we find only a single reference to taxes paid in the 1930s at one baht per rai (LMH 8/7/57). This was for some of the best land in Bang Chan but at a time when rice prices were low.

10. We have estimated the number of Bang Chan men who served in the armed forces or police. Of 263 men in the age group 25–54 at the time of the 1953 research census, 66 (25 percent) served in the army, 22 (8 percent) in the police, and 4 (1.5 percent) in the navy; 171 (65 percent) never served. Conscription officers at the district office rejected the physically unfit. Those who paid a certain minimum tax were exempted (Graham 1913:247). There was a local tale of a sister who "gave" her land to a brother in order to render him exempt (SM 3/31/49). A household that might be severely handicapped by loss of a member could petition the district officer for exemption. Then the choice of some among those remaining was made by lot, for military facilities could not handle all the eligible men.

11. Certain names are quickly recognized by Bangkok people as those of farmers. Among them are those that combine the personal names of two parents or grandparents: Maūmsīlā and Kongiam, made up from two personal names. Others take the name of one parent or grandparent, usually male, and add an embellishment implying progeny: Sumhiran or "Sum's riches"; Khlājsuan or "Khlāj's garden." City people have taken names of more abstract elegance: Ditmonkon or "way of auspiciousness" (McFarland 1944:329, 619).

12. In 1954 members of the research group visited thirty-eight households in one

of Bang Chan's administrative hamlets. Of these households, four did not grow rice but earned their living by wage work in Bangkok, in highway maintenance, and so on. In the thirty-four households of rice growers, agricultural ceremonies were carried on in the following frequencies:

First plowing	33
First sowing of grain	33
First transplanting	33
Offerings to Rice Mother (*tham khwan khāw*)	
done once	16
done twice	1
First harvest	33
First padi to threshing floor	33
Make merit before eating first rice	34
First rice to rice bin	33
First rice taken from bin	33
Call Rice Mother from fields	33
Request rice spirit from buyer	33

Thus, except for the offerings to the Rice Mother in the midst of the growing season, nearly everyone observed these ceremonies. The one person who did not perform them rented only two rai, probably to grow rice for his own consumption. He earned his livelihood as a hired laborer working for other growers. Three other farm laborers in approximately the same circumstances, however, performed all ceremonies.

We would further call attention to variations in the invocations of the guardian spirits. One example is the following address to the Rice Mother at the first appearance of the grain (JRH 8/27/53):

Mother of Rice, mothers Prasī, Chenthī, and Sīdā,
Come, mothers, come,
Receive the offered fruit.
Up and down the field
Come and clothe yourselves.

The ceremony is conducted, like other rites for the Rice Mother, on Friday (*wan sūk*), day of happiness, day of grain and fruits and of Agni or Sukara, associated with fire and the planet Venus. The informant explained that Prasī, Chenthī, and Sīdā are servants of the Rice Mother. We note from McFarland (1944:292, 868) that Chānakī (called Chenthī by our informant) is a patronym for Sīdā, heroine of the Ramakian (the Thai version of the Ramayana), who in the Veda is identified with the furrow dug by the plow and is a deity of cereals and fruits. The invocation may originally have addressed not the Rice Mother but Sīdā. If Pōsob derives from the Pali word *posōk*, meaning guardian (ibid.:537), then the invocation might have run something like this:

Guardian mother, mother of regal splendor, Chānakī Sīdā,
Come, mother, come . . .

For a fuller description of agricultural rites see Anuman Rajadhon 1961 and Textor 1960:412–434.

13. The word for ancestral spirits in the Thai language is a compounding of the words for the entire range of grandparents: pū = father's father, his brothers, and the brothers of his wife; jā = father's mother, her sisters, and the sisters of her husband; tā = mother's father, etc.; jāj = mother's mother, etc.

One evening during the course of an interview with the head priest at the temple, a woman came asking his help. A "brother" was sick; he had something wrong with his mind; he laughed, sometimes wept, and uttered strange cries. The head priest without hesitation said his illness was caused by ancestral spirits and recommended an offering. On the following day he was recovered (LMH 7/13/53). We did not inquire how the diagnosis was made. The symptoms of the patient are those frequently associated with spirit possession. Also the priest may have employed *jām*, a system of diagnosis whereby the day of the visit and the particular period of the seven that make up the day and the direction from which a patient (or the communicator of the illness) comes furnish the clues for diagnosis (LMH 6/21/53).

14. Textor (1960) lists a considerable number of these beings under "ghosts" (*phī*), supernatural objects related to the natural environment, supernatural objects from the Brahmanic tradition, and other complex supernatural objects. Even his extensive census is not exhaustive.

A number of guardian spirits have their own particular temperaments and special appetites and demands, which a supplicant does well to know. Thus Lord Paternal Grandfather (Chao Phāū Pū) protects against stealing and helps recover lost boats. Formerly he kept elephants away from the house and fields. He likes pigs' heads and liquor, but in addressing a request to him one should not use the ordinary words to promise these delights, but should use special words—not *hua mū* (pig's head) but *sī sak mongkhon*; not *lao* (liquor) but *nāmchan*. An informant stated that her parents also appealed to Lord Paternal Grandfather, so that an introduction is desirable (JRH 12/18/53). It is reported that a man addressed the Emerald Buddha in Bangkok (Phra Kaew) with a petition and became mad (LMH 7/7/53). We infer that the Emerald Buddha was offended. In addition a guardian spirit who fails to receive a promised offering may remind the petitioner of his delinquency. A protector against snakes permitted a cobra to approach to remind his charge of some forgotten offering (JRH 12/18/53). Another informant reported that the guardian spirit possessed her husband and said through him that he wanted drink (JRH 12/12/53).

15. We believe that the top price given here is high, since other informants (LMH 12/6/53, 8/17/57) spoke of 80–100 baht per kwian for the year following the flood.

16. The Laotians named not only the Bang Chan hamlet where they lived for a decade or so, but also other hamlets on Saēn Saēb canal. We have the name for one: Village Receiving Splendid Bounty (Bān Lāb Siri Khun) (LMH 7/29/57). Northern and northeastern peoples build and live in collective and more corporate villages that are protected by village ancestral spirit guardians (LS 11/7/57; Kingshill 1960:180; Keyes 1966). This practice contrasts with the Bang Chan custom of living in isolation on one's own land with a guardian spirit (phra phūm) for each household or compound.

The individualistic, dispersed, and mobile population of Bang Chan resembles the Cambodian *phum* (Delvert 1961:201–204), which is an administrative unit of government. The term *phum*, like the Thai *mūbān*, designates no sociologically collective entity but, according to Delvert, means to the populace only an inhabited area.

17. The "special people" chosen to help vary widely, as may be seen from the following example, given by a woman whose household was situated close to the homes of many kinsmen:

> My husband's older brother's wife will look after the baby when I ask her, but she never offers to. My mother lives nearby but never comes, and I never take the children there to be watched. . . . I looked after the children of my husband's older brother when they were small. Sagnuan [husband's father's older brother's son's wife] once helped take care of the children when they were small but does not help any more since the oldest ones can now look after the younger ones. [JRH 10/11/55]

The husband's father, father's younger brothers, and some of their children lived nearby, but only certain ones assisted in the fields. A buffalo was rented from the wife's younger brother at twenty-five thang per year. The cooperative labor group consisted of the following persons (JRH 11/26/53):

Chan called nā (honorific but just an elder friend)

Mong called nā (husband's mother's sister's husband)

Chȳn called nā (husband's father's younger brother's wife's brother)

Prasoed called naung (not close; Prasoed's father called nā by husband's father)

Sawong called nāung (husband's father's younger brother's son)

Rag called friend

Jū called friend (though a distant relationship can be traced by marriage)

When a buffalo died, this household invited two of the foregoing persons (Mong and Chȳn) to assist in the butchering and share the meat. In addition two persons described as nāung were invited, though we could not trace the precise relationship of these two.

Selection of another for a common undertaking depends upon the type of job to be done, the individual's resources and circumstances, and mutual compatibility.

18. In the 1930s Bang Chan parents allowed a lock of a child's hair to continue growing until the boy or girl reached the age of eleven or thirteen, when the danger of loss of soul was considered past. An odd year of age was chosen for the cutting since auspicious influences are stronger in odd years. The tonsure ceremony might be carried out quite simply by taking the child with an offering to some itinerant priest (*phra thudong*), who then cut off the lock. Or the ceremony might be more elaborate, with priests and guests invited for a feast. Kamnan Phlym had a dance troupe at the tonsure ceremony for one of his daughters (LMH 7/30/54). Phūjaj Wek spent 2,800 baht for such a rite for his daughter in 1949 (KJ 6/9/49). More recently Bang Chan parents were allowing the lock to grow only when a child was sickly; otherwise the lock was cut off when the child was five or seven years old and about to enter school. The style was determined by the child: when a child was one to three years old he or she was allowed to choose among three or four dolls with various arrangements of one, two, and three topknots made of clay; the one chosen determined the style (JRH 7/17/54). The cutting of the topknot "helps the child to grow" (JRH 2/23/54).

19. We believe that 900 baht for a ceremony is too high. Another informant stated that 400 baht was a high price to pay for a ceremony during this period (JRH 12/3/53). On the basis of statements made concerning this period by Bang Chan people (JRH 12/3/53), we estimate that an income of 1,000 baht per year would be high for a farmer. Let us assume the most favorable circumstances: a man can work 50 rai and reap 30 thang of padi per rai. At this rate he would harvest about 15 or 16 kwian. If one uses the top price of 80 baht per kwian, the total gross income from selling all the padi would be 1,280 baht. Even with such a high income, it would take a family several years to save enough for a major ceremony. Rarely would funds be borrowed for such a purpose.

20. The titles refer to long epic narratives in verse. The actors select an episode from the narrative, assign roles, and improvise (Schweisguth 1951:61–63). They play as long as anyone wishes to continue. "Khun Chang Khun Phaen" is a well-known Thai epic (ibid.:205–211). "Phrām Kae Saun" and "Laksanawong" appear to be episodes from a larger narrative, which we have not identified.

21. A kamnan's duties appear approximately the same under law then as they do today. Wealth enhanced a hamlet headman's chance of being chosen as kamnan. We have been unable to determine precisely when kamnans became salaried and ceased to pay themselves solely from tax receipts. The change appears to have occurred

during the reign of Rama VI but is not specifically mentioned in the Local Reorganization Act of B.E. 2440 (Laws 1935b). Frederick Horrigan describes the contemporary position and duties of the kamnan:

> The kamnan is not a civil servant, but is entitled to wear a uniform, receives some official benefits, and is paid an honorarium of some 140 baht per month for his services. Election of the kamnan is conducted under the supervision of the district officer who delivers to him his warrant of appointment from the governor. . . . The prescribed duties of the chief headman (kamnan) include: assisting in keeping the peace, recording vital statistics within his jurisdiction, and reporting to the district officer on matters of government interest. He also performs certain duties relating to the recording of land ownership and collecting taxes, for which he receives a small commission. As chief agent of the government within the commune, he is the "eyes and ears" of the district officer in criminal investigation and suppression. . . . [1959:221–222]

22. Our observations of clients and patrons suggest two elements of the traditional Thai concept of sovereignty. First, sovereignty was personal. Though kings, by granting titles, minimized the person of the title bearer and sought to maximize the impersonal continuity of the office, the rules of patronage seem to have emphasized the person of the patron. When a patron left office, the clients who sustained him also departed, and the new appointee brought in his own clients. A person wishing to petition the new appointee needed a personal introduction, for his relation to the former appointee did not carry over to the new one.

Second, sovereignty was unlimited. A client seeking aid from an official placed all of his resources at the official's disposal and expected assistance in all areas. Kamnan Phlym treated his clients' health as well as their land disputes. The division of affairs into private and public matters applied at no level. Kings ruled as readily on matters of dress as on public safety.

These concepts of the nature of sovereignty become important in accounting for certain peculiarities of the shift from a personal to a functional government and from absolute to constitutional monarchy. We have noted the following four characteristics: (1) The predilection of cabinet-level officers to build autonomous units. A certain amount of overlapping and duplication of function occurs in any bureaucratic organization, but the Thai system of organization goes beyond these minimal levels. During the 1950s, for example, the police were equipped with their own tanks, airplanes, and gunboats, as if they were the army. Easy communication between these branches of government can be accomplished only at the cabinet level. (2) The difficulty of delegating powers. Top officials complain that their desks are overcrowded with routine matters that only they can handle. Most Western officials would have turned these less important decisions over to subordinates. The locus of the difficulty may lie in the organization of the bureaucracy, the authority of the signature on the order, or elsewhere. (3) The welfare and ceremonial obligations of high officials. A former prime minister stated in conversation that his home and office were filled every day with petitioners who sought his aid on all kinds of household, health, and financial matters. Another prime minister organized a welfare agency in order to be relieved of this phase of his work. Horrigan (1959:156–161) confirms that provincial governors in the 1950s were thus occupied and also were expected to carry on a host of honorary tasks, as if a committee or organization could not exist without their presence. (4) Advancement of civil officials by rank rather than by function. With certain exceptions men are promoted from department to department or even across ministry boundaries. Their training and experience are not considered limitations. As individuals they work toward higher rank in any department or ministry rather than rising through a particular functional line, such as agriculture or finance (Mosel 1957).

Doubtless students of the transition from one type of government organization to another would find further survivals of the earlier prebendal system and the pervasive patron–client relationship in recent Thai political culture. What we consider to be the corporate state operating for the public welfare was regarded in Thailand as the personal business of the king. Now the cabinet and the extensive civil service, still called "servants of the king," operate the business.

Chapter 7: *Years of Austerity*

1. The merit accruing to the sponsors of an ordination is not lightly treated in Bang Chan. Parents feel aggrieved if a son becomes ordained only after marriage, for the merit then accrues to the wife rather than to the parents. A wealthy household increases its merit by including a poor young man, or several, in the ordination ceremonies intended primarily for its own child. A dispute over the sponsorship of a younger brother's ordination led to a rift between brothers:

> My husband's younger brother lived nearby but did not visit because my husband quarreled with him. This younger brother had wanted to become a priest, and so my husband invited him to come and live at this house with us [so that we could sponsor his ordination]. He refused saying he did not like me. Once I had criticized him for smoking opium. So my husband and he quarreled, and the young brother went to live with a friend. My husband was very angry. We did not attend his ordination, nor did any other relatives, because he did not respect his older brother. [JRH 6/25/53]

Failure to appear at the ordination or cremation of a kinsman is a profound rebuff, seen as diminishing both the religious and the social claims of the sponsors. For these rites not only elevate the position of participants on the religious scale of merit mobility but also obviously improve their secular position or social merit. Indeed, it is this latter reward which is the more tangible and immediate. In this sense, these and other family-sponsored public ceremonies are functionally similar to the "feasts of merit" found among so many non-Buddhist groups in Southeast Asia, in which the entire community participates and benefits but the sponsors gain the greatest social status or prestige increment.

Investment in Buddhist ceremonies for conspicuous consumption may be relatively large in Bang Chan (Janlekha 1957:149). While participating guests make five- or ten-baht contributions, the net expense for the sponsor may be as much as 15,000 baht, and the original capital involved is, of course, much more. In 1949 a hamlet headman, only moderately well off, spent some 3,200 baht on the ordinations of his youngest brother and four other young men whose families stood as his clients. From Bang Sȳ he imported two dramatic troupes, including a sixteen-piece orchestra. A dozen drummers were recruited from neighboring hamlets. A famous seventy-four-year-old priest walked the fourteen kilometers from his temple in Bāngkapi District to officiate. A dozen vendors appeared to sell snacks, beverages, and toys. People said two thousand guests attended during the two-day event, each efficiently fed by the headman's family and helpers. In 1953 the same headman sponsored the ordination of his eldest son, again with others included. One thousand formal printed invitations were issued. Costs by then were higher. A ceremony (*ngān*) on such a scale, it was said, gave the headman's family "much face" (*nā jaj*) (SM 4/6/49; LS 4/15/53).

2. The obligations of child to parent are terminated just as effectively when a child is lent to serve some kinsman, unless the parent is in a position to recall the child to the parental home. Typically a son's obligations to his parents are terminated when he enters military service, is ordained, reaches his twentieth birthday, gets his first job, or marries. A parent's wealth often determines whether the time of separation will occur early or late in the child's life. In the following rather standard case a son left home after ordination: "My son Thiang attended school as far as the fourth grade. I then taught him carpentry, and he worked for seven or eight years with me. We worked together until he became a priest. After that he went to live with his mother's younger sister in Sāmsen as a hired hand. He happened to meet a girl who was working there, too. They married, and he stayed at his wife's home. His mother-in-law gave him some land, and now he earns a little from this farm" (LMH 8/31/53). The son had worked with his father from the age of fourteen until his ordination at twenty-one. Thereafter he was on his own and could contract with whomever he wished.

The parent in the following case seems to have obliged a kinsman with the loan of a child and did not necessarily end his expectation of service from the child: "My son Prasert is sixteen years old and lives with my wife's younger sister. He farms as a laborer but has received no pay for two years. That woman is married but has no children and invited Prasert to come and live on the farm. She gives him food and clothing only" (LMH 12/8/53). This young boy did not receive a hired man's pay beyond his keep. Though he left home at the invitation of his mother's younger sister, his father probably could have recalled him if he wished. In fact, the father was poor and benefited from being relieved of his support.

A girl ordinarily terminates obligations to her parents at marriage. Before their daughters marry, poor families may find it expedient to farm them out along with their sons to households that have greater need for help or are better able to provide for them. After marriage at least a token stay with the bride's parents is expected. About two-thirds of the young couples in Janlekha's sample left the bride's parents' household by the end of one year (1957:37). Thereafter the couple chose its residence in accordance with its best opportunities for becoming independent.

3. An example of Buddhist depersonalization of the body appears in the following quotation (Warren 1921:158):

> The windy element is characterized by its activeness and its ability to prop up, and courses through every member of the body. Resting in the earthy element and held together by the watery element and preserved by the fiery element, it props up the body . . . [so] that it does not fall over, but stands upright. And it is when the body is impelled by the windy element that it performs its four functions of walking, standing, sitting, or lying down, or draws in and stretches out its arms, or moves its hands and its feet. Thus does this machine made of four elements move like a puppet and deceive all foolish people with its femininity, masculinity, etc."

Even the will is depersonalized as a "windy element."

Not only is the newly ordained priest transformed in body, but his entire social being is transformed by a cultural redefinition of his personality. He undergoes a rite of passage in which his accustomed secular social roles are discarded or radically altered. He is no longer considered an ordinary person (*khon*), but is now placed in a special superior category reserved for priests and royalty (*ong*), which implies, as Thomas Kirsch has suggested to us, that he is a being "full of mana" or special sacred power, which is thus seen as related to increased merit.

4. Phillips' findings raise important questions for comparative psychology

(1965:61). He found no "oughts" or "shoulds" acting to stimulate or inhibit Thai behavior, and similar observations have been suggested by Hanks for Burma (1949:298). Is the ethical component of behavior missing, or does it take some less obvious form? Is the familiar "sense of sin" limited to certain parts of the world?

The case for personality without superego may be made on these grounds. We are already familiar with societies in which shame seems to be the chief deterrent force, rather than guilt. Thus guilt may not operate in certain societies. Can guilt occur where the idea of binding membership in a corporate group or community is lacking? Without the idea of responsibility to superior rules that have been assimilated into the self, guilt cannot operate. As we have noted, Thai groupings, including the family, are loose associations of individuals without a corporate superstructure or definite corporate boundary. One can escape them easily, even in childhood, and thus perhaps escape guilt.

Self-inhibition comes from at least two other sources. Shame is one, and we have seen Thai hesitate to perform in the presence of a critical audience. Another is the realization of the likelihood that an act may fail to achieve its ends. Here we note Thai sensitivity to the consequences of action and relative unconcern for the causes of action. People vary between impotence and omnipotence in their ability to effect a given end, much as the Chinese emperors of the mythical age differed from the ordinary emperor: one could separate the earth from the sea, the other was barely able to separate the barbarians from the civilized Chinese.

5. Carle Zimmerman (1931:48) states that in 1931, the year of his survey, the average income for farmers in central Siam was 279 baht. In the province of Bangkok (Phranakhāun) the income from crops was 166.31 baht and from other sources 113.78 baht, altogether totaling 280.09 baht; cash expenditures per family totaled 375.37 baht for farming costs, taxes, interest, etc. (ibid.:53–54). The difference was made up by loans from neighbors, rice buyers, or others. People borrowed, Zimmerman reports, because of lack of thrift, free spending, and gambling as well as because of losses in crops or animals. The average family was overspending after years of easy living. Bang Chan was not atypical.

6. In the late 1940s and 1950s small sums of money were still freely handed back and forth between kinsmen without interest. The size of the sums varied with the availability of money, the warmth of relations between kinsmen, and the ability to continue reciprocation of such services (Sharp et al. 1953:235; Janlekha 1957:155; JRH 2/5/54). When larger sums were needed than a kinsman could be expected to provide, one approached a known neighbor, who usually asked for security but who might ask little or no interest: "I used to own land but sold it to Chyam. I owed Sud a lot of money and had to sell the land. I had put the money he loaned me into farming, but the crop was not good. The debt built up over ten years. I had pawned the land to Sud. The loan had gone on for a long time. Then Sud wanted the money back and urged me to change title, selling the land. So I sold it to Chyam" (JRH 1/28/54). This loan was made with no written agreement and with low or negligible interest. If interest were at the usual commercial rates, varying between 12 and 60 percent, this man could not have postponed payment for a decade (LS 12/28/48). One or two years is about as long as the professional lender permits a debt to remain outstanding.

7. A declining yield of padi over the years has been widely discussed (Ingram 1955:48; Min. Ag. 1957:2). The cause is unclear. Were marginal lands brought into cultivation? Has the fertility of the old lands decreased? Was the decline only apparent, the result of more accurate figures? Or are there other explanations of the reported decline in yield?

In Bang Chan many farmers speak of a decline in yields. They recall years in which as much as forty thang per rai were grown on new land with the broadcast method. This figure must be stereotyped, however. They also report that rats and fish were continuously thinning the broadcast crop, and that more would be lost in the harvesting. A yield of forty thang per rai would be exceptional indeed.

Though an increase is not reflected in the general statistics for the nation as a whole, a rise is reported for the central plain in recent years (Min. Ag. 1965, Table 12). The increase in Bang Chan's yields over the past four decades, we believe, is due primarily to the change from broadcasting to transplanting and to the use of natural manures (LS 6/18/49). The average yield increased from ten or fifteen thang per rai to nearly thirty thang with the extension of transplanting (Janlekha 1957:52). In 1963 we heard of yields of fifty thang per rai with transplanted rice, presumably new varieties, and with the aid of commercial fertilizer.

The Mission of the Bank for International Reconstruction and Development affirms a 2 percent annual increase in yields since 1950, when marginal lands in the northeast began to be converted from padi to other crops (IBRD 1959:34). Fragmentation of lands is also held to be a factor. IBRD statistics on yield show, moreover, that the only decline occurred in the central plain, where there was a poor crop for two years (ibid.:272). Certainly it is not yet clear that marginal lands alone are responsible.

Nor is the case for a change in soil fertility clear. The annual flooding and silting is said to replace the needed nutrients. Even as late as 1957 few farmers in Bang Chan were using commercial fertilizers, and then only in the seedbeds. Yet intensive cultivation of a single crop may have resulted in an annual net loss of certain important nutritive elements. The obvious answer, addition of fertilizer, is complicated by flooding and resultant washing away of fertilizer (ibid.:67; LS 6/18/49). Studies reported by the Department of Agriculture (Min. Ag. 1957:20) showed that fertilizer increased the yields of padi, as one might expect. However, attempts to isolate particular fertilizing elements that might be missing from the soil proved inconclusive.

8. In Bang Chan during the 1950s slaughtering was done by Moslems, who killed bullocks for their feasts. Buddhists disapproved but were willing to eat the meat, if someone else soaked up the sin from killing the animal. During the 1930s the Buddhists overcame their reluctance to take life when they were in the pig-raising business, but by 1949 only two households still had pigs (Sharp et al. 1953:199).

Bang Chan Buddhists are perfectly willing to eat the meat of animals killed by accident. The death of a buffalo results in a work session in which the meat and skin are divided among households. The question of how much aid a buffalo should receive in the act of dying caused a rift in one household and apparently the loss of the buffalo:

> One day while her husband was away, Saeng got into a quarrel over a yearling buffalo which had fallen into the canal. She asked her brother-in-law to cut the tether rope so that it could get out. He said he wanted it to drown so that he would be able to eat meat. Saeng asked again, and the brother-in-law replied that if she continued asking, he would beat her. She said she was ready. He started to beat her when his older sister intervened. He then seized a knife to go after her, too. His younger brother intervened and took the knife away, saying, "You cannot use this on your sister." The brother-in-law continued fighting with a stick. Saeng's mother was fishing nearby, heard the quarrel, and called the village headman, who stopped the fight. After that Saeng and her husband moved out. [LMH 12/6/53]

9. We have no direct evidence of precisely when the present poultry, fish, and garden production began. Concerning the early Depression years Zimmerman observed: "The chief source of miscellaneous income in the Center are wages and rentals in cash from farms" (1931:49). Further: "The proportions of the food expenditures used for rice declined with the approach to the commercialized farming districts. The home production of other food items was neglected more and more as these were purchased in larger quantities from the markets" (ibid.:108). Our impression, however, is that these home industries peripheral to rice growing began in Bang Chan sometime between 1931 and 1948. Evidence places pig raising in Bang Chan during the 1930s, though it died out (Janlekha 1957:22). We believe it reasonable to place such home production at the time when people were particularly thirsty for cash and were seeking ways of earning extra money.

10. Though Minburī had been reduced by Rama VI in 1913 to a district of Phra Nakhaūn Province (Lumbini 1925:191), it seems still to have maintained some trappings of a province (changwat) until 1932, the date for effecting the change to a district (amphoē) under a royal order of the preceding year.

11. Public secular education began under the Compulsory Education Act of 1921 but did not reach Bang Chan until 1932 (SM 3/25/49; Jumsai 1951:39). The curriculum of the school soon followed the Primary Education Act of 1935, requiring children between the ages of eight and fifteen to attend school (ibid.:42). Children completing the four grades of the curriculum were released. The financial support from Bangkok could be augmented by the collection of a head tax by the district office; no tuition was charged.

12. That Jum's husband was being groomed to assume the kamnan's duties is an inference not directly substantiated by our notes. Conceivably this educated man aspired to higher official office than kamnan. In fact, a kamnan could not appoint his successor, though his recommendation of a successor to the headmen of the hamlets in his commune and to the district officer would have gone far toward establishing the young man's credentials. Phlym doubtless influenced the choice of an administrative hamlet in the vicinity of his property, Bang Chan 5. We do not know who succeeded Phlym as hamlet headman or kamnan in 1928. We do know, however, that Kamnan Phlym sought to retire on his sixtieth birthday, about 1918 (LMH 7/30/57). At that time a son by his second wife, the eldest of his male children, was still an adolescent. None of the other sons-in-law had sufficient personal stature for the position. It thus seems likely that Jum's husband, had he lived, would have succeeded him as kamnan; possibly his death helped reverse Phlym's decision to retire.

13. Division of property into equal shares does not preclude preferential treatment for the child who has cared for the deceased through his or her old age. Jum, in speaking of her lioness' share, emphasized these tasks in justification:

> After my father's death, my husband's relations persuaded me to come [and stay in Prapadaeng] because I was not happy with my own relatives here in Bang Chan. They envied me. I had more land than they did; it came from my father, and he gave more to me than to his other children, six hundred rai of land. My older sister did not get this much. I was not a favorite child, but was still living at home when my mother died, and so I helped my father at the end of his life. My older sister had already married and left. I stayed with father until his death. Before his death he made it known how his property was to be divided. Every wife got something and their children got land, more than twenty rai, according to how much he loved them. There was much envying and petty stealing from each other. [JRH 7/23/57]

Six years later, in the late 1930s or early 1940s, she returned to Bang Chan.

14. The vernacular "chickens" and "ducks" have several shades of meaning. Sharp et al. (1953:31) observed that the terms distinguish between "progressive" and "traditional" within Bang Chan: "The majority are 'chickens' or progressive farmers who actively seek to improve their economic status; the others are 'ducks' or laggards satisfied with traditional or 'poor' standards. A 'chicken' hopes that his daughter will not want to marry a 'duck.' It is clear that the former group, which includes local leaders and persons with high prestige, is on the increase." The words also refer to urban–rural differences and to differences of occupation, interests, and values; ducks are simply farmers, chickens are interested in business or government (KJ 4/9/49). The following passage from field notes amplifies these meanings:

> Farmers' children are used to hard work and have more tolerance than the children of these special families who cannot work hard. It is a difference in habit [*nitsaj*]. The headman's family has two daughters who are not used to working hard; so farmers' sons cannot marry them. They are different, like a duck, which cannot mate with a chicken. [*Where will these girls marry?*] The parents of some boys are afraid their sons will have to work alone because the girls cannot help, but the daughter of a farmer can marry a clerk, school-teacher, or gardener. Farmers' daughters are used to working hard and have experience. A duck is a farm person and a schoolteacher is a chicken. A duck can live in any place that is wet or dry. [*Ducks marry chickens?*] Many cases of daughters marrying city people . . . but there are few cases of a chicken marrying a duck boy. The headman's daughter married out. I never saw a boy from Bangkok come and take up farming. Many local boys want to marry the daughters of the headman, but the parents of these boys object, saying they cannot marry chickens. . . . They are not used to hard work. If the husband were sick, she could not do farmwork. A farmer's life is different from that of a government official. If he is ill, the official can stay home; but a farmer must work all the time. [LMH 2/8/54]

15. According to our field notes, a portable gasoline engine was reported stolen from the compound of Kamnan Phlym at the time of his death in 1928 (JRH 8/7/53). If this is true, the first engine reached Bang Chan in the 1920s rather than in the late 1930s, as Janlekha (1957:93) suggests. Rich farmers tend to lead the community in trying out new devices. Phlym's purchase of an engine is consistent with his leadership in the community. The windmill seems to have appeared suddenly in the late 1930s and rapidly spread throughout the lower central plain. According to local tradition, it was "invented" by three Bang Chan brothers (LS 11/4/48; KJ 3/12/49).

16. It may be no more than a coincidence that both of the most recent major floods (1917 and 1942) occurred immediately after Thailand became involved in an international war. Not only was the 1942 crop ruined in the lower central plain, but poor seed rice distributed by the government produced a poor 1943 harvest also. Fishing, however, was improved after the flood in Bang Chan; and only after the flood could salt shellfish sauce (kapi) be produced locally in quantity and with quality (LS 12/31/48).

17. Though deYoung (1955:50) does not report the practice of lying by the fire in northern Thailand and affirms that it is dying out generally, it occurs regularly in Bang Chan (J. R. Hanks 1963) and has been reported from a wide range of locations in Thailand, Southeast Asia, and beyond.

18. Gerini (1904:13) quotes the proverb "Man is padi, woman hulled rice." He explains that men take root and settle by themselves in life, whereas women are not self-supporting. We would add that padi symbolizes male hardness and somber color in contrast to female softness and lightness of color.

19. Responses to Phillips' sentence completion item "He was most afraid of . . ." disclosed that in Bang Chan "they specify such threats as poverty (15 informants), not having enough to eat (11), illness (4), flood and fire (3), death (3), and being bitten by poisonous snakes (2) (1965:356). When asked to complete the sentence "His greatest problem . . .," 57 percent spoke of well-being and survival. "Twelve villagers phrase their replies in terms of worrying about obtaining money, being rich, having money to spend. . . . Thirteen informants say they are worried about making a living or their work. . . . Nine say they are worried about starving, one is worried about illness; one about floods. . ." (ibid.:360–363). In response to "If one is frightened, the best thing to do is . . ." 40 percent of the informants respond by saying they would keep cool and calm (*chōej*). The other major response, by 31 percent of the villagers, expressed dependency. "However, what is important is that this is a metaphorical dependency seeking help from the Lord Buddha or from Allah (for Moslems) or from one's soul stuff rather than human beings" (ibid.:366).

These responses obtained from 111 adults in Bang Chan indicate worries not only over food but especially over money. The people of Bang Chan seek help mainly from their own resources, less often from guardian spirits. Though food and dependence appear as themes, they seem subordinated to money and self-reliance. We suggest the possibility of changes in response over the years from food anxieties toward job and money anxieties as well as changes toward increased self-reliance. Making rough calculations of the age of respondents in Phillips' data, we find that for "His greatest problem . . ." the average age of respondents who mentioned food was 41 years; of those who mentioned money, 31 years. For the item on fright, those who referred to a guardian averaged 41 years, while the majority who looked to their own resources averaged 33. If these changes do not reflect solely the effects of aging but changes in the historical scene, some slight evidence exists for a change in attitudes between pre- and postwar worlds.

Chapter 8: *Transformation Scene*

1. In northern Thailand, cremation customarily takes place within a few days of death (see Wells 1960:212; Kingshill 1960:164–165; deYoung 1955:69), but in the central plains a delay of at least 100 days is customary, except in cases of extreme poverty or of violent death (KJ 12/1/49; KY 12/1/49; LS 12/3/49, 7/10/52).

2. Like most of the traditional skills of Bang Chan, those of the undertaker require the learning of verbal formulae from a teacher. An important preliminary qualification is lack of fear of corpses. Having learned his skills, the practitioner is obligated to pay annual respects to his teacher in order to renew the effectiveness of the verbal formulae.

One of the three undertakers of Bang Chan described some of his duties (LS 2/5/53; CIW 3/13/54; LMH 3/31/54). First he must obtain a new or used coffin at the temple at a price varying between five and ten baht. Second, he drives lurking ghosts from the coffin and gives it to the deceased. Third, as if the corpse were a newborn child, he bathes it with water (*nām koed*), then dresses it, binds the hands and legs, inserts a coin in the mouth, and presses a solid wax mask without holes in it over the face. Fourth, he places the body in the coffin slightly on its side, combs the hair, breaks the comb, and nails the lid shut. At the proper hour of the proper day he assists in removing the corpse from the house of death and rents a space for storage at the temple from its ghost keeper, called Jāj Kālītikala.

On the day of cremation the undertaker fetches the body from the storage place to inspect it. A corpse less than one year old must be stripped of its soft parts, which are burned separately at a special ceremony attended by only a few kinsmen. The undertaker places the bones in a new box for formal cremation. After supervising the cremation of the bones at the funeral pyre, he forms two manikins from the ashes, one with a head facing east and a second with a head facing west, while a priest chants. One or more bones may be taken by a survivor. The rest are discarded onto a heap. This concludes the undertaker's duties. Our notes tell nothing of his fees or earnings, but none of Bang Chan's undertakers depends wholly on his profession for his living.

3. Less expensive cremations are also available. A group of kinsmen may simply cremate the corpse at the temple in the presence of a few priests. Here the entire body is burned at once without separation of flesh from bones. A poor person may petition a wealthy household about to undertake a major cremation to allow the simultaneous cremation of his own kinsman. The body of the poor man receives a less favorable place in the rites that build merit for the departing soul and is burned at a secondary pyre near the main cremation platform. The costs of cremation are also decreased through such expedients as inviting few guests and providing them with simple food and entertainment.

4. The host at a festival of any size writes a permanent list of the donors and the amount that each gives. This he keeps for reference so that when any person named on the list holds a festival, he may return the exact sum that was given him. The host at such a festival is patron only for a day, for tomorrow he returns to his role of participator in long-range exchange (tog raeng, chaj raeng: offer strength, use or return strength).

Janlekha (1957:149) found that between March 1948 and February 1953 his 96 sample families held 36 festivities with an average net expense of 4,361 baht. This sum represents the host's outlay minus contributions from the guests, ranging from a net gain of 10 baht to a net loss of 15,000.

5. The concept of death sometimes appears as the opposite of life, the mirror image, but in this locality not as the negation of living. The living circumambulate a ·building clockwise, as at Wisākhabūchā (Buddha's Birthday) or at a priest's ordination; the cremation procession moves counterclockwise. The living enter a sanctuary from the east, while the dead mount the funeral pyre from the west. The head and feet of a ghost are said to be turned backward; the ghost lurks only at night, while the living work in the day.

6. Until 1952 taxes were based on whether or not the land was cultivated (Ingram 1955:75–79). Taxes generally were low, though the rate of one baht per rai during the dropping prices of the 1930s made some hardship in Bang Chan until it was reduced (see LMH 7/17/57). In 1951 the tax became based on the approximate market value of the land (LS 9/19/52, 2/12/53; CIW 7/14/54), and the new rate, about one-quarter of 1 percent of the assessed value, kept the land tax low. Ingram (1955) and Silcock (1970) discuss the rice premium, gained by the government through its export monopoly, as an indirect tax on farmers.

7. Janlekha (1957:25) refers to corrections he has made in the census data, and some of these changes have been incorporated in our figures.

8. We would like to be able to demonstrate from our data that the central Thai, lacking fixed roots in any plot of land, are more mobile than, say, people of Italian or French agricultural communities of comparable size. Our data do not permit us to test this hypothesis, since the various censuses were not strictly comparable. More important, an answer to the question requires the development of an index of population mobility, a kind of measure of a community's metabolism. This becomes

a rather technical operation needing special study, rather than just another study of in- or out-migration.

9. Besides such improvisation of kinship relations, there are some indications of a shift. Formerly children of parents' older siblings were called *phī* regardless of age with reference to ego. Today there is a tendency to call all cousins *phī* who are older than ego, whether their parents are older or younger than ego's parents. If true, this may reflect neighborhood instability.

10. By the late 1960s the aging abbot of Wat Bang Chan saw before his death the realization of a dream he had persistently pursued for more than two decades. The old *bōt*, its plaster cracking, its bricks falling down, hazardous and stylistically outmoded, was being replaced by a new and larger sanctuary built on the same site. Local rumor put the cost at some 800,000 baht ($40,000), half coming from Bangkok, where the abbot—or, more likely, his superiors—had easy contact with city people of means and piety as well as with the Department of Religious Affairs, and the other half from neighborhood people who invested in this worthy enterprise their profits from recent land sales. With its large temple rivaling many a monastic institution in the city, Bang Chan had ceased to be a little-known and unmarked rural community standing alone on the central plain of Thailand.

Chapter 9: *Five Perspectives*

1. We may have narrowed our definition of historical orientation too severely in excluding China. Certainly all of the cultural symptoms of historical orientation occur there, with the possible exception of rites of reenactment. Similarly most of the criteria for ordering experience historically are present. We would underscore the lack in China of a concept that occurs in historically oriented societies: change was abnormal rather than a "fact" of nature. Like a fire, change could be prevented, the damage could be repaired, and life could go on as before. Thus history, instead of lying central to social existence, became an agent like the army or police force, for use in emergency.

2. Immutability and change are persistent concerns of our Western tradition. Unlike Indian religions, which have accepted (or negated) change, occidental thinkers have resisted it. From Judaism to Communism, all have stated the conditions of losing or gaining or regaining paradise. All these paradises, whether in heaven or of this world, have one characteristic in common: the essential characteristic, whatever it is, is immutable. So in our tales Croesus was tormented lest his good fortune end and Faust would continue to taste experiences until he found the one he wished to have linger. Even today, when the concept of evolution in limitless time encourages us to accept the inevitability of change, we do so only halfheartedly. We make it palatable by proclaiming it "progress" toward an ideal; we like to write books on utopias.

3. We should not stray near the fields where Kluckhohn and Strodtbeck (1961) worked effectively without comparison. Here we proceed from their classification of world outlooks, in particular their classification of temporal orientation toward the past, present, or future. Having found people who live with reference to the past, we ask what are the cultural concomitants that distinguish those with an orientation toward the past from those with an orientation toward the present or future. Our working hypothesis, like theirs (ibid.:3), is that all peoples are problem-oriented, but only some draw upon a temporal order to give their problems meaning.

4. A. Irving Hallowell observes (1955:94–95):

> If we wish to postulate a sense of self-continuity as a generic human trait, a culturally constituted temporal orientation must be assumed as a necessary condition. This seems to be a reasonable hypothesis in view of the fact that self-identification would have no functional value in the operation of a human social order if, at the same time, it was not given a temporal dimension. Who I am, both to myself and others, would have no stability.

Bang Chan people appear to have a sense of self-continuity, but of much smaller magnitude than ours. Their continuity is broken by life-cycle rites that are thought to alter the individual. Their games of spirit possession suggest that personal continuity is less important than for us, who feel a threat in hypnotic adventures. Change of status also implies a change of identity; under the monarchy official promotions carried change of name. Buddhism always emphasizes the transience of all things, including the ego, though in actual practice the Thai tend to play down the discontinuity of the ego.

In Bang Chan people lived linear lives but time offered no necessary continuity for the ego. As people grew up, the past died away quickly by neglect. The temporal present always shrank by comparison with eternity. As old age mounted, people did not look back to childhood; they thought of the hereafter and their next life.

The Thai have little sense of personal continuity and this seems unrelated to time. We believe that Hallowell's problem needs exploration and suggest an alternative hypothesis: a sense of personal identity is a concern only to people with a large Western-styled and centrally placed ego. Since Hellenic times we have been obsessed with questions of identity, continuity, and consistency of person; this concern seems to reflect our heritage of historic thinking.

5. We hold that Western European civilization is historic-minded and in this sense operates within past, present, and future. This view differs from the "traditional" society of David Riesman (1950), who emphasized an orientation toward the past rather than the future. He dwells on a social polity, either conserving institutions of the past or building the brave new world. From our point of view both are historic-minded, whether they date all goodness from a more or less remote ancestor or the revolution of tomorrow. Economists, too, write of "traditional" societies (e.g., Lerner 1958, Hagen 1962, Pye 1964), yet their quite different aim is to contrast a nonindustrial with a "modern" industrial type of social organization. They seem to have chosen the word "traditional" not to refer to temporal orientation but to avoid the contaminated word "underdeveloped."

6. Some indirect evidence for this assertion may be found in the following observations:

Unlike American society, Thai society does not attempt to cure its deviants of a sickness, to purge them of alien influences, or to change their hearts. Instead it makes them suffer through exile, if imprisonment or corporal punishment does not suffice. Conversely, the rewards of society go to those best able to muster men and sustain a group. Civilization is a populous city, barbarity the jungle.

Religion is praised for its value in promoting social living; in the words of a middle-aged Bang Chan man:

> Religion seems to be useless sometimes. If we look at spending money for making merit such as presenting robes to priests, it seems to be useless. But if we use money to buy arms or to promote other things than religion, the country will become uncivilized. Then we can see that religion is the main thing. Then the Thai people will promote religion. The people of Russia have no religion and do not know how to act toward each other. All people, even the king, must promote religion. [LMH 11/24/53]

Here religion becomes the socializing influence, the ingredient that makes group living possible. .

We have observed Thai students at American colleges and universities. When such a student finds himself the sole Thai at his school, the situation seems more than ordinarily difficult, particularly for young males. Academic difficulties are forerunners of severe depression, homesickness, sleeplessness, and other psychic disturbances. In discussing these symptoms, one Thai student pointed to the isolation of these individuals and said that in a group this effect would not have occurred.

7. Daniel Lerner (1958:96–97) prompted us to look for the symptoms of modernization that he found in a Turkish community near Angkara, and we found them. In Bang Chan we would never have phrased them, in Lerner's term, as "increasing empathy," for placing oneself imaginatively in another's position is a poorly developed faculty among Thai farmers. Awareness of affairs in a larger world they had, and a farmer's children easily thought of themselves as future doctors, teachers, and government officials. Participation in a larger scene had increased.

Lerner's "transitional" type (ibid.:101–102), whose newly gained aspirations were frustrated and who became unhappy, also has counterparts in Bang Chan. We describe two. Both had education sufficient to become schoolteachers, were heads of households, and belonged to the broader circle of relatives of the former kamnan.

M. in the 1950s was in his forties, had married a daughter of a wealthy woman, and had become a teacher in the local government school. During the 1930s he resigned his teaching post and became manager of inherited orchard property in another community. This venture failed after a few years and he returned to work his mother-in-law's lands in Bang Chan. Bang Chan farmers deemed him a poor manager and he had a heavy turnover of hired labor. Nevertheless, he sent his children to be educated in Bangkok, where some reached the university level. Bang Chan sources further reported that in competition for the favors of his mother-in-law he was losing to the husband of another daughter. At the time of interview he was very depressed and had sought the interviewer's assistance. He complained of not having sufficient money to pay for the education of his children and was seeking additional employment. He sold his buffalo to buy the facilities for raising mushrooms; when the mushroom business failed, he was left without farming tools. Four years later he was reported to have failed and avoided meetings with the interviewer.

S. in the 1950s was in his thirties and lived in the household of his mother-in-law. He had received sufficient education to become a local schoolteacher, though he worked in the fields during periods of heavy labor. Many times he approached various members of the research team for assistance in English. He was one of a handful of persons in Bang Chan who subscribed to a magazine, and through his hands daily papers were passed around. Unlike M., he wore modern clothes on most occasions. He was reported to be drinking excessively, and researchers confirmed this report. As a teacher he was said to be lax in his duties, arriving at school late, missing classes, and the like. After the completion of the new school building in 1956 he was transferred to a neighboring school. A letter from him spoke of the hardship of having to travel more than an hour by boat to reach his work. When we returned to Bang Chan in 1957, this man avoided us.

Both men failed to advance themselves to desired social positions and appear to have been shamed by failure. Both were unable to maintain their positions securely.

Thai society has always permitted and at times encouraged upward social mobility. Thus we cannot state that these failures are clearly the products of modernization. Western influences in both Turkey and Thailand did open the way to many new occupations, including teaching. Both men aspired to more than life in a farming community. We suggest that the presence of Americans and educated urban Thai in the community reminded these men of their failure to achieve and aggravated their shame.

8. The organic image of society appears and disappears in the writings of most anthropologists. A. R. Radcliffe-Brown, whose theories stand near an organic conception of society, states (1952:190–191):

> Social structures are just as real as are individual organisms. A complex organism is a collection of living cells and interstitial fluids [just as a cell is] a structural arrangement of complex molecules. The physiological and psychological phenomena that we observe in the lives of organisms are not simply the result of the nature of the constituent molecules or atoms of which the organism is built up but are the result of the structure in which they are united.

The organic image, never quite firmly fixed, disappears a few pages later (pp. 197–198) when he turns to economic "machinery" and "mechanism." Few anthropologists strayed nearer, though A. L. Kroeber, speaking of *Oikumene* as a "web of culture growth" (1952:392), often treated the superorganic in organic language. Biologists, too, shy away from organic images, preferring to consider society as an implement of man rather than a living species. Yet Teilhard de Chardin's phrasing of the "noosphere" uses organic idiom (1959:207):

> There is no need for me to emphasize the reality, the diversity and continual germination of human collective unities, at any rate potentially divergent; such as the birth, multiplication and evolution of nations, states and civilizations. . . . However hominised the events, the history of mankind in this rationalized form does prolong—though in its own way and degree— the organic movements of life.

9. Julian Steward's (1955:64–77) vision of the nation-state posits three kinds of structure: vertical local communities, horizontally dispersed classes, and an interlocking institutional network. Robert Redfield (1956:57–66), observing comparable subject matter, found territorially based groups, independent economic activity, and networks of relationship. Converting these views into our organic metaphor would not be difficult. However, we have not stressed the social connections of kinship, marriage, and so on. These problems of organic continuity lend themselves nicely to such metaphors as cell division.

While Steward's and Redfield's integrative features doubtless operate in Thai society, two special characteristics may lead to a genetic scheme for the nation-state on quite a different basis than a gradual integration of locally fixed villages. In Thailand the people are not rooted to a particular piece of land. They move at will; villages appear and disappear. In addition, people are linked together through relations to a leader. The resulting pattern is radiate rather than a network. The European type of network, firmly rooted in a given territory, is better coordinated and probably hardier. Yet a radiate type easily integrates new cells and recovers more quickly from a lethal blow. For many centuries Asian cities have formed the centers for the settlement and integration of populations. Though urban-rural polarity, certain facets of a class structure, and other characteristics of a peasant society can be found here, a folk-urban transition would have had to take place centuries ago, if it had occurred. Indeed, Robert Braidwood and Gordon Willey (1962:350–358) observe a differing genesis of cities in the old world as compared with the new. Since then in Southeast Asia the Oikumene has furnished a mud in which cities grew, absorbing all manner of persons (Hewes 1961). Certainly the century in Bang Chan was only a facet of urban growth.

10. Current interest in economic development and more recently in political development is directly related to the organismic metaphor. Here we think not only of the imagery implied in such terms as "growth" but more concretely of systematic development of the science. The day of abstract model building (e.g., Rostow 1960, Hoselitz 1960) has given way to comparisons of concrete examples (e.g., Ayal 1963, Von Vorys 1964). If more is to come of these comparisons than a set of contrasts, we must be able to see societies as a whole. Only then will it be possible for anthropologists to address such generalized questions as the shapes of "dual societies" (Nash 1964). Conceivably the organic metaphor offers a scheme of sufficient flexibility and clarity to accomplish this end. One merely needs, like cartographers making maps, to establish certain conventions; e.g., the political system is equated with the muscular system, communications with the nervous system, economics with the nutritive system, and so on. This accomplished, one can see the interrelations between systems, chart changes, and study the effects upon the whole. Any scientific ordering needs a metaphor of this serviceability, be it a mechanical or a mathematical one. All metaphors have limitations, but only by adopting some guiding metaphor can we pass beyond description.

Bibliography

Alabaster, Henry
    1871 *The Wheel of the Law: Buddhism, Illustrated from Siamese Sources*. London: Trubner.
Anuman Rajadhon, *Phya*
    1955 *The Life of the Farmer in Thailand*, trans. William J. Gedney. Translation series. New Haven: Yale University Southeast Asia Studies.
    1961 *Life and Ritual in Old Siam: Three Studies of Thai Life and Customs*, trans. and ed. William J. Gedney. New Haven: HRAF Press.
Ayal, Eliezer B.
    1963 "Value Systems and Economic Development in Japan and Thailand." *Journal of Social Issues* 19:35–51.
    1969 "Thailand." In Frank H. Golay et al., *Underdevelopment and Economic Nationalism in Southeast Asia*, pp. 267–340. Ithaca: Cornell University Press.
Bangkok Calendar (English-language periodical). Bangkok: American Missionary Press, 1859–1872.
Barnett, Homer G.
    1953 *Innovation: The Basis of Cultural Change*. New York: McGraw-Hill.
Bastian, Adolf
    1867 *Reisen in Siam in Jahre 1863*, vol. 3 of *Die Völker des östlichen Asien*. Jena: Hermann Costenoble.
Beals, Ralph
    1962 "Acculturation." In *Anthropology Today*, ed. Sol Tax, pp. 373–395. Chicago: University of Chicago Press.
Bernatzik, Hugo Adolf
    1958 *The Spirits of the Yellow Leaves*. London: Robert Hale.
Bisolyaputra, Uthai
    1949 "A Brief Study of the Diets of Minburi People in Thailand (Siam)." *Journal of the Medical Association of Thailand* 32:45–67.
Bock, Carl
    1884 *Temples and Elephants: The Narrative of a Journey of Exploration through Upper Siam and Lao*. London: Sampson, Low, Marston, Searle & Rivington.
Bowring, John
    1857 *The Kingdom and People of Siam, with a Narrative of the Mission to That Country in 1855*, 2 vols. London: John W. Parker & Son.

Braidwood, Robert J., and Gordon R. Willey
    1962 *Courses toward Urban Life: Archaeological Considerations of Some Cultural Alternates.* Viking Fund Publications in Anthropology no. 32. New York: Wenner-Gren Foundation for Anthropological Research.
Bunker, Robert, and John Adair
    1959 *The First Look at Strangers.* New Brunswick, N.J.: Rutgers University Press.
Chakrabongse, Chula, *Prince*
    1960 *Lords of Life: The Paternal Monarchy of Bangkok.* New York: Taplinger.
Chandruang, Kamut
    1938 *My Boyhood in Siam.* New York: John Day.
Credner, Wilhelm
    1935 *Siam, das Land der Tai.* Stuttgart: J. Engelhorn.
Damrong Rajanubhab, *Prince*
    1919 "Siamese History prior to the Founding of Ayudhya." *Journal of the Siam Society* 13, pt. 2:1–66.
Davenport, William
    1959 "Nonunilinear Descent and Descent Groups." *American Anthropologist* 61:557–572.
Delvert, Jean
    1961 *Le Paysan Cambodgien.* Paris and Le Haye: Mouton.
deYoung, John E.
    1955 *Village Life in Modern Thailand.* Berkeley: University of California Press.
Dhani Nivat, *Prince*
    1955 "The Reconstruction of Rama I of the Chakri Dynasty." *Journal of the Siam Society* 43, pt. 1:21–48.
Dilock, *Prince*
    1908 *Die Landwirtschaft in Siam: Ein Beitrag zur Wirtschaftsgeschichte des Königreichs Siam.* Leipzig: C. L. Hirschfeld.
Duplatre, Louis
    1933 Review: "L'esclavage privé dans le vieux droit siamois," by Robert Lingat. *Journal of the Siam Society* 26, pt. 1:103–124.
Fraser, Thomas M., Jr.
    1960 *Rusembilan: A Malay Fishing Village in Southern Thailand.* Ithaca: Cornell University Press.
Gerini, G. E.
    1904 "On Siamese Proverbs and Idiomatic Expressions." *Journal of the Siam Society* 1:11–168.
Goldsen, Rose K., and Max Ralis
    1957 *Factors Relating to Acceptance of Innovations in Bang Chan, Thailand.* Data paper no. 25. Ithaca: Cornell University Southeast Asia Program.
Goodenough, Ward H.
    1963 *Cooperation in Change.* New York: Russell Sage Foundation.
Graham, W. A.
    1913 *Siam: A Handbook of Practical, Commercial, and Political Information,* 2d ed. Chicago: G. G. Browne.
Haas, Mary R., and Heng R. Subhanka
    1945 *Spoken Thai.* Washington, D.C.: Published for the U.S. Armed Forces Institute by the Linguistic Society of America and the Intensive Language Program, American Council of Learned Societies.

Hagen, Everett E.
1962 *On the Theory of Social Change: How Economic Growth Begins.* Homewood,
Ill.: Dorsey Press.
Hall, D. G. E.
1955 *A History of South East Asia.* New York: St. Martin's Press. (Rev. ed. 1970.)
Hallowell, A. Irving
1955 *Culture and Experience.* Philadelphia: University of Pennsylvania Press.
Hanks, Jane R.
1959 "Thai Character and Its Development." Burg Wartenstein Conference on
Stability and Change in Thai Culture. Unpublished paper, Cornell
Thailand Project.
1960 "Reflections on the Ontology of Rice." In *Culture in History: Essays in Honor
of Paul Radin*, ed. Stanley Diamond, pp. 298–301. New York: Columbia
University Press.
1963 *Maternity and Its Rituals in Bang Chan.* Data paper no. 51. Ithaca: Cornell
University Southeast Asia Program.
Hanks, Lucien M., Jr.
1949 "The Quest for Individual Autonomy in Burmese Personality with Particular Reference to the Arakan." *Psychiatry* 12:285–300.
1957 "Modified TATs of 47 Thai Children and Adults." In *Primary Records in
Culture and Personality*, vol. 1, ed. Bert Kaplan. Madison, Wis.: Microcard
Foundation.
1958 "Indifference to Modern Education in a Thai Farming Community."
Human Organization 17, no. 2:9–14.
1959 "Changes in Family Life." Burg Wartenstein Conference on Stability and
Change in Thai Culture. Unpublished paper, Cornell Thailand Project.
1962 "Merit and Power in the Thai Social Order." *American Anthropologist*
64:1247–1261.
1972 *Rice and Man in Southeast Asia.* Chicago: Aldine, 1972.
Hanks, Lucien M., Jr., and Jane R. Hanks, with the assistance of Kamol Janlekha,
Aram Emarun, Jadun Kongsa, and Saovanee Sudsaneh
1955 "Diphtheria Immunization in a Thai Community." In *Health, Culture, and
Community*, ed. Benjamin D. Paul and Walter B. Miller, pp. 155–185.
New York: Russell Sage Foundation.
Hanks, Lucien M., Jr., and Herbert P. Phillips
1961 "A Young Thai from the Countryside: A Psycho-social Analysis." In
Studying Personality Cross-culturally, ed. Bert Kaplan, pp. 637–656. Evan-
ston, Ill.: Row, Peterson.
Hauck, Hazel M., with the assistance of Anusith Rajatasilpin, Sapha Indrasud,
Chumlong Kittivija, and Saovanee Sudsaneh
1956 *Aspects of Health, Sanitation, and Nutritional Status in a Siamese Rice Village.*
Data paper no. 22. Ithaca: Cornell University Southeast Asia Pro-
gram.
Hauck, Hazel M., with the assistance of Anusith Rajatasilpin, Sapha Indrasud,
Saovanee Sudsaneh, Sylvia de la Paz, and Barbara J. Smith
1959 *Maternal and Child Health in a Siamese Rice Village: Nutritional Aspects.* Data
paper no. 39. Ithaca: Cornell University Southeast Asia Program.
Hauck, Hazel M., Saovanee Sudsaneh, and Jane R. Hanks
1958 *Food Habits and Nutrient Intakes in a Siamese Rice Village.* Data paper no. 29.
Ithaca: Cornell University Southeast Asia Program.

Heine-Geldern, Robert
  1956 *Conceptions of State and Kingship in Southeast Asia.* Data paper no. 18. Ithaca: Cornell University Southeast Asia Program.
Hendry, James B.
  1964 *The Small World of Khanh Hau.* Chicago: Aldine.
Hewes, Gordon W.
  1961 "The Ecumene as a Civilizational Multiplier System." In Kroeber Anthropological Society, *Papers,* no. 25, pp. 73–109.
Horrigan, Frederick James
  1959 "Local Government and Administration in Thailand: A Study of Institutions and Their Cultural Setting." Ph.D. thesis, University of Indiana.
Hoselitz, Bert F.
  1960 *Sociological Aspects of Economic Growth.* Glencoe, Ill.: Free Press.
Ingersoll, Jasper C.
  1963 "The Priest and the Path: An Analysis of the Priest's Role in a Central Thai Village." Ph.D. thesis, Cornell University. Ann Arbor, Mich.: Xerox University Microfilms.
Ingram, James C.
  1955 *Economic Change in Thailand since 1850.* Stanford, Calif.: Stanford University Press.
  1971 *Economic Change in Thailand, 1850–1970.* Stanford, Calif.: Stanford University Press. (Rev. ed. of Ingram 1955.)
IBRD
  1959 *A Public Development Program for Thailand: Report of a Mission Organized by the International Bank for Reconstruction and Development at the Request of the Government of Thailand.* Baltimore: Johns Hopkins University Press.
Janlekha, Kamol Odd
  1957 *A Study of the Economy of a Rice Growing Village in Central Thailand.* Bangkok: Division of Agricultural Economics, Ministry of Agriculture. (Title page dated 1955.)
Jumsai, Manich, *M.L.*
  1951 *Compulsory Education in Thailand.* Paris: UNESCO.
Kaufman, Howard Keva
  1960 *Bangkhuad: A Community Study in Thailand.* Locust Valley, N.Y.: J. J. Augustin.
Keyes, Charles F.
  1966 "Peasant and Nation: A Thai-Lao Village in a Thai State." Ph.D. thesis, Cornell University. Ann Arbor, Mich.: Xerox University Microfilms.
  1970 "Local Leadership in Rural Thailand." In *Local Authority and Administration in Thailand,* ed. Fred R. von der Mehden and David A. Wilson, pp. 92–127. Report no. 1. Los Angeles: Academic Advisory Council for Thailand.
King, D. O.
  1860 "Travels in Siam and Cambodia." *Journal of the Royal Geographic Society* 30:177–182.
Kingshill, Konrad
  1960 *Ku Daeng–The Red Tomb: A Village Study in Northern Thailand.* Chiangmai, Thailand: Prince Royal's College.
Kluckhohn, Florence R., and Fred L. Strodtbeck, with the assistance of John M. Roberts and others
  1961 *Variations in Value Orientations.* Evanston, Ill.: Row, Peterson.

Kroeber, A. L.
    1952   *The Nature of Culture*. Chicago: University of Chicago Press.
Kruger, Rayne
    1964   *The Devil's Discus*. London: Cassell.
Lajonquière, E. Lunet de
    1906   *Le Siam et les siamois*. Paris: Libraire Armand Colin.
Laws
    1935a "Phrarātchabanyat laksana pogkhrāung thāung thī" [Local Administration
           Act (1896)]. In *Prachum kodmāj pracham sog* [Collection of laws of the year],
           comp. Sathian Lailak et al., 16:22–67. Bangkok: Siam Free Press.
    1935b "Phrarātchabanyat laksana pogkhrāung thāung thī phraphutthasagkarād
           2457" [Local Administration Act 1914]. In *Prachum kodmāj pracham sog*
           [Collection of laws of the year], comp. Sathian Lailak et al., 27:210–251.
           Bangkok: Nītiwēd.
    1936   "Prakād ryang jub ruam thāung thī bāng monthon lae bāng changwat"
           [Announcement dissolving or establishing the jurisdiction of some prov-
           inces]. In *Prachum kodmāj pracham sog* [Collection of laws of the year],
           comp. Sathian Lailak et al., 44:443–445. Bangkok: Rongphim Sayām
           Witthayākāun.
    1953   "Phrarātchabanyat kaekhaj phoēmtoēm pramuan radsādakaun (chabab thī
           9) ph. s. 2495" [Amendment of the revenue code (no. 9), 1952]. In *Prachum
           kodmāj pracham sog* [Collection of laws of the year], comp. Sathian Lailak et
           al., 65, pt. 1:128–136. Bangkok. Nītiwēd.
Leach, Edmund Roland
    1961   *Rethinking Anthropology*. University of London, School of Economics and
           Political Science, Monographs on Social Anthropology no. 22. London:
           Athlone Press.
Lee, Dorothy
    1959   *Freedom and Culture*. Englewood Cliffs, N.J.: Prentice-Hall.
Leighton, Alexander H., and Lauriston Sharp
    1952   *Cornell University Thailand Project: Notes for Field Research Workers*. Bangkok:
           Cornell Research Center.
Lerner, Daniel
    1958   *The Passing of Traditional Society: Modernizing the Middle East*. Glencoe, Ill.:
           Free Press.
Lingat, R.
    1931   *L'Esclavage privé dans le vieux droit siamois*. Paris: F. Leviton.
    1950   "Evolution of the Conception of Law in Burma and Siam." *Journal of the
           Siam Society* 38, pt. 1:9–31.
Love, H. H.
    1954   *A Report on Plans and Progress with Rice Improvement in Thailand*. Natural
           History Bulletin no. 16. Bangkok: Siam Society.
Lumbini
    1925   *The Souvenir of the Siamese Kingdom Exhibition at Lumbini Park, B.E. 2468
           (1925)*. Bangkok, 2470 (1927).
McClelland, David C.
    1963   "Motivational Patterns in Southeast Asia with Special Reference to the
           Chinese Case." *Journal of Social Issues* 19, no. 1:6–19.
McFarland, George B.
    1944   *Thai-English Dictionary*, 2d ed. Palo Alto, Calif.: Stanford University
           Press.

Malinowski, Bronislaw
    1927   *Sex and Repression in Savage Society.* London: K. Paul, Trench, Trubner.
    1929   *The Sexual Life of Savages.* London: G. Routledge & Sons.
Min. Ag. See Thailand, Ministry of Agriculture.
Moffat, Abbot Low
    1961   *Mongkut, the King of Siam.* Ithaca: Cornell University Press.
Moore, Frank J., with Clark D. Neher
    1974   *Thailand: Its People, Its Society, Its Culture.* New Haven: HRAF Press.
Mosel, James
    1957   "Thai Administrative Behavior." In *Toward the Comparative Study of Public
            Administration,* ed. William J. Siffin, pp. 278–331. Bloomington: Indiana
            University Press.
Murdock, George P., ed.
    1960   *Social Structure in Southeast Asia.* Viking Fund Publications in Anthropol-
            ogy no. 29. Chicago: Quadrangle Books.
Nash, Manning
    1964   "Southeast Asian Society: Dual or Multiple." *Journal of Asian Studies*
            23:417–423.
Notton, M. Camille
    1926   *Annales du Siam,* pt. 1. Paris: Imprimeries Charles-Lavauzelle.
Paauw, Douglas S.
    1963   "Economic Progress in Southeast Asia." *Journal of Asian Studies* 23:69–92.
Pallegoix, Jean Baptiste, *Mgr.*
    1854   *Description du Royaume Thai ou Siam,* 2 vols. Paris: La Mission de Siam.
Pendleton, Robert L.
    1962   *Thailand: Aspects of Landscape and Life.* New York: Duell, Sloan & Pierce.
Pfanner, David E., and Jasper Ingersoll
    1962   "Theravada Buddhism and Village Economic Behavior." *Journal of Asian
            Studies* 21:341–361.
Phillips, Herbert P.
    1958   "The Election Ritual in a Thai Village." *Journal of Social Issues* 14, no.
            4:38–50.
    1963   "Relationships between Personality and Social Structure in a Siamese
            Peasant Community." *Human Organization* 22:105–108.
    1965   *Thai Peasant Personality.* Berkeley and Los Angeles: University of Califor-
            nia Press.
Potter, J. M., M. N. Diaz, and G. M. Foster, eds.
    1967   *Peasant Society.* Boston: Little, Brown.
Pramoj, Kukrit, *M.R.*
    1955   "The Social Order of Ancient Thailand." *Thought and Word* 1, no. 4:10–15.
Pye, Lucian W.
    1962   *Politics, Personality, and Nation Building: Burma's Search for Identity.* New
            Haven: Yale University Press.
    1964   "Perspective Requires Two Points of Vision." *Journal of Asian Studies*
            23:429–432.
Rabibhadana, Akin, *M.R.*
    1969   *The Organization of Thai Society in the Early Bangkok Period, 1782–1873.* Data
            paper no. 74. Ithaca: Cornell University Southeast Asia Program.
Radcliffe-Brown, A. R.
    1952   *Structure and Function in Primitive Society.* Glencoe, Ill.: Free Press.

Redfield, Robert
  1956 *Peasant Society and Culture: An Anthropological Approach to Civilization.*
        Chicago: University of Chicago Press.
  1962 *Human Nature and the Study of Society.* Chicago: University of Chicago
        Press.
Riesman, David
  1950 *The Lonely Crowd: A Study of the Changing American Character.* New Haven:
        Yale University Press.
Rostow, W. W.
  1960 *The Stages of Economic Growth: A Non-communist Manifesto.* Cambridge: At
        the University Press.
Rowe, John Howland
  1962 "A Social Theory of Culture Change." In Kroeber Anthropological Soci-
        ety, *Papers*, no. 26.
Schweisguth, P.
  1951 *Etude sur la littérature siamoise.* Paris: Adrien Maisonneuve.
Sharp, Lauriston
  1950 "Peasants and Politics in Thailand." *Far Eastern Survey* 19:157–161.
  1951 "Experimental Field Research in Thailand." *International Social Science
        Bulletin* 3:218–225.
  1960 "Foreword." In Thomas M. Fraser, Jr., *Rusembilan.* Ithaca: Cornell Uni-
        versity Press.
  1963 "Thai Social Structure." *Proceedings, Ninth Pacific Science Congress, 1957* 3.
        129–130. Bangkok.
  1967 *Cornell Thailand Project: Bibliography of Materials Relating to Thailand and
        Project Personnel.* Ithaca: Cornell Thailand Project.
  1968 "Cultural Differences and Southeast Asian Research." In *American Re-
        search on Southeast Asian Development: Asian and American Views*, pp. 65–79.
        New York: Asia Society.
Sharp, Lauriston, Hazel M. Hauck, Kamol Janlekha, and Robert B. Textor, with
        the assistance of John Brohm, J. Marvin Brown, and Singto Metah
  1953 *Siamese Rice Village: A Preliminary Study of Bang Chan, 1948–1949.* Bangkok:
        Cornell Research Center.
Siam Repository (weekly), vols. 1–6 (1869–1874). Bangkok: S. J. Smith's Place.
Silcock, T. H.
  1970 *The Economic Development of Thai Agriculture.* Ithaca: Cornell University
        Press.
Skinner, G. William
  1957 *Chinese Society in Thailand: An Analytical History.* Ithaca: Cornell University
        Press.
Smith, Robert J.
  1951 "A Comparative Study of the Shift in Six Selected Villages from Eco-
        nomic Self-sufficiency to Dependence on the Larger Unit." M.A. thesis,
        Cornell University.
  1955 "Outline for Discussion of Change Materials." Unpublished paper, Cor-
        nell University, Comparative Studies of Cultural Change.
  1956 "Working Papers on Bang Chan Materials." Unpublished paper, Cornell
        University, Comparative Studies of Cultural Change.
Spengler, Oswald
  1926 *The Decline of the West.* New York: Knopf.

Spicer, Edward
    1952 *Human Problems in Technological Change: A Casebook.* New York: Russell Sage Foundation.
Steward, Julian H.
    1955 *Theory of Culture Change: The Methodology of Multilinear Evolution.* Urbana: University of Illinois Press.
Teilhard de Chardin, Pierre
    1959 *The Phenomenon of Man,* trans. Bernard Wall. New York: Harper & Row.
Textor, Robert Bayard
    1960 "An Inventory of Non-Buddhist Supernatural Objects in a Central Thai Village." Ph.D. thesis, Cornell University. Ann Arbor, Mich.: Xerox University Microfilms.
    1961 *From Peasant to Pedicab Driver.* Cultural Report series no. 9. New Haven: Yale University Southeast Asia Studies.
    1973a *Roster of the Gods: An Ethnography of the Supernatural in a Thai Village,* 6 vols. New Haven: Human Relations Area Files.
    1973b *Patterns of Worship: A Formal Analysis of the Supernatural in a Thai Village,* 4 vols. New Haven: Human Relations Area Files.
Thailand, Ministry of Agriculture (cited as Min. Ag.)
    1950 National FAO Committee, *Thailand and Her Agriculture Problems,* rev. ed. Bangkok.
    1956 *Prawad Krasuang Kaset* [History of the Ministry of Agriculture]. Bangkok, 2499 (1956).
    1957 *Agriculture in Thailand.* Bangkok.
    1965 *Agricultural Statistics of Thailand.* Bangkok.
Thailand, Ministry of Public Instruction
    1912 *Report, 1911/12.* Bangkok.
Thailand, National Archives
    Raīngān Monthon Krungthēp Kān Khana Song [Reports on ecclesiastical affairs in Monthon Krungthēp], 5 S, 26/12, R.S. 118, 119, 121, 122, 127 (1899, 1900, 1902, 1903, 1908).
Thailand, Royal Academy
    1957 *Watthusathān thī Phrabāt Somdet Phra Nang Klao Chaoyūhūa Song Sathāpanā* [Royal works constructed under King Rama III]. Bangkok: S. Kānphim, 2500.
Thiphakarawong, Chaophrayā (Kham Bunnag)
    1934a *Phrarātchaphongsāwadān Krung Rattanakosin Rātchakān Thī 4* [Chronicle of the Fourth Reign]. Bangkok: Hausamud haeng chad, 2477.
    1934b *Phrarātchaphongsāwadān Krung Rattanakosin Rātchakān Thī 3* [Chronicle of the Third Reign]. Bangkok: Rongphim Srīhong, 2477.
    1937 *Phrarātchaphongsāwadān Krung Rattanakōsin Rātchakān Thī 3* [Chronicle of the Third Reign]. Bangkok: Sophonphattanākon, 2480.
Thompson, Virginia
    1941 *Thailand: The New Siam.* New York: Macmillan.
    1948 "Governmental Instability in Siam." *Far Eastern Survey* 17:161, 185–189.
Thornton, H., and A. Thornton
    1962 *Time and Style.* London: Methuen.
Tirabutana, Prajuab
    1958 *A Simple One.* Data paper no. 30. Ithaca: Cornell University Southeast Asia Program.

Van der Heide, J. Homan
  1906 "Economic Development of Siam during the Last Half Century." *Journal of the Siam Society* 3, pt. 2:74–101.
Vella, Walter F.
  1955 *The Impact of the West on Government in Thailand.* University of California Publications in Political Science 4, no. 3:317–410. Berkeley and Los Angeles: University of California Press.
  1957 *Siam under Rama III, 1824–1851.* Locust Valley, N.Y.: J. J. Augustin.
Von Vorys, Karl
  1964 Review: "Old Societies and New States: The Quest for Modernity in Asia and Africa," ed. Clifford Geertz. *Journal of Asian Studies* 23:290–291.
Wales, H. G. Quaritch
  1931 *Siamese State Ceremonies: Their History and Function.* London: Bernard Quaritch.
  1934 *Ancient Siamese Government and Administration.* London: Bernard Quaritch.
Warren, Henry Clarke
  1896 *Buddhism in Translation.* Harvard Oriental Series, vol. 3.Cambridge: Harvard University Press.
  1921 *Buddhist Legends.* Cambridge: Harvard University Press.
Wells, Kenneth E.
  1958 *History of Protestant Work in Thailand, 1828–1958.* Bangkok: Church of Christ in Thailand.
  1960 *Thai Buddhism: Its Rites and Activities.* Bangkok: Christian Bookstore.
Wilson, David A.
  1959 "Thailand." In *Governments and Politics of Southeast Asia,* ed. George McT. Kahin, pp. 1–72. Ithaca: Cornell University Press.
  1962 *Politics in Thailand.* Ithaca: Cornell University Press.
  1970 *The United States and the Future of Thailand.* New York: Praeger.
Wilson, David A., and Herbert P. Phillips
  1958 "Elections and Parties in Thailand." *Far Eastern Survey* 27:113–119.
Wittfogel, Karl A.
  1957 *Oriental Despotism: A Comparative Study of Total Power.* New Haven: Yale University Press.
Wolf, Eric R.
  1966 *Peasants.* New York: Prentice-Hall.
Wyatt, David K.
  1963 "Siam and Laos, 1767–1827." *Journal of Southeast Asian History* 4, no. 2:13–32.
  1969 *The Politics of Reform in Thailand: Education in the Reign of King Chulalongkorn.* New Haven: Yale University Press.
Young, Ernest
  1907 *The Kingdom of the Yellow Robe,* 3d ed. Westminster: Archibald Constable.
Zimmerman, Carle C.
  1931 *Siam: Rural Economic Survey, 1930–1931.* Bangkok: Bangkok Times Press.

Index

Library of Congress Cataloging in Publication Data
(For library cataloging purposes only)

Sharp, Lauriston.
  Bang Chan: social history of a rural community in Thailand.

  (Cornell studies in anthropology)
  Bibliography: p.
  1. Ethnology—Thailand. 2. Bang Chan, Thailand—Social conditions. 3. Bang Chan,
Thailand—Social life and customs. 4. Villages—Thailand. I. Hanks, Lucien Mason,
1910–   joint author. II. Title. III. Series.
GN635.T4S52   301.29'593   77-90910
ISBN 0-8014-0858-X